All or Nothing

An Autobiography

W AYNE K USCHEL

Order this book online at www.trafford.com
or email orders@trafford.com

Most Trafford titles are also available at major online book retailers.

Printed in the United States of America.

ISBN: 978-1-4269-5936-3 (sc)
ISBN: 978-1-4269-5937-0 (hc)
ISBN: 978-1-4269-5938-7 (e)

Library of Congress Control Number: 2011902958

Trafford rev. 12/08/2011

 www.trafford.com

North America & international
toll-free: 1 888 232 4444 (USA & Canada)
phone: 250 383 6864 ♦ fax: 812 355 4082

I want to thank Kristine T and Julia L for their outstanding action's on assisting me in completing this book.

"Thanks to Kristine and Julia"

Wayne A. Kuschel

DEDICATION

TO MY WIFE MARIE FOR THIRTY FOUR YEARS AND TO MY OLDER BROTHER DONALD C. KUSCHEL

I want to dedicate this book to two of my dearest friends.

From my whole heart in memory of my wife, Marie Kuschel, for thirty four years she was the best companion that anyone on this earth could have had. She was a remarkable gal. When I was at Roswell AFB, New Mexico I met Marie and we immediately began dating.

When I finished my B-29 Flight Engineer Transition Course at Roswell AFB, New Mexico my assigned aircraft crew were transferred to Lincoln AFB, Nebraska, where numerous B-29 crews were awaiting official travel orders and B-29's to fly toward the Pacific Islands sufficient in size to hold our aircraft.

However on 6 August 1945 the "Little Boy" atomic bomb was dropped on Hiroshima, Japan by Colonel Paul W. Tibbetts "Pilot of Enola Gay".

Then on 15 August 1945 the second Atomic Bomb "Big Boy" was dropped from "Box Car" by Captain Sweeney on the city of Nagasaki, Japan commencing all the surrendering of World War II activities and exercise's.

Regardless, I asked Marie to come to Lincoln Nebraska and visit with me, in the mean-time not knowing what the future held for us bomber flyers, Marie and I were married on the15th September 1945. I was assigned to a ground school in Lowry AFB, Colorado and before the ink was dry on my orders I was transferred to Wright Field, Dayton, Ohio and assigned to the Flight Test Division, duties with Cargo Test and Maintenance Directorate (C T & M) as a Flight Engineer.

From this assignment we completed over 34 harmonious and glorious years together.

When I was away on official duties in the service she had to take my place in running the family and when I was assigned to the Republic of Vietnam for a year she never got upset at all, it was my duty call.

In addition, I would also like to dedicate this book to my older brother Donald C. Kuschel, who constantly keeps pushing me to do something with my life besides talking about our childhood. Both of us are well acquainted with each other's heart attack episodes. We debate who takes the worst pills for health reasons. By the way, my brother Don is 88 years young and I follow him at 85 years young (2008).

Don enlisted in the Civilian Conservation Corp (CCC) in 1937 and went on to a tour in the Minnesota National Guard 216th—Anti Aircraft Artillery from Red Wing Minnesota. He didn't like cold weather, so he traded in his heavy winter clothes for a tour of the South Pacific Ocean with the invasion of Bougainville and later with General McArthur in the Philippines, received numerous medals and was discharged in 1946. It's too bad he wouldn't write a book of his enduring experiences with the Japanese soldier escapades, twenty four hours a day and for many months.

My thanks go out to all you good people who liked my first book "Against All Odds", and would like a follow-up of my second career episodes. By the way "All or Nothing" will point out the importance of having an education, and I do believe that you can achieve your own desired goals by using good judgement and putting education as #1 in your life.

In order to read my commendations I may elect to put them side ways so they won't appear squeezed up and be more clear to read. There are only two (2) sections that will be affected.

Marie Kuschel, My wife of 34 glorious years

My Older Brother Donald C. Kuschel

Contents

PREFACE

MY SECOND CAREER COMPACTED WITH MY FAMILY

After my twenty year career in the United States Air Force and retiring at age 36, I just couldn't stop being active and had to continue with some type of a likeable business or trade, so for six years I accomplished nothing that I really could enjoy. That is why I began looking for something in the aviation line, which I eventually found with the United States Army Aviation Material Command, Civil Service Commission in St. Louis, Missouri. I had to do something reasonable, rational and affordable to satisfy the family. One reason is that I came from a very patriotic family. My father, Ertman M. Kuschel, was in World War I and married my mother, Esther Emma Kuschel (Nadeau) on Christmas Eve, 24 December 1918, and from this marriage came five boys. Their service careers are as follows: (1) Robert enlisted in United States Army Air Corp (1942). (2) Donald enlisted in United States National Guard, 216th Army Anti-

Aircraft Artillery from Red Wing, Minnesota (1940). (3) I enlisted 12 June 1940 and retired 30 June 1960. (4) Earl enlisted in United States Navy (1942) and our youngest brother (5) Everal enlisted in the United States Air Force (1949) for the Korean War.

CHAPTER 1-
DID I QUALIFY FOR A POSITION?
YES!

After my retirement, decisions had to be made to exist in this society. Immediately after receiving my first official United States Air Force retirement check of $315.00, it wasn't enough money to buy a tooth pick to go with a glass of water, let alone enough change for a tip to leave for the waitress. The family and I talked freely of what had to be done to pay the basic bills. One consolation was that my wife was a qualified California Real Estate Broker, but that often didn't provide enough money to buy a loaf of bread and butter to put on the table, unless she closed some large real estate sales package. We had a give and take ordeal and had to weigh each option or requirement for funds. After researching all the choices of acceptable approaches, I elected to enter the electronics field using my VA education bill. My first step was to visit the Veterans Administration within the Los Angeles area. Many attempts were made because of changing government requirements on submission of required correspondence. Numerous forms had to be filled out correctly, because the amount of support would be based on the input information. So I lucked out for the maximum amount to be paid for attending. It was a good start for entering the electronics field and providing for the family. The Veterans Administration sent me an acceptance letter, so I applied to the Western Electronics Institute for a nine and a half months electronics course totaling 1,059 hours, this was for both class work and laboratory time.

I began my new 1960 civilian career by driving daily from Riverside, California to Western Electronics Institute located in Hollywood, California. [Photo 1-1] That was 52 miles one way. I did this for a while before I decided that a cheap hotel or motel would be a better solution. From the Riverside highway to Hollywood, California there was a bumper to bumper situation for no less than 39 miles, very monotonous and time consuming each day. I would arrive at Western Electronics Institute (WEI) minutes before the daily class was scheduled to start. No time to study the new notes on the blackboard or speak with the instructor. However, to change my driving habits I found a nice one room efficiency apartment one block from Western Electronics Institute that solved my problem.

If my wife wanted to visit me in Hollywood, California she had a choice of several things to do, the WEI school allowed visitors to attend classes and enjoy the technical briefings or laboratory work. This allowed the days to go by fast and allow your mind to absorb the information provided by the instructor.

The third one, go shopping, the City was large enough to engage in any of your choices. Culinary, clothing, sightseeing or be lazy, watch television, read and relax.

My old stand-by when my wife had things to do in Riverside, California was to relax in the apartment, review my notes, or go over laboratory work this was from Monday through Friday then return to Riverside, California for the weekend, which was a lots of turmoil with the heavy traffic.

After a couple of months, approximately August 1960, The Western Electronics Institute, Director Mr. George I. Alagna appointed me to be their Honor student and be on their Western Electronics Institute servicing calls, they were proud of the end results. I maintained a highly successful rate of achievement. In turn they could advertise as to the schools ability for electronic training under the G.I. Bill. All of us students were warned to prepare for the final exam on Thursday—prepare how? We all were present for 9 ½ months so what was the last day going to involve.

When I walked into the class room my attention was directed on the four class room "black boards" the test involved a continuous chain of questions, around the room, diagrams the such I had never seen before. It was a whole day of completing the electronics test!

At the end of the day it was like I was dragged, through a key hole, drained of all energies that I had at the start of the day. WHAT A TEST!

I graduated with a grade average of 90 ½. [Photo of Diploma 1-2]

A couple of days after graduating, 10 April 1961, I applied at the Sears, Roebuck & Company in Riverside, California for an electronics position and was accepted two days later. The manager gave me a top dollar position and training for two weeks. Then Sears gave me a raunchy route, reason being there were two employees that would do anything to complete an electronics service call on their route. Guess who always got the two employees customers from the previous day to correct their electronics problems? So I would get my fanny chewed royally from each of the disgruntled customers. Consequently, I had to remove each chassis and take it into the shop for repair, which should have been the responsibility of the two employees. Within two weeks I was the number one man on all of the Sears routes. In one day I sold 12 service maintenance contracts, serviced seven homes and traveled over two hundred miles. It pleased the management personnel highly and I was presented with a fairly large bonus. Because I was very conscientiously doing my Sears job and serviced several areas belonging to the Sears old fogies (20-25 years of faithful Sears service), there was no sense in me fighting with Sears managers over their favorite employees work performance. So I talked it over with my family about going into my own business near March Air Force Base, California. On my time off I surveyed the areas around the base for an ideal site. I gave Sears two week's notice. I then decided on Sunnymead, California. I had found a real nice building, reasonably priced. The owner really wanted someone available to repair his older model televisions and electronic gear that he had stored in his supply room and would sell in his store.

One of my buddies at Sears, qualified in washing machines, dryers and such, decided also to go in business in the building next to the one I contracted for. He signed the contract and we thrived in the area business. The service fees were very low keyed for the United States Air Force (USAF) personnel, so as a result the volume was tremendous. But the same thing happened with the owner; he started arguing on getting cheaper prices for his repair cost on TVs, electronics, and raising the building rent to where we were working for low wages. We could not survive. We began to look for new locations. I found one in Edgemont, California, approximately a half-mile from March Air Force Base. I took the building because of the space and availability to the highways. I didn't know the exact layout of March Air Force Base and wasn't thinking of runways heading towards the front of our new building, but they say lightning and accidents never strikes twice in the same location, so I took a chance that no aircraft would fall onto or into our building. Besides all of these things, nobody advised us about bad weather and the consequences of too much rain.

Three months later I opened Kuschel's TV, my own electronics service shop and began experiencing what it takes to be the civilian boss. Our business increased tremendously, we began selling several different named sets, Zenith, Admiral, Philco and Emerson. With numerous March Air Force Base personnel knowing of my USAF background and a former service member, I had more than enough work to do. In fact business was so good I had my Western Electronics Institute supervisor Harold

Pillsbury help to troubleshoot sets on Saturday and Sundays. I averaged eleven sets coming in each day and I repaired about the same number. There was one problem that I couldn't take much longer. On rainy days, the awful rain storms in that area would make my store leak like a sieve. Water would run down the electrical leads onto my test instruments and with the amperage and voltage on the test bench and in the walls and ceiling it was unsafe for a human being to be inside the building. So I gave up the shop and took four months off for some rest. My current TV and electronics business location had been in a precarious area as March Air Force Base runways ran right toward my entrance door. I can't give the exact date or time, but a navigator friend on a B-47 aircraft was scheduled to fly an early flight. From the knoll in front of the business you could see part of the runway. When I exited my service truck after a service call a B-47 was approximately halfway down the runway coming toward me when the next thing I saw, was a ball of flame and oil-fuel smoke went up several hundred feet and I said a silent prayer for the crew. No one was saved from the B-47 accident. It was only a short distance in a straight line to my business from where the accident happened, so we had a possible problem for any future accidents that might occur. But the scientists say lightning doesn't hit in the same place twice. That may be true, but how about an aircraft accident, what would the chance be then? That was a big question only the man above could answer.

Then the March Air Force Base Exchange manager came to me and requested that I become the first Electronics Servicing Company on any United States Air Force Base. We discussed the contract between the base and myself. It was based on a percentage factor, electric heat and maintenance was in addition.

After opening my base business I got around to mowing the grass late at night because of house calls and installing antennas after work hours.

My business needed to have a good appearance, not to look like a junk shop. I can vouch on the appearance as going beyond my efforts.

All of my electronics gear and television sets were inside the building. Then one night a burglar broke into my shop and stole all the expensive testing equipment. I had my Jackson oscilloscope in my truck so I saved that item. But the problem was my insurance company never had the chance to record serial numbers so I lost insurance funding on all the equipment. Being on March Air Force Base whoever thought this would happen, not me! So I began slowly to get necessary equipment to resume operation on base, doing a large volume of business satisfying everyone. A lot of my friends would come over and talk over old times at my shop location on the base. What happened to some of my old supervisors and working buddies?

This position lasted until the end of July 1963, when I started to get sick from working sixteen to eighteen hours per day, seven days a week. I contacted another electronics shop in Edgemont, California to take over the concessions. I didn't like this guy but he was the only one that was able to take over the business. He would present the customers with large repair bills that would choke a horse. He had no conscience problems; he only wanted to make money.

Then I went to the March Air Force Base flight surgeon Dr. Boyles. My system was all messed up. I could sleep twenty-four or more hours and never fully wake up. Dr. Boyles tested me for everything possible to get to the bottom of it. Since 1963 I had been plagued by health problems and taken many different tests, glucose testing, and physicals, that was almost my middle name, "Tests". Then I began to get well or feeling better as the end of 1963 was coming up.

When my health began to improve and I felt better I began to think of my future and what to do. Then I saw an advertisement in the Riverside newspaper that a new class for students was starting at California School of Automation specializing in International Business Machine (IBM) for computer programmers. I applied, took all the aptitude tests, passed and I enrolled for night classes. My thinking was the automation would be an enterprising experience for me. I learned that computer programmers were scarce and a premium position to hold. The school kept advising us of the position held. It would be more of a secret type of operation where you worked for one boss of that organization. He received all the IBM results and no one else; he disseminated the information to other personnel himself.

Regardless, I enjoyed each and every class gaining more knowledge of the program criteria. When the whole class was very sufficient in preparing programs, we would drive to the Lockheed Aircraft Company at the Ontario Airport and apply all the technical material into the IBM machines and behold, a typed and workable program would be available after a short time. Then we would apply all the machine information to a large sheet of program material so it made sense to whatever you decided to schedule into a feasible program, and disseminate the readable language to the workers or manager's for their input and control of any subject they required. When I became efficient in my work I graduated with honors on 3 June 1963.

One of my buddies asked me to go into the IBM School, teaching data processing to Arizona students. So a survey was ongoing, with Phoenix, Arizona as being the ideal area, so we found the correct building and leased IBM equipment. We were doing fine until the Republican Presidential candidate Barry Goldwater (R) was not doing so well. Upon winning the presidential position the Democrats took all defense work out of the state of Arizona. This time I had to declare the school closed, there was no way to get around the debts that I had accumulated. So our lawyers, accountants, and various companies did one outstanding job of clearing up all the problems with the funds I had, whereby everyone could get on with their lives. My seven employees acquired positions in schools within the Phoenix area. I stayed in Riverside, California and took a service manager position with Luds TV electronics and did very well financially, in addition, I also serviced stock machines that had input from the New York Stock Exchange to the customer.

I continued exploring civil service testing. There were no positions available and I was getting disappointed by all the turn downs. Sometime during November 1964 I put my name on a vacancy hiring list at March Air Force Base, Civilian Personnel Office (CPO) for a GS-11 position as a jet propulsion specialist. The CPO office contacted me and said I had the position and that the paperwork would be forthcoming to my residence. Before the week went by I again received word that a Lieutenant Colonel (LTC) had retired more recently than I, and might be more experienced.

In this case my name would be with-drawn, however, I kept looking, not getting depressed and wished the new propulsion person the best in that position. I knew some bases have their own rules and regulation on hiring. I believe I could have kept that position if I wanted to use Civil Service rules and sue for that job. It didn't mean that much for my ego factor, easy come, easy go. I never got discouraged and continued searching for a position by visiting all the post offices in or around Riverside, California.

To keep busy I took a temporary security guard position until 1 January 1966, then went back to be being retired. After so long showing my loyalty I had the opportunity to stay on but you can only do so much in a guard's position because the pay was small, so I moved on for greener grass.

I never gave up on getting a position that I would enjoy, there were several bases to visit and acquire information, besides I had a very experienced career in the Air Force, however, I doubt if anyone in my position would put up with my problem of not getting along with your boss for three years and not retire. Of course you can cut off your nose to spite your face, but I wasn't to give in all the time because a person doesn't understand the basic facts of management and takes the word of his "Yes" buddies to stop all sound maintenance decisions.

This was the main reason I wanted a challenging position in whatever field I elected to enter for a second career.

To enable me to stay ahead of any available positions in the government, especially Federal Government employment, I subscribed to a magazine "The Government Employee Exchange" which provided a person with available positions at bases in the Continental United States (CONUS) and overseas with the technical data required for each qualifying position. When I read the column, Technical, Professional Jobs that were open, with the United States Army Aviation Systems Command (AVSCOM) at St. Louis, Missouri, I proceeded to the Riverside Post Office for a copy to review. Upon receipt, I began to review the Aviation announcements. There were 25 aircraft equipment specialist GS-12 positions open for qualified personnel to submit correspondence.

In my case the statement was a broad view of the grades and positions available. The AVSCOM CPO was the deciding office to determine the position and grade level anyone would be offered in response to the bulletin.

When I arrived at my home in Riverside, I began a thorough research for items regarding the United States Civil Service Commission announcement #388-B, issued January 4, 1966, with no closing date. [Document Equipment Specialist 1-3] There were several options in Group I for aircraft air delivery, Aircraft Propulsion, airframe and airframe equipment, machinery, electrical and avionics. I analyzed every paragraph in my mind and realized that I was qualified for several positions. Of course I didn't know exactly how the Army worked and how they might react to my resume from my former United States Air Force career. I had my resume updated and sent to the Army Board of Civil Service

Commission, Room 410, Federal Building, 208 N. Broadway, St. Louis, Missouri, 63102. After the board's examination of my resume, I received a notice of rating from the board dated 25 March 1966, #62220 that I was eligible, that my numerical rating was for a GS-11 (90) aircraft and GS-9 (100) aircraft. [Document Notice of Rating 1-4]

For any of you that want to or who would like to be qualified in Civil Service in any form, can follow my lead or input. I was accepted into an Equipment Specialist position in aviation. Step by step it would take several paragraphs of my writing for you to be able to see the method I employed to get an approved position. Of course this day and age, everyone utilizes the computer to accomplish what I had to do in the olden golden days, using the yellow pencil with lead and eraser since changes do take place and you have to follow the rules and regulations when you decide to request a Civil Service position.

The orange colored form, announcement #388-B for a "career as an Equipment Specialist" had all the information on what experience was required for input into your resume. It also had all the pertinent information concerning all available positions that a person might want to apply for, so get out your pen or pencil and update your resume concerning your job ability and how it fits in with the United States Army, or whatever government service you want to apply for. Then dispatch it into the United States mail system to the proper addressee. (Make sure you keep a copy of your resume in case the mail is lost). Then you begin to sweat it out and wait for an answer. When the Civil Service commission sends you a notice of a rating, such as mine, dated 25 March 1966, then it's up to you to decide on your future. Remember, be sure you understand the current regulations governing the position you applied for.

To prevent any misunderstanding you will receive another letter or correspondence such as the one I received on 20 April 1966 from AVSCOM's CPO explaining all of the commands qualification requirements in great detail of what the position consists of, saying my name was certified and being considered to fill GS-1670-11, salary $8191.00 per annual as a propulsion specialist. [Letter certified 1-5] The CPO was more interested in assuring that you knew what was expected of you in the event you accepted the Equipment Specialist position. No hanky-panky when you're on the job, it's official business. Hence training and qualified, then placed in a vacant position in the United States of America, or more of a probability overseas than in the continental United States. Most generally the CPO will alert you and follow up with another letter regarding this position, title, grades and the salary.

Now it's up to you to accept or reject the offer. In the CPO letter sent to me, there was a job description outlining all future assigned duties and all other correspondence necessary to get you on board. The St. Louis CPO seemed like they were burning up the Post Office route, on 11 May 1966, I received another official letter informing me of my selection for Equipment Specialist (Aircraft Propulsion Equipment) in grade GS-11. [Letter selection 1-6]

Enclosed were several items, don't ask me what each stands for: SF78, SF79, SF514a, SF519a, Statement, Job Description, and a return envelope. The physical examination was completed at March Air Force Base, California and returned promptly to AVSCOM CPO. I filled in all blank areas requested in the letter and returned it to Department of the Army CPO for their action. Then on 24 May 1966 they replied to me that I had a confirmed selected position as an Equipment Specialist position (aircraft propulsion equipment) GS-1670-11 and all the information required to fulfill the job and what to expect. [Letter confirming 1-7]

So on 27 May 1966 I called Mr. Stein and told him that I would be at AVSCOM on 6 June 1966, and I was immediately accepted based on all information sent in and that I would be in St. Louis, Missouri on 6 June 1966 to be sworn in that day. The government would not pay for moving my household goods unless I had a permanent change of station (PCS) further than Riverside to St. Louis. I had a specific thirty day time limit to accept the equipment specialist position, reason being that AVSCOM had a world-wide commitment to provide trained personnel for the United States Army Aviation Units. The position, if I accepted, required me to be fully trained and qualified to instruct the T-55 Gas Turbine Engine on the CH-47 (Chinook) helicopter.

One of the prerequisites was to take inoculations required for world-wide assignment. I drove to Norton Air Force Base, California. The doctor advised me I would have to get approximately twenty-one shots.

A few days later I got up enough courage to begin the shot ordeal and went to Norton Air Force Base and reported into the Inoculation Clinic. There was a doctor and a nurse on duty. After a few minutes of discussion regarding my worldwide assignment, the nurse opened up a large cabinet type locker on the wall that had maps showing around the world locations, that all armed forces personnel honored with different required inoculations for each country. Low and behold, in my case I would still be required the twenty-one shots, no change in my status or locations. The shots had to be taken within twenty days and some of them were wicked or rough ones to endure. I just knew that taking the shots would please Norton Air Force Base and AVSCOM. So I told the nurse to begin, that twenty days was too short of a period to complete twenty-one shots, and immediately my arms began to feel like a pin cushion and sore as boils. The nurse had a smile on her face to show her satisfaction. After my first few shots were began to be administered and be on a time schedule for more, to enable me to report into St. Louis, Missouri on 6 June 1966. So I advised the doctor I would return for the easier shots if there was such a thing. I asked, "Was there an easier way to take shots?" and the doctor said, "NO!"

But the fact is while assigned to the Strategic Air Command (SAC), I was given inoculations every six months regardless of any scheduled duties, and yes, I hated those shots. My tour of duties in SAC was twelve years so you can guess the number of shots that I had to take. By the time I got home that day, my arms were twice the size of normal ones and if anybody would slap you on the arm or shoulder area it would be war, or plain stomp day. So before I left Riverside, I had the required twenty-one shots that was stipulated and completed for any location around the world. I felt safe and AVSCOM could assign me to any area they desired.

One thing I found out was if a need for a specific technical specialty was required by any country worldwide you had to be available for a twenty-four hour departure, including a valid passport with visa for that area. Again I kissed the wife good-by and departed Riverside 2 June 1966 for St. Louis, Missouri in my little yellow American Motor Corporation (AMC) station wagon which was packed for the trip. Little did I know what the future held for me and where I was going to be sent for assignment.

Gas for the wagon varied from twenty-two to thirty-eight cents a gallon. Then when I arrived in Flagstaff, Arizona it was really atrocious at forty-five cents per gallon. That was the going price in Flagstaff. My feelings were the people were being gouged and the oil companies were getting rich. (Look at today's 2009 prices, over $3.00 per gallon.) What an experience you achieve driving, eating and sleeping in run down motels and restaurants, but I was saving money, ha ha! You were plain uncomfortable, with not even fans or any type of air conditioning. Since I didn't know the highway or weather routes a person could think that these were the comforts of home. I suffered with the heat since no motel had air conditioning on this road. Truthfully the motels were saving money on their electric bills.

The third day on the highway I arrived on the outskirts of St. Louis, this was on the 5th of June 1966 so I was in good shape, time wise. Since I could not sleep the morning of the 6th because of the anxiety of a new position or job, my wake up sense had my internal alarm set for five o'clock. My breakfast was a fast one, and I arrived at the United States Army Aviation Systems Command, Mart Building, 12th and Spruce at 0700 a.m. There were a few early birds going into their offices, like all eager beavers in Federal Service, be it military or civilian. Of course traffic might be the culprit for early arrival times.

I reported into the United States Army Aviation System Command (AVSCOM) Civilian Personnel Office (CPO) at 0730 a.m. where they provided me with all kinds of manuals, army regulations, and local AVSCOM information to be used in my new position. My assigned escort Charley Cox was a member of the Maintenance Director for Technical Assistance where I was to be assigned, he took me to all the AVSCOM offices I would be working with and introduced me to their personnel, those I might have to touch base with, when and if I was permanently assigned to the Republic of Vietnam (RVN). This statement about Vietnam was lightly discussed until about 4:00 p.m. on 6 June 1966 (1600 hours military time) I was escorted into a room that AVSCOM CPO was assigned, that had the United States and United States Army flags in one corner of the room. There were upwards to twenty personnel, that were to be sworn in at one time and since I was of a higher grade Civil Service employee I was going to be the last one that day. My swearing in ceremony took place at 1630 on 6 June 1966, then everyone shook hands and departed. On this special occasion, time and date, the CPO presented me with correspondence of an Official PCS order effective in six months to Saigon, RVN for a one year tour of duty. One stipulation, I had to be completely and well qualified to instruct the T-55 Gas Turbine Engine utilized on the CH-47 (Chinook) helicopter prior to December 1966, pending departure from Travis AFB, California, to Vietnam. [Notice of Personnel Action 1-7a] [Job Description 1-7 b&c]

Since I had an approved United States of America, Department of Commerce, Civil Aeronautics Administration #641863 dated 5/27/48 for

Aircraft Engine Mechanic, I was assigned to the AVSCOM gas turbine propulsion section, because when I was assigned to the pilot training class at Randolph Air Force Base, Texas, a group of us became interested in fulfilling an aircraft engine mechanics course. That was for our intent to have something to fall back on besides the pilot training. There was always a chance of failing the course or washing out. [Document CAA 1-8]

The Mart building was a large, permanent structure 18 floors high for approximately 7,000 personnel, numerous agencies, and Directorates. It was centrally located with a police station next door, mayor's office a few blocks away, the baseball stadium five blocks away. I was surprised it was so large. When you were in the interior, there were so many agency offices and Directorates that it was confusing to understand. However, with so many personnel being assigned to the United States Army Aviation Systems Command in St. Louis, they had representatives all over the world on any type of aviation equipment with the Mart building being the hub of them all. [Photo Mart Building 1-9]

The Directorate of Maintenance kept me in St. Louis for a familiarization period to acquaint me with the complete command structure and who the various Directorates were that would intertwine with my duty assignment in CONUS or overseas, and whom I would contact in the event of any problems that developed. I will say one thing, the AVSCOM personnel were well adjusted in supporting all aircraft, equipment and troop requirements regardless of what or who in the Directorate was responsible. The command staff had their fingers on the organizations pulse, which made me feel comfortable in accepting this position and being assigned as an AAMTAP instructor in CONUS or assigned to Vung Tau, Vietnam.

WESTERN *Electronics* INSTITUTE

Photo 1-1 Western Electronics Institute

Western Electronics Institute
Vocational School

This Certifies that **Wayne A. Kuschel**
has satisfactorily completed the requirements for Graduation in
Radio-Television-Electronics
and is therefore awarded this

Diploma

Given at Los Angeles, California this 10th day of April 1961

_____
Director

_____
Associate Director

Document 1-2
Western Electronics Institute Diploma

UNITED STATES CIVIL ⬤RVICE COMMISSION
Washington, D. C., 20415

⬤ Announcement No. 388-B
Issued: January 4, 1966
No Closing Date

CAREERS AS AN

EQUIPMENT SPECIALIST

FOR EMPLOYMENT THROUGHOUT THE UNITED STATES AND OVERSEAS

IN THE FOLLOWING OPTIONS:

GROUP I	Aircraft Specialties GS-9, GS-11, GS-12
	Electrical GS-9, GS-11, GS-12
	Machinery GS-9, GS-11, GS-12
GROUP II	Electronics GS-9, GS-11, GS-12
GROUP III	Automotive GS-9, GS-11, GS-12
GROUP IV	Missile Maintenance GS-12 only

AT THE FOLLOWING SALARIES:

GS-9	$ 7,479
GS-11	$ 8,961
GS-12	$10,619

See page 5 for Instructions on WHERE TO APPLY

Document 1-3
Equipment Specialist

APPLICANT MUST FILL IN ALL BLANKS DOWN TO HEAVY BLACK LINE

EXACT TITLE OF EXAMINATION	DATE OF EXAMINATION
EQUIPMENT SPECIALIST	UNASSEMBLED

NAME: Mr. Wayne A. Kuschel

ADDRESS:

CITY, STATE AND ZIP CODE: 4175 Adams Street

Riverside, California 92204

This is not a notice of appointment. It is a record of your rating. It is important that you keep it. It is noted that your application was not rated for any position with a lower entrance salary than that which you indicated thereon.

Your Rating is — ELIGIBLE

☐ This examination is not rated on a numerical basis
☒ Your numerical rating is: GS-11   90.   Aircraft
                                              GS-9   100.   "

Your Rating is — INELIGIBLE for the reasons checked below:

☐ The lowest acceptable salary indicated on your application is higher than the salary shown on our announcement.
☐ You did not pass the written test. All competitors must attain an earned rating of 70 without regard to veteran preference. When an applicant's paper falls below the passing mark it is not scored further. Ineligibles do not receive a numerical grade.
☐ Your application does not show that you meet the minimum requirements as to experience (or education) which were specified in the examination announcement.
☐ Your eligibility is suspended pending your furnishing the Commission proof of correction of physical condition, as shown on the attached notice.
☐ Failed to reply to official correspondence.

☐

IF THERE IS A CHECK BELOW, IT INDICATES THE AMOUNT OF VETERAN PREFERENCE CREDIT INCLUDED IN YOUR RATING

☒ 5 POINTS—IF YOU ARE APPOINTED YOU WILL BE REQUIRED TO FURNISH TO THE APPOINTING OFFICER EVIDENCE OF HONORABLE SEPARATION FROM THE ARMED FORCES.   ☐ 10 POINTS

If you have received an eligible rating, be sure to read the important message on the back of this form.

MAR 25 1966

ARMY BOARD, U.S. Civil Service Examiners
Room 410 Federal Building
208 North Broadway
St. Louis, Missouri 63102

Document 1-4
Notice of Rating March 25, 1966

DEPARTMENT OF THE ARMY
U.S. ARMY AVIATION MATERIEL COMMAND
12TH AND SPRUCE STREETS
ST. LOUIS, MISSOURI 63166

20 April 1966

Mr. Wayne A. Kuschel
4175 Adams Street
Riverside, California 92504

Dear Mr. Kuschel:

Your name, among others, has been certified by the U. S. Civil
Service Commission for consideration in filling a position as Equipment Specialist (Aircraft Propulsion Equipment), GS-1670-11, $8961
per annum, with this Command.

The U. S. Army Aviation Materiel Command is a logistical command
providing global support for the Army Aviation mission, including the
gamut of aeronautical engineering, plus procurement, inventory management, depot maintenance, including aircraft and aerial delivery equipment.

In the position of Equipment Specialist the incumbent maintains
continuing contact with the command and close liaison with the U. S.
Air Force, the U. S. Navy, and aircraft manufacturers to assure constant cognizance of the latest maintenance engineering data, such as
engineering change proposals, blueprint changes, microfilm, factory
bulletins, and other data pertinent to his assigned type of equipment.
Investigates, analyzes, and corrects diverse and complicated operational and mechanical problems requiring intensive knowledge covering
maintenance and construction of his assigned types of equipment. Makes
occasional flights as technical observer to determine causes of malfunctions. Researches and assembles information for classroom training
purposes and based on practical experience and ingenuity, conducts
classes for maintenance and operational personnel. Represents the
command at Army supply and maintenance conferences, National Guard
conferences, and other top level meetings and conferences to discuss
maintenance and operating procedures. Prepares and submits written
reports at predetermined intervals to the command, indicating clearly
and factually the nature of tasks accomplished, trouble encountered,
and corrective measures taken or adopted.

Letter 1-5
Certified Letter 20 April 1966 page 1

19

This position for which you are being considered is under the Command's Technical Assistance Program and requires that all candidates be available for world-wide assignment and frequent travel, and selected candidates will be required to sign a statement to this effect as a condition of employment.

You are requested to complete and return the attached Optional Form 5 by 27 *April 1966* to insure further consideration. Candidates finally selected will be required to be available to enter on duty within 30 days after notification of final selection, and in any event no later than 30 June 1966.

Sincerely yours,

EUGENE W. MEYER
Chief, Employment and
Services Branch

2 Incl
1. OF-5
2. Return Envelope

Letter 1-5
Certified Letter 20 April 1966 page 2

20

DEPARTMENT OF THE ARMY
U.S. ARMY AVIATION MATERIEL COMMAND
12TH AND SPRUCE STREETS
ST. LOUIS, MISSOURI

MAILING ADDRESS
P.O. BOX 209
ST. LOUIS, MO 63166

IN REPLY REFER TO
SMOSM-RCS

11 May 1966

Mr. Wayne A. Kuschel
4175 Adams Street
Riverside, California 92504

Dear Mr. Kuschel:

This is to inform you of your selection for the position of Equipment Specialist (Aircraft Propulsion Equipment), GS-1670-11, $8961 per annum, with this Command, contingent upon satisfactory completion of physical examination, pre-employment inquiries, and security check.

Inclosed are the physical examination forms which must be completed by yourself and the physician conducting the examination. This examination can be given by any currently licensed doctor of medicine or osteopathy. You may also arrange to have the physical examination conducted by a Federal medical facility or U. S. Public Health Service. Upon completion of the examination, the forms are to be returned to this office, ATTENTION: F. J. Steins, as soon as possible. Any expense incurred in this matter must be borne by yourself.

This position is in this Command's Directorate of Maintenance and selected candidates such as yourself will serve in the Army Aircraft Mobile Technical Assistance Program (AAMTAP). Attached is a recently developed job description for the position in question to provide you with some advance information. The position requires world-wide availability for assignment and travel. Also inclosed is a Statement of Availability which all selected candidates must complete.

After receipt of all the preceding material by this office, you will be contacted concerning a starting date.

Sincerely yours,

EUGENE W. MEYER
Chief, Employment and
Services Branch

7 Incl
  1. SF-78
  2. SF-89
  3. SF-514A
  4. SF-519A
  5. Statement
  6. Job Description
  7. Return Envelope

Letter 1-6
Selection Letter May 11, 1966

DEPARTMENT OF THE ARMY
U.S. ARMY AVIATION MATERIEL COMMAND
12TH AND SPRUCE STREETS
ST. LOUIS, MISSOURI

MAILING ADDRESS
P.O. BOX 209
ST. LOUIS, MO 63166

IN REPLY REFER TO
SMOSM-RCS

24 May 1966

Mr. Wayne A. Kuschel
4175 Adams Street
Riverside, California 92504

Dear Mr. Kuschel:

This is to confirm your selection for the position of Equipment Specialist (Aircraft Propulsion Equipment), GS-1670-11, $8961 per annum, with this Command.

Initial processing has been satisfactorily completed and you are now asked to contact Mr. Francis J. Steins, this office, MAin 2-3772, and inform him of the date you will be available to begin work with this Command.

You are advised that since you are a new appointee to Federal civilian service, this office does not have authority to provide you or your dependents with transportation or for movement of your household goods. Since you will be in St. Louis for a short period for orientation prior to proceeding TDY for training, it is suggested that you do not relocate your family at this time.

Inclosed for your information is a map of St. Louis and the surrounding area.

This office looks forward to your entrance on duty with this Command.

Sincerely yours,

EUGENE W. MEYER
Chief, Employment and
Services Branch

1 Incl
as

Called Mr. Stein 1300, 27 May 66 stated I would be thru on Monday 6 June 1966

Letter 1-7
Confirmation Letter May 24, 1966

STANDARD FORM 50—Rev. December 1961
U.S. Civil Service Commission
FPM Chap. 235

6 June 66
5 PART
50-126-02

NOTIFICATION OF PERSONNEL ACTION

(EMPLOYEE — See General Information on Reverse)

P298-65   vs

(FOR AGENCY USE)

1. NAME (CAPS) LAST—FIRST—MIDDLE	MR.—MISS—MRS.	2. (FOR AGENCY USE)	3. BIRTH DATE (Mo., Day, Year)	4. SOCIAL SECURITY NO.
KUSCHEL, WAYNE AUGUST	MR.	36617	12-06-23	████████

5. VETERAN PREFERENCE	6. TENURE GROUP	7. SERVICE COMP. DATE	8. PHYSICAL HANDICAP CODE
2 1—NO 3—10 PT. DISAB. 5—10 PT. OTHER 2—5 PT. 4—10 PT. COMP.	2	02-01-56	00

9. FEGLI	10. RETIREMENT	11. (FOR CSC USE)
1 1—COVERED 2—INELIGIBLE 3—WAIVED	1 1—CS 3—FS 5—OTHER 2—FICA 4—NONE	

12. CODE	NATURE OF ACTION	13. EFFECTIVE DATE (Mo., Day, Year)	14. CIVIL SERVICE OR OTHER LEGAL AUTHORITY
101	Career Conditional Appointment-RETO	06-06-66	Cert. #D66-91 St. Louis Army Bd of CSC Exam 04-18-66

15. FROM: POSITION TITLE AND NUMBER	16. PAY PLAN AND OCCUPATION CODE	17. GRADE OR LEVEL	18. SALARY

19. NAME AND LOCATION OF EMPLOYING OFFICE

20. TO: POSITION TITLE AND NUMBER	21. PAY PLAN AND OCCUPATION CODE	22. GRADE OR LEVEL	23. SALARY
Equipment Specialist (Aircraft Propulsion Equipment) JN 9561	GS-1670	11/1	pa $8961

24. NAME AND LOCATION OF EMPLOYING OFFICE
U.S. Army Aviation Materiel Command, Directorate of Maintenance, Technical Assistance Division, Technical Support Branch, St. Louis, Missouri

25. DUTY STATION (City—county—State)	26. LOCATION CODE
Republic of South Vietnam	95-7000-945

27. APPROPRIATION	28. POSITION OCCUPIED	29. APPORTIONED POSITION
23L0.10223.A011MA UMA OK	1 1—COMPETITIVE SERVICE 2—EXCEPTED SERVICE	FROM: TO: STATE 1—PROVED-1 2—WAIVED-2

30. REMARKS:	X	A. SUBJECT TO COMPLETION OF 1 YEAR PROBATIONARY (OR TRIAL) PERIOD COMMENCING	06-06-66
	X	B. SERVICE COUNTING TOWARD CAREER (OR PERMANENT) TENURE FROM:	06-06-66

SEPARATIONS: SHOW REASONS BELOW, AS REQUIRED. CHECK IF APPLICABLE: C. DURING PROBATION   D. FROM APPOINTMENT OF 6 MONTHS OR LESS

Selected from AVCOM Career Referral List 212-66 dated 04-28-66.

Leave Category - 0

RETO/AF/06-30-60/A02099311/0-4/nonreg/20/noncmbt

Entrance Performance Rating: Satisfactory

31. DATE OF APPOINTMENT AFFIDAVIT (Accessions only)	34. SIGNATURE (Or other authentication) AND TITLE
06-06-66	**FOR THE APPOINTING OFFICER**
32. OFFICE MAINTAINING PERSONNEL FOLDER (If different from employing office)	*Katherine R. Greer* KATHERINE R. GREER, Act Appointment Unit Supv Employment and Services Branch

33. CODE	EMPLOYING DEPARTMENT OR AGENCY	35. DATE	
AR 12	DEPARTMENT OF THE ARMY	06-03-66	2298

1-7a Notice of Personnel Action

DEPARTMENT OF THE ARMY **JOB DESCRIPTION** (DA CPPM I and CPR P30)	1. INSTALLATION OR HEADQUARTERS OFFICE **U.S. ARMY AVIATION MATERIEL COMMAND**		2. JOB NUMBER **9561**
3. CITATION TO APPLICABLE STANDARD AND ITS DATE OF ISSUANCE	4. TITLE Equipment Specialist (Aircraft Propulsion Equipment)		
	5. PAY SCHEDULE GS	6. OCC. CODE 1670	7. GRADE 11
8. EVALUATION APPROVAL Title, pay schedule, code and grade of this job have been fixed in accordance with Department of the Army official policy and grade level standards.	SIGNATURE *M. Lawrence Shannon* M. LAWRENCE SHANNON		DATE 29 Mar 66

9. SUPERVISORY CONTROLS, DUTIES, AND WORKING CONDITIONS (Indicate percent of time for each duty, where pertinent.) (Continue statement of duties, etc., on reverse side if necessary.)

SUPERVISORY CONTROLS

Work is performed in an assigned area overseas or within CONUS under the general direction and administrative supervision of a supervisor located in St. Louis, Missouri and under the general guidance of a higher graded Equipment Specialist. Detached duty station results in incumbent's receiving broad policy guidance outlines on objectives to be accomplished at time of assignment. Has wide latitude in exercising independent judgment in accomplishing assignments which are clearly covered by applicable maintenance policies and procedures. Confers with higher graded employee in the solution of the most difficult problems or unprecedented matters. Adequacy of performance is judged through analysis of written reports, oral reports, and personal visitation.

MAJOR DUTIES

As a representative of the command with duty station located overseas or within CONUS, incumbent serves as a technical expert and advisor in the maintenance of a specific series of reciprocating or turbine propulsion equipment used in the make-up of Army aircraft. Under the guidance of a higher graded employee, furnishes specialized advice, assistance, and instructions to Department of the Army personnel in maintenance, adjustment, repair, servicing, testing, processing, packaging, preservation, assembly, in-storage maintenance, and modification of his assigned aircraft propulsion equipment.

1. Maintains continuing contact with the command and close liaison with the U. S. Air Force, the U. S. Navy, and aircraft manufacturers to assure constant cognizance of the latest maintenance engineering data, such as engineering change proposals, blueprint changes, microfilm, factory bulletins, and other data pertinent to his assigned type of aircraft propulsion equipment. Assists in the development of proposed changes to DA maintenance publication, maintenance procedures, and practices. Investigates, analyzes, and corrects diverse and complicated operational and mechanical problems requiring thorough knowledge covering maintenance and construction of his

10.	JOB-CONTENT APPROVAL (Complete on organization file copy only.)	
ORGANIZATION LOCATION		
	THIS STATEMENT ACCURATELY DESCRIBES THE WORK REQUIRED IN ONE POSITION OR IN EACH OF A GROUP OF POSITIONS IN THE ABOVE ORGANIZATION.	THE ABOVE DESCRIPTION, WITH SUPPLEMENTAL MATERIAL, IS ADEQUATE FOR PURPOSES OF EVALUATION.
	SIGNATURE OF APPROVING SUPERVISOR	SIGNATURE OF ANALYST

11.		REAUDIT APPROVAL			
DATE					
SUPERVISOR'S APPROVAL					
ANALYST'S SIGNATURE					

DA FORM 374   PREVIOUS EDITIONS OF THIS FORM ARE OBSOLETE

1-7 b Job Description #9561 page 1

assigned type of Army aircraft propulsion equipment. Participates in the investigation of deficiencies for the purpose of establishing areas that should be reported for equipment improvement. Makes occasional flights as technical observer to determine causes of malfunctions, such as improper fuel adjustment or flow, improper ignition system operation, origin of unusual noises, unusual vibrations, improper valve train adjustment or functioning, abnormal rpm indications, etc.

2. Assists in the research and assembly of information for classroom training purposes and based on practical experience and ingenuity, conducts classes (including lectures and demonstrations) for maintenance and operational (military and civil service) personnel in the maintenance and operation of assigned type of aircraft propulsion equipment. Further, effects training required by instructing all Department of the Army personnel or by training of maintenance personnel and overseeing their subsequent training of other troops. Assists in conducting on-the-job training by demonstration and/or overseeing troops conducting maintenance at actual site to insure proper methods and techniques are used. Slants training toward preventive maintenance to avert engine breakdown and deadline of equipment. Also, assembles and prepares on request of installation commanders, direction from higher authority, or observation in the field, a wide variety of information from technical and administrative publications (including TO's, TM's, SB's, TAB's, AR's, SR's, etc.).

3. As required, represents the command at Army supply and maintenance conferences, National Guard conferences, and other top level meetings and conferences to discuss maintenance and operating procedures and is empowered to make commitments and decisions which are normally accepted as final. Renders technical advice and assistance to accident investigation boards in determining cause or probable cause of accidents, corrective and/or preventive action to be taken, and recommends applicable product changes and modifications. As required, inspects and furnishes analysis of engine damage and recommends repair methods, repair levels, and/or engine salvage. Makes periodic trips to manufacturers or training agencies to maintain current knowledge of assigned propulsion equipment and to keep abreast of the latest maintenance and operating procedures.

4. Prepares and submits written reports at predetermined intervals to the command, indicating clearly and factually the nature of tasks accomplished, trouble encountered, corrective measures taken or adopted, recommendations made and to whom made, and any other pertinent information related to the general adequacy of maintenance facilities, parts supply, tools, and publications.

Performs other duties as assigned.

NOTE: Travel for TDY will be made by commercial or military aircraft as directed by superiors. Involves temporary assignments requiring world-wide travel.

(Title and grade are established in accordance with position classification standards and guides. These materials are available for your review in the Civilian Personnel Division.)

1-7c Job Description #9561 page 2

1	2	3	4	5	6
80 A	90 A	87 A	83 A	83 A	

WAYNE AUGUST KUSCHEL

UPO 1, BOX 1285

RANDOLPH FIELD, TEXAS

Director, Airman Service

C GPO-769926

Document 1-8
Department of Commerce, Civil Aeronautics Administration,
Aircraft Engine Mechanic May 27, 1948

Photo 1-9 Mart Building

CHAPTER 2-
TRAVELING FOR TRAINING,
COAST TO COAST

I was using the accommodations at the YMCA for my stay in St. Louis, Missouri. The facility was wonderful and well located near the Mart building. The Technical Assistance Office on Friday, 10 June 1966, provided me with travel orders to be at Fort Sill, Oklahoma, Monday, 13 June 1966, to attend a ten day course on the T-55 Gas Turbine Engine installed on the CH-47 (Chinook) helicopter. [Document Travel Orders 2-1]

In all my years of service, my experience was always "jet engines" on all the aircraft that I have flown or maintained. This was going to be a real challenge. One other area I was never told anything about was my college degree. However, I believe I was a threat to a lot of managers that did not have one, because at that time education was on everyone's mind, or it was being pushed for filling some sensitive positions. But it seemed like management had high ideas for my skills, experience, knowledge and other education factors.

I reported at 0800 on 13 June 1966 to the big hangar at Fort Sill, Oklahoma which was next to the flight line for the ten day course of instruction with Mr. Charles Gerau being the T-55 engine instructor. Chuck Gerau and I became good friends. He taught me additional items to keep me one step ahead of the normal attendees. Chuck's family was my family away from home. It was nice to have these friends and I appreciated this short tour of duty.

On duty I met the other members of my team, and it became an all-day study, lecturing and instruction for the United States Army Aviation personnel. After ten days of instruction, I graduated 24 June 1966 and I was told to stay on at Fort Sill and assist the instructor on the T-55 gas turbine engine by going to the flight line and applying our knowledge to the actual T-55 engine installed on the CH-47 (Chinook). It was a joy for hands-on learning, of what I would encounter in the field. My Department of Army certificate of training is being shown as an example of the good work involved by AVSCOM personnel. [Document Certificate of Training 2-2]

Since I completed the T-55 Gas Turbine Course on CH-47 (Chinook) aircraft 24th day of June, 1966, at no time was any other requirements for additional gas turbine engine courses conveyed to me or any consideration of such. However, as time went by the Technical Assistance personnel kept advising me that I had the education and experience on reciprocating engines, jet engines and now on T-55 gas turbine engines to qualify on any additional training on T-53 utilized on UH-1 (Huey) helicopters. It didn't dawn on me that I was being considered for the new T-53—L-13 which was beginning entry into the United States Army Supply System.

I received word that my request for Visas was submitted to Washington, D. C. on 27 June 1966 and would be required by 1 August 1966. Mr. Gerau also advised me that he was to provide AVSCOM Technical Assistance Office a report on my progression for instructing and any special abilities I had shown. This requirement would be an ongoing requirement until I finished training and became a fully qualified instructor. This involved only the T-55 gas turbine engine. After my T-55 gas turbine engine course and becoming a qualified instructor, I was provided sufficient graduation certifications (DA Form 87, 1 September 54) to sign, the Commanding General would have already signed the certificate, and in turn the United States Army units would recognize the certificate and would be recorded on the soldier's records as qualified. [Document Certificate of Training 2-3]

To have maintenance management personnel begin thinking of my future, in any special executive job, when and if I returned from an overseas assignment sounded great. Little did I know that Vietnam would escalate my career into a grade of GS-12 prior to returning, and I was just then to begin my Civil Service career to a final GS-14 grade. Then I would be sent to the pasture for a permanent spot to enjoy life. The Fort Sill gas turbine engine school that I had attended was so easy to understand that it was like second nature to me. The easy part I liked was to instruct, which I had plenty of in the Air Force, and with a good propulsion engine curriculum to teach from, it was the one thing that kept me going. Each time I began to research the technical manuals I gained a tremendous wealth of mechanical theory and applications abilities. It didn't seem like I had been at Fort Sill fifteen days, but it was time. My oral orders on 25 June 1966 were changed, so I began my return travel to AVSCOM St. Louis for more coordination efforts and work in the office, plus visiting all the Directorates again for more input from engineering, procurement, maintenance and the Project Manager's Office (PMO).

Everyone gave a special effort to acquaint me with any possible T-55 gas turbine engine problems that might arise in any of my assignment's or duty stations. After my short stay at AVSCOM, guess what? I received my letter dated 28 June 1966, with travel orders for sixty days to Fort Rucker, Alabama, and Fort Benning, Georgia. [Document travel orders 2-4] I was in contact with my office in AVSCOM for any changes that would be involved during my travel. It was time for temporary duty (TDY) training at Fort Rucker, Alabama. I proceeded and was given sufficient travel time to arrive on time for the scheduled date. This time frame was soon after Dr. Martin Luther King, Jr. situation in Selma, Alabama. When I arrived in Memphis, Tennessee, there were no demonstrations but the closer I got to Selma it looked like a tender situation. Early in the afternoon I pulled into a restaurant on the outskirts of Selma, Alabama. When I walked into the restaurant there were both white and African-Americans sitting around. There was no chit-chat going on, but I could feel that there were sympathy and remorseful feelings within the café. I had my meal, without any talking going on. It looked like the people were being hit with reality of King's ordeal, and what course would have to be taken in order for all people to come together and work together. I was real shook up because of the rumors and possible repercussions from statements made over the airways. It didn't appear like there would be any problems, Thank God!

There was another Fort to be included in my new travel itinerary. That was Fort Eustis, Virginia, for the T53—L13 Lycoming Factory Engine Course. This location was on the coast of the Atlantic Ocean. So I've come from California to St. Louis, back to Fort Sill, Oklahoma return to St. Louis, Missouri then to Fort Rucker, Alabama, Fort Benning, Georgia and then to Fort Eustis, Virginia coast to coast. All of this would occur during a six-month training episode, June to December 1966, and I would be qualified on three different gas turbine engines. And then during December 1966, I would travel to Travis AFB, California then to Republic of Vietnam (RVN).

About seventy miles from Dothan, Alabama, I pulled into a motel as it was warm and the road was getting longer ahead of me. I could not afford an accident. After daybreak the next day, I got on the road again and pulled into the motel in the big city of Dothan, Alabama population about 50,000. I believe it was structured around Fort Rucker Army Air

Base. The army personnel were the only thing keeping the town operating, doing business of housing personnel. I arrived at Fort Rucker, Alabama on 5 July 1966, and went into more training on the Chinook helicopter's T-55 gas turbine engines.

Things were looking up. We would solve one problem and another problem would appear. But time was getting short so all of us worked extra hours to complete the discrepancies. All the United States Army Aviation Maintenance personnel were happy with the end results, because of the expertise provided by the team members.

A couple of weeks later we had an unexpected guest, a supervisor from the AVSCOM Technical Assistance team. They called a meeting and told me I was definitely going to instruct on the CH-47 (Chinook) helicopter, T-55-L-11 gas turbine engine and in addition, the old T-53-L-11, plus the new Lycoming engine T-53-L-13 used on various UH-1 (Huey) aviation assigned units. This would be called a triple threat and I would be utilized more effectively on three propulsion systems. I was the only AVSCOM Technical Assistance person qualified on three different engines.

While at Fort Rucker I worked in conjunction with our AVSCOM Technical Assistance team. There was another Huey T-53-L-11 propulsion specialist by the name of Steve Bilinsky. He took me in hand and showed me the ropes of how and why you did things by the book.

Our duty station was on Cairns Army Air Field, all of us were residing at various spots. I found a very nice, clean motel in Enterprise, Alabama, about eighteen miles away. You could never get lost whichever direction you drove, you would be at the monument in the center of the town. It was an awful quiet town, but I really did enjoy it.

On weekends of course, our buddies always had a barbeque that got us all together and talking shop. All this time I gained more knowledge on the propulsion equipment. The Huey propulsion team instructed me on the older model T-53-L-11 engine. I received as many manuals as I could scrounge from everyone. When I would get back to my motel room I would read, and go over all the sections on what had to be accomplished in troubleshooting and mechanically repairing all gas turbine engines to keep the helicopters in the air.

When Chuck Gerau submitted my first progress report on 31 August 1966 to AVSCOM, it sounded like I was doing things correctly. A copy was sent to my Fort Rucker address. [Letter Progress Report 2-5]

On my fourth week at Fort Rucker, my buddy Steve Bilinsky was going to have a small party for all of us "experts". His motel was in the center of Dothan, a town with a "dry" drinking law for the county. Most of us never paid any attention to it, as the beer would be purchased when you went near the strip and taken to the motel on your return there. So this one night the sheriff converged on our social party since we were sitting in full view of the residence, people in cars traveling up and down the streets notified us that we were in violation of the city ordinance and would have to do our beer drinking inside. The police officer whom visited us was very polite and understanding, so to prevent any further complications we went into the motel. By the way, I am a social drinker, one is enough for me.

On Monday, 1 August 1966, I was on the road again to Fort Benning, Georgia. Utilizing a verbal go-ahead from AVSCOM. (Then on 8 September 1966 AVSCOM amended my Letter Order 9-17 for a complete trip to Fort Rucker, Alabama, Fort Benning, Georgia and Fort Eustis, Virginia for 150 days).

It wasn't too far and once more I reported in to headquarters Fort Benning with assignment to a CH-47 (Chinook) special aviation unit. [Document travel orders 2-6]

There was an ad in the local paper about a house trailer for rent so I searched out the owner and rented it. I found out he was a real friendly person. After leasing it, then unloading my clothes and equipment, it felt like home. The owner liked to fish, so on Saturdays or Sundays he would take me out in the country to his ponds or lakes. Heck, we caught so many fish it got to where there was no fun in fishing! Then we would have a big catfish fry and everyone in the neighborhood was invited.

The people all locals, were very friendly and would help you in anyway required if you asked them. Eating places were outstanding for any type of food you wanted.

In touring around, they had acres upon acres of property that were stacked with piles of pine trees that looked like fence posts but they were being used for many products. Driving near the saw mill area, you had to be very careful as the roads were very narrow and winding. The big trucks with trailers carrying logs were transporting them all over the state, to various destinations for all types of wood products and usage. The trucks desired the whole road for maneuvering the trailers. If you were careful no accidents happened, and no filling out of accident reports which would be time-consuming action and expensive.

Mr. Gerau submitted my ongoing progress report dated 30 September 1966 that was very satisfactory and he felt I would be eligible for overseas duty by December 1966. [Letter progress report 2-7]

After two months here, at Fort Benning, Georgia I again was given AVSCOM's verbal orders on 28 October 1966 to proceed immediately to Fort Eustis, Virginia be there no later than 31 October 1966 to attend a Lycoming Factory engine course on the T-53-L-13 turbine engine. This was the latest and newest gas turbine engine configuration to enter the army supply system or inventory during 1966. I did not learn what the reason was for my expedited departure from Fort Benning, Georgia to Fort Eustis, Virginia. My oral communications with AVSCOM personnel were always correct, because my typed orders was an estimate date and unreliable, only general terms.

When I began the 15 day or 120 hour Fort Eustis propulsion turbine T-53—L-13 school, taught by Lycoming factory personnel, they were not too happy or friendly with us, so we had to take it one day at a time. We were tested and verbally questioned all through the course. It wasn't a difficult course as long as you paid attention in the classroom. But it appeared to me like the Lycoming personnel were making it as difficult on the AVSCOM personnel as possible. I knew no reason for this problem or happening as the AVSCOM had a paid contract with Lycoming for instructing army personnel. I called my supervisor in St. Louis to ascertain what the problem was. Mr. Bartley advised me that the Army was to inventory everything in order to take over the Lycoming engine contract immediately in Vietnam since it had been over a year, but it was up to the Army to make the final decision one way or the other. So that was the main reason that I was attending the T-53-L-13 course at Fort Eustis. At this time Bernie Reece was at Fort Eustis tentatively as my teammate to instruct in Vietnam. Then at Vung Tau we would team up and instruct the T-53-L-13 course at the AAMTAP School.

However, I heard through the grapevine, the rumor was true that the United States Army Aviation Systems Command was not going to renew Lycoming's T-53-L-13 gas turbine engine contract, and that I would report to the AAMTAP school in Vung Tau as a triple threat, so to say, and could be used in several areas of instruction, research on gas turbine problems with resolution to the satisfaction of the United States Army Aviation Command, Directorate of Maintenance, and the Commands, Engineering Directorate. My team would be the only Qualified Instructor team in Vietnam at Vung Tau on the T-53-L-13 gas turbine engine. This would align up and conform to AVSCOM's ideas about the termination of Lycoming's contract.

My feeling was our team would be ready for the challenge and time would tell how well we instruct personnel on the new engine. In my opinion our team was ready for anything that would be thrown at us. My confidence factor was at 100 percent for a perfect score for our team

(Bernie Reece and myself). In addition, I could assist either the CH-47 (Chinook) or UH-1 (Huey) units in the field to alleviate problems that were hindering the availability of aircraft for missions. One reason the aircraft could not be grounded, whenever the Viet Cong (VC) would attack unannounced, the aircraft had to be combat ready or on the line ready and available for any type of operation or catastrophic ordeal that could happen to the ground personnel, without air support.

Before I left Fort Benning I called my wife in Riverside and asked her if she could meet me in Fort Eustis, VA. She could not fly due to health problems, so she took a fast cross country train and within three days I picked her up at the station. Then we proceeded to the Officer Billeting at Fort Eustis. They provided us with real nice quarters with messing facilities next door. In addition, the post had a very efficient hospital for her medical needs or medicine.

My final grade was very high according to Army standards. My comment on this course was that no one received specific technical answers when you asked the Lycoming instructors. They gave you nothing; you had to delve into the engine technical manuals or listen exceptionally well or ask to repeat the question to the specific Lycoming instructor giving the lectures. The Lycoming T-53-L-13 engine team was excellent because they had firsthand knowledge provided directly from the Lycoming factory on the latest updates and of problem areas from the field on the T-53-L-13 gas turbine engines and all corrective actions or problems to be resolved. The United States Army Aviation System Command would have to devise a new reporting system for any field problem that occurred and that all United States Army technical systems personnel worldwide would be advised as expeditiously as possible to prevent any reported problems to eventually accelerate into a highly technical unsolved subject matter, whereby the personnel in the field were without the proper solution or guidance so the aircraft could be grounded until communication was received from AVSCOM with the necessary corrective action. If anything had a high impact on the command, information would be put in the communications channel to AVSCOM like yesterday. There could not be any delay of any sort in disseminating information to or from the field.

After graduating from Lycoming T-53-L-13 class at Fort Eustis, we were to report back to AVSCOM in St. Louis. [Diploma Lycoming Course T-53-L13 2-8]

We left on 18 November 1966, because we didn't know the specific date of departure from CONUS for the Republic of Vietnam. When we reported into the Directorate of Maintenance, Technical Assistance Office, I was immediately put to work finalizing my training information and readying myself to depart from St. Louis, Missouri.

When I first reported this problem to AVSCOM, before leaving Fort Benning, Georgia personnel from all Directorates were solving the new reporting system, and had to be in place before I arrived December 1966, to begin processing out of AVSCOM on PCS status to Republic of Vietnam (RVN).

I requested a short leave of absence at my home in Riverside, California. Because of my wife's health she had to carry an Oxygen breathing case at all times to prevent any emergency. So this was of primary importance to what type of transportation to utilize for our trip from Riverside to Travis Air Force Base, California. I decided to use my automobile.

I contacted the United States Air Force doctors and hospital of my wife's illness for heart, lung problems.

The Oxygen specialists were appraised of the seriousness of my wife's health requirements and would give her a high priority servicing for liquid Oxygen needs at our residence on a 24 hour basis.

The AVSCOM Civilian Personnel Office would be advised on how to contact me or vice-a-versa in case anything happened while in RVN. All of AVSCOM offices were cooperating exceptionally well.

REQUEST AND AUTHORIZATION FOR MILITARY PERSONNEL TDY TRAVEL AND CIVILIAN PERSONNEL TDY AND PCS TRAVEL
(AR 310-10 and CPR T-3)

1. TYPE OF TRAVEL ORDERS
☒ TDY: UCMR PROPER STA. ☐ PCS (Civilian only) ☐ CONFIRMATORY ORDERS

2. NAME OF REQUESTING OFFICE			3. TELEPHONE EXT.	4. DATE
Dir of Maintenance, Tech Asst Div			2593/3632	10 Jun 66

5. FIRST NAME - MIDDLE INITIAL - LAST NAME	GRADE	SERVICE NUMBER	ARM OR SERVICE (Military) POSITION OR TITLE (Civilian)	SECURITY CLEARANCE
WAYNE A. KUSCHEL	GS-11	DAC	Equip Spec	

6. ORGANIZATION AND STATION	9. ITINERARY ☐ CIPAP
USAAVCOM (MI-4021), St. Louis, Mo.	WP from St. Louis, Mo. to Ft Sill, Okla and return to St. Louis, Mo.

7. TO PROCEED O/A	8. APPROXIMATE NUMBER OF DAYS
12 Jun 66	14

10. PURPOSE OF TEMPORARY DUTY
To attend course of training on T-55 turbine engine conducted by T-55 AAMTAP Team

11. TRANSPORTATION AUTHORIZED
☐ COMMON CARRIER: ☐ AIR ☐ SURFACE ☐ WATER ☐ AS DETERMINED BY TRANSPORTATION OFF. (Military only)
☐ GOVERNMENT OWNED: ☐ VEHICLE ☐ AIRCRAFT ☐ VESSEL
☒ PRIVATELY-OWNED VEHICLE AT RATE OF_____ CENTS PER MILE ☐ TPA-TMDAG
☒ REIMBURSEMENT LIMITED TO COST TO GOVT OF TRAVEL BY USUAL MODE OF TRANSPORTATION, INCLUDING PER DIEM. (Civilian only)

12. PER DIEM AUTHORIZED (Civilian Personnel only)
☒ MAXIMUM AUTHORIZED BY CPR T-3 ☐ OTHER RATES OF PER DIEM (Specify)

13. TRANSPORTATION OF DEPENDENTS (Civilian Personnel only)
☐ EMPLOYEE REQUESTS TRANSPORTATION OF DEPENDENTS WHOSE NAMES(S) AGE(S) AND RELATIONSHIP(S) APPEAR UNDER REMARKS
☐ TRANSPORTATION AUTHORIZED BY GOVERNMENT ☐ VEHICLE ☐ AIRCRAFT ☐ VESSEL
☐ TRANSPORTATION AUTHORIZED BY COMMON CARRIER (Commercial Air, Rail, Bus, Vessel)
☐ TRANSPORTATION AUTHORIZED BY PRIVATELY-OWNED CONVEYANCE

14. SHIPMENT OF HOUSEHOLD GOODS (Civilian personnel only)
☐ EMPLOYEE HAS DEPENDENTS AND IS AUTHORIZED MOVEMENT OF HOUSEHOLD GOODS NOT IN EXCESS OF 7000 POUNDS NET WEIGHT ☐ EMPLOYEE DOES NOT HAVE DEPENDENTS AND IS AUTHOR-IZED MOVEMENT OF HOUSEHOLD GOODS NOT IN EXCESS OF 2500 POUNDS NET WEIGHT

15. REMARKS (Use this space for special requirements, delay, authority for issuance, names of dependents, designation as courier, superior accommodations, excess baggage, etc.)

Reporting time: 0800 hours, 13 Jun 66

Traveler must proceed within 7 days of WP date or the order becomes invalid.

TRAVELER IS DIRECTED THAT HE WILL COMPLY STRICTLY WITH THE PROVISIONS OF DOD Dir 5500.7 REGARDING ACCEPTANCE OF GRATUITIES IN ANY FORM.

16. ADMINISTRATIVE APPROVAL

MARION F. HIGIERE, Deputy Director
Directorate of Maintenance (IMP)

17. FISCAL APPROVAL (Chargeable to)
2162020 64-3040 P2300-21 S23-204
cc 14 23L0.10223.A011MA UMA

NAME, GRADE OR TITLE
BV 606472

FOR USE OF APPROVING OFFICE ONLY

18. AGENCY

19. ORDER NUMBER/REFERENCE U. S. ARMY AVN MATERIEL COMMAND
SOMBM 66-3923

20. DATE 10 June 66

21. APPROVED. TRAVEL TO BE PERFORMED IS NECESSARY IN THE PUBLIC SERVICE. WP.

FOR THE COMMANDER:

NAME, GRADE OR TITLE
S. E. Byrne,
Asst to Ch of Syms Div

DA FORM 662 1 OCT 61   PREVIOUS EDITIONS ARE OBSOLETE.

2

Document 2-1
Travel Orders 14 June 1966

Department of the Army

Certificate of Training

This is to certify that

WAYNE A. KUSCHEL
DAC ST. LOUIS, MO.

has successfully completed

T-55 LYCOMING GAS TURBINE
OPERATION & MAINTENANCE COURSE
CURRICULUM II

Given at

FORT SILL, OKLA.
24 JUNE 1966

HOWARD F. SCHILTZ
Brigadier General, USA
Commanding

DRM
' 56 87   REPLACES DA FORM 87, 1 JAN 49, WHICH IS OBSOLETE

Document 2-2
Certificate of Training

Department of the Army

Certificate of Training

This is to certify that

has successfully completed

Given at

JOHN MORTON
Major General, USA
Commanding

DA FORM
1 SEP 56   REPLACES DA FORM 87, 1 JAN 48, WHICH IS OBSOLETE.

Document 2-3
Certificate of Training

**REQUEST AND AUTHORIZATION FOR MILITARY PERSONNEL TY TRAVEL
AND CIVILIAN PERSONNEL TDY AND PCS TRAVEL**
(AR 310-10 and CPR T-3)

1. TYPE OF TRAVEL ORDERS
☐ TDY, UCMR PROPER STA. ☐ PCS *(Civilian only)* ☐ CONFIRMATORY ORDERS

2. NAME OF REQUESTING OFFICE			3. TELEPHONE EXT.	4. DATE
Dir of Maintenance, Tech Asst Div			7632/7624	28 Jun 66

5. FIRST NAME - MIDDLE INITIAL - LAST NAME	GRADE	SERVICE NUMBER	ARM OR SERVICE *(Military)* POSITION OR TITLE *(Civilian)*	SECURITY CLEARANCE
WAYNE A. KRUCHEL	GS-11	DAC	Equip Spec	Interim Secret

6. ORGANIZATION AND STATION	9. ITINERARY ☐ CIPAP
USAAVCOM (MI-4021), St. Louis, Missouri	WP from St. Louis, Mo to Ft Rucker, Ala

7. TO PROCEED O/A	8. APPROXIMATE NUMBER OF DAYS	to Ft Eustis, Va to Ft Rucker, Ala and
4 Jul 66	60	return to St. Louis, Mo.

10. PURPOSE OF TEMPORARY DUTY   To attend and participate in trainee status, the functions
and procedures of a T-55 AMTAP training team.

11. TRANSPORTATION AUTHORIZED
☐ COMMON CARRIER: ☐ AIR ☐ SURFACE ☐ WATER ☐ AS DETERMINED BY TRANSPORTATION OFF. *(Military only)*
☐ GOVERNMENT OWNED: ☐ VEHICLE ☐ AIRCRAFT ☐ VESSEL
☐ PRIVATELY-OWNED VEHICLE AT RATE OF_____ CENTS PER MILE ☐ TPA-TMOAG
☐ REIMBURSEMENT LIMITED TO COST TO GOVT OF TRAVEL BY USUAL MODE OF TRANSPORTATION, INCLUDING PER DIEM. *(Civilian only)*

12. PER DIEM AUTHORIZED *(Civilian Personnel only)*
☐ MAXIMUM AUTHORIZED BY CPR T-3 ☐ OTHER RATES OF PER DIEM *(Specify)*

13. TRANSPORTATION OF DEPENDENTS *(Civilian Personnel only)*
☐ EMPLOYEE REQUESTS TRANSPORTATION OF DEPENDENTS WHOSE NAMES/ AGES/ AND RELATIONSHIPS/ APPEAR UNDER REMARKS
☐ TRANSPORTATION AUTHORIZED BY GOVERNMENT ☐ VEHICLE ☐ AIRCRAFT ☐ VESSEL
☐ TRANSPORTATION AUTHORIZED BY COMMON CARRIER *(Commercial Air, Rail, Bus, Vessel)*
☐ TRANSPORTATION AUTHORIZED BY PRIVATELY-OWNED CONVEYANCE

14. SHIPMENT OF HOUSEHOLD GOODS *(Civilian personnel only)*
☐ EMPLOYEE HAS DEPENDENTS AND IS AUTHORIZED MOVEMENT ☐ EMPLOYEE DOES NOT HAVE DEPENDENTS AND IS AUTHOR-
OF HOUSEHOLD GOODS NOT IN EXCESS OF 7000 POUNDS NET   IZED MOVEMENT OF HOUSEHOLD GOODS NOT IN EXCESS
WEIGHT   OF 2500 POUNDS NET WEIGHT

15. REMARKS *(Use this space for special requirements, delay, authority for issuance, names of dependents, designation as courier, superior accommodations, excess baggage, etc.)*

Reporting time: 0800 hours, 5 Jul 66
* Due to rescheduling of classes and changes in itinerary

Traveler must proceed within 7 days of WP date or the order becomes invalid.
TRAVELER IS DIRECTED THAT HE WILL COMPLY STRICTLY WITH THE PROVISIONS OF DOD
Dir 5500.7 REGARDING ACCEPTANCE OF GRATUITIES IN ANY FORM.

16. ADMINISTRATIVE APPROVAL	FOR USE OF APPROVING OFFICE ONLY
(signature)	18. AGENCY Jrs
WAYNE Y. HINES, Deputy Director	19. ORDER NUMBER/REFERENCE CONTROL 20. DATE
17. FISCAL APPROVAL *(for Maintenance (JBP))*	21. APPROVED/TRAVEL TO BE PERFORMED IS NECESSARY IN THE PUBLIC SERVICE. WP.
2172020 64-5040 P2300-21 S23-204	
oc 14 2310.10223.AO11PA UPA	
Subject to availability of funds	
	FOR THE COMMANDER:

NAME, GRADE OR TITLE	NAME, GRADE OR TITLE
BY A 10116	WALTER J. TOBIN Trans Officer (civ)

DA FORM 662   PREVIOUS EDITIONS ARE OBSOLETE.
1 OCT 61

5

Document 2-4
Travel Orders 28 June 1966

31 August 1966

SUBJECT: AAMTAP Progress Report of Wayne A. Kuschel

TO: Leonard E. Bartley
        USAAVCOM Technical Assistance
        Program Manager

FROM: Charles J. Gerau
        T-55 AAMTAP AVCOM

This Report is compiled and submitted by the writer in accordance with verbal orders issued by the addressee May 1965. Period covered, 1 August thru 31 August 1966.

The past month of August Mr. Kuschel has made excellent as well as extraordinary progress. He not only attended all lectures given by Mr. Birch and myself but satisfactorrily taught numerous subjects. At the present time he has three more subjects to teach which will comprise the entire course material for curriculum II. In addition Mr. Kuschel has spent many extra hours and without our aid comprised his personal supplemtary lesson plans, training aids and researched the latest technical information available.

It is my opinion that Mr. Kuschel will be fully qualified after teaching two more classes or by the end of September.

May I recall to your attention our discussion concerning qualification of trainees prior to my departure from St. Louis. We agreed that before an individual is fully qualified, he should be able to teach an entire course without assistance. This is the goal we will achieve in the best interest of AVCOM.

cc
D. Efinger
file

Charles J. Gerau DAC
T-55 AAMTAP AVCOM

Letter 2-5 Progress Report

42

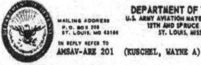

DEPARTMENT OF THE ARMY
U.S. ARMY AVIATION MATERIEL COMMAND
12TH AND SPRUCE STREETS
ST. LOUIS, MISSOURI

MAILING ADDRESS
P. O. BOX 209
ST. LOUIS, MO 63166

IN REPLY REFER TO
AMSAV-ARE 201 (KUSCHEL, WAYNE A)

LETTER ORDER 9-17

SUBJECT: AMENDMENT OF TRAVEL ORDERS   8 September 1966

TO: Mr. Wayne A. Kuschel
          Dir of Maint

     TC 379. DA Form 662 (Req and Auth for Mil Pers TDY Tvl and Civ Pers
TDY Tvl and PCS Tvl) for fol indiv sta is AMENDED

KUSCHEL WAYNE A 11 Equip Sp Dir of Maint Interim Secret
     SMO: Sec 8
     As reads: "60 days
     IATR: 150 days
     SMO: Sec 9
     As reads: "WP from St. Louis, Mo to Ft Rucker, Ala to Ft. Eustis
               Va to Ft Rucker, Ala and return to St. Louis, Mo."
     IATR: "WP from St. Louis, Mo. to Ft. Rucker, Ala to Ft. Eustis Va
            to Ft Rucker, Ala to Ft Benning, Ga and rtn to St. Louis, Mo."
     WP date: 4 Jul 66
     Eff date: 29 Jun 66
     AMSAV Order No: 66-3328
     Acct Clas: 2172020 64-8040 P2300-21 S23-204 OC 14 23L0.10223.
                A011MA UMA

     FOR THE COMMANDER:

OFFICIAL: FLOYD W. CROUCH, JR.
                                   Lt Colonel, GS
                                   Acting Chief of Staff

R. B. JANUARY
Asst to Chief
Admin Svc Ofc

DISTRIBUTION:
     6 - Indiv named
     3 - Fin & Acct Ofc
     2 - Trans Div
     2 - Editorial Br

2-6 Travel Orders

30 September 1966

SUBJECT: AAMTAP Progress Report of Wayne A. Kuschel

TO: Leonard E. Bartley
USAAVCOM Technical Assistance
Program Manager

FROM: Charles J. Gerau
T-55 AAMTAP AMSAV

This Report is complied and submitted by the writer in accordance with verbal orders issued by the addressee May 1966. Period covered, 1 September thru 30 September 1966.

Mr. W. Kuschel this period has successfully completed his training as a T-55 AAMTAP Instructor.
His capability as an instructor as well as helping train Mr. E. Cox is highly commendable. In addition, requiring many extra hours, he has personally compiled a complete updated set of lesson plans, technical literature, training aids and new transparancies. Of particular interest and note of his ability, is a layover transparancy he manufactured to teach the use of a Vernier Depth Gage. This subject has always required many hours of hard work which has now been reduced to a relatively short period of time easily accomplished with his new aid.
It is the writers opinion that Mr. W. Kuschel will perform to the highest degree in any position assigned to him by AMSAV.

Charles J. Gerau DAC
T-55 AAMTAP AMSAV
Ft. Benning, Georgia

cc.
T.L. Clemens
file

2-7 Progress Report

44

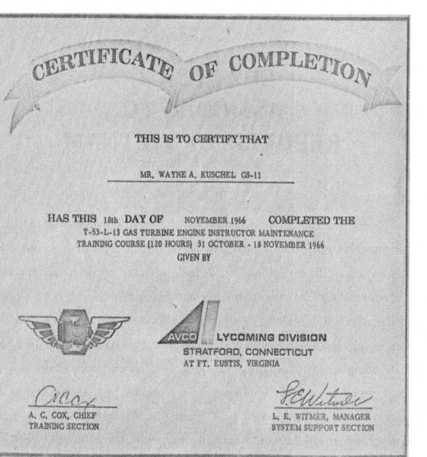

CERTIFICATE OF COMPLETION

THIS IS TO CERTIFY THAT

MR. WAYNE A. KUSCHEL GS-11

HAS THIS 18th DAY OF NOVEMBER 1966 COMPLETED THE
T-53-L-13 GAS TURBINE ENGINE INSTRUCTOR MAINTENANCE
TRAINING COURSE (120 HOURS) 31 OCTOBER - 18 NOVEMBER 1966
GIVEN BY

AVCO LYCOMING DIVISION
STRATFORD, CONNECTICUT
AT FT. EUSTIS, VIRGINIA

A. C. COX, CHIEF
TRAINING SECTION

L. E. WITMER, MANAGER
SYSTEM SUPPORT SECTION

2-8 Diploma Lycoming Course T-53-L13

CHAPTER 3-
ASSIGNED TO
REPUBLIC OF VIETNAM

Guess I made an impression on the Maintenance Management personnel because prior to my trip to Travis Air Force Base Mr. Leonard E. Bartley, Chief, Technical Support Branch provided me with a letter dated December 1966. The subject was "Appointment of AAMTAP Team Leader in Vietnam." It contained specific instructions for me to follow, and the four team members to submit correspondences that AVSCOM required on team compliances. [Letter appointment of AAMTAP team leader 3-1]

Letter Order 11-62, Subject: Travel Orders permanent change of station (PCS) to Tan Son Nhut, Republic of Vietnam (RVN) also gave orders for port call date and time and all types of instruction to be carried out these orders were dated 23 November 1966.

There were four of us Department of the Army Civilian (DAC) employees, all GS—11's: George Dikum, Preston S. Russell, Bernard D. Reece and myself Wayne A. Kuschel on the correspondence. My T-53-L-13 team member was Mr. Bernard D. Reece, since we both attended the Lycoming factory school at Fort Eustis, Mr. Russell and Dikum were the T-53—L-11 team members. [Document Travel Orders 3-2]

The T-53—L-13 was the most recent gas turbine engine the United States Army put into the inventory valued at nearly $100,000.00 each, incorporating numerous updated systems like extra power for lift-offs in case of emergency requirements that set a precedence for its mechanical ability to have sufficient power for the UH-1 (Huey) flying performance in any situation. However, our field aviation maintenance personnel had to have the specific technology know how to keep the helicopters in the air or flyable.

Finally we arrived at our home in Riverside, 27 November 1966 to begin our very short leave together and try to rest for the upcoming year in Vietnam. My thoughts were playing havoc with my mind as I had never been in an actual ground fighting combat war zone before. However, I was in the United States Army and United States Army Air Corp in Newfoundland 1942-1944 fighting the Germans or Nazis if and when required. With all the rumors that can and do play tricks on your mind, how do you sift through the residue and come up with only facts? Would there be any type of accident happen to me? The closer to the departure date the more your tension begins building up. Then, on 15 December 1966, we were on the road to Travis Air Force Base, California. The wife wanted to go because a year is a long time to be away from each other. I can truthfully say I had a 100% perfect wife devoted to keeping a harmonious man and wife relationship. In my entire United States Air Force career she kept my life worthwhile. If I had to get up for any 24-hour flight or mission she prepared a perfect meal regardless of the time I had to depart company, she was always there to greet me on my return to earth or base and have a delicious lunch ready regardless if she was up to par, sick or not. Besides her niece, Tina, she was near Travis Air Force Base. California so she would visit her for a few days then return to Riverside. The trip was a relaxing one. At Travis Air Force Base, we were provided with real nice quarters. The only thing annoying was base operations kept calling me regarding the chartered flight, Continental Airlines (H241), which was very nerve wracking. At Base Operations the Chief advised me that the flight to Vietnam would be as scheduled on Continental Airlines scheduled for a late afternoon flight to Honolulu for refueling, then on to Clark Air Force Base, Philippines for refueling, then onto Saigon, Tan Son Nhut airport.

My wife Marie and I enjoyed each other's company; it was like our second honeymoon. However, it all had to come to an end with the bubble or balloon bursting. The dream was over, and the event became a reality. We kissed and gave each other a big hug and it was time to board the Continental flight (H241). At least we were together for a while, because a year would be an extra-long time to be separated. Being on several United States Air Force temporary duty (TDY) assignments while on active duty was easier understand, but this was for an extended period in the southwest Pacific and not on Guam or other SAC base. So we said our farewells, boarded and I departed on my Continental Flight (H241). All I can say it was a short second honeymoon.

Our first stop at Honolulu, Hawaii was relaxing and we stayed on the ground two hours. Then all the passengers re-boarded and we were en-route to Clark Air Force Base. The time seemed to get longer, everyone was getting somber, tired, time-wise and realizing it wouldn't be too long before we would be at Tan Son Nhut Airport in Republic of Vietnam. The pilot called and advised the passengers that we were over the Republic of Vietnam's east coast and that we would be flying over a certain route, in my pilot term a "race track pattern" to help waste time for landing approval. At this time the pilot stated that Tan Son Nhut airport was under a Viet Cong attack and the United States Army Assault Aircraft was counter-attacking them. There were approximately two hundred Viet Cong in their force. My mind went back trying to visualize the seriousness of being in Vietnam. Oh! well, I am as safe as anyone else was my feelings! The aircraft made a very steep approach and finally landed and we disembarked. We were then escorted into the Operations Section. I thought it might be relevant, in my first contact of being in Vietnam, in the restroom we all got into a urinal and began relieving ourselves mighty fast, and at the same time it was falling out on the concrete flooring because the brass tubing was missing. Must have been someone stealing them for brass sale or junk. Just like what is happening in the good old United States of America. Today, numerous people steal copper and sell to junk dealers for money. After a few laughs and some chuckles we all departed for our own hotel area to think for ourselves and perhaps realize this incident could happen anywhere in the world.

The military police escorted us to our quarters for a few hours rest. The next morning our MACV-Technical Assistance team began helping us process and sign in, then we traveled to all areas within Saigon, personnel office, pay records and then to our AVSCOM Technical Assistance supervisors. That first night we were driven from MACV to our temporary billets, and then we waited until transportation to Vung Tau was arranged. We walked from the billets to our officer's mess hall, the path was filthy with trash all over the area, air smelled bad, dirt paths was all sand and rocks, barbed wire fencing on both sides of the walk, all the comforts of home, what an imagination! Along the way, when the mom-a-sons would have to do a #1 or #2, they would stop next to the road, roll up their bell bottom black pajamas or pants and do their thing right there. Then numerous vehicles would come along, roll over the #1 or #2 scene and then there would be dust for all of us to breath in and get some type of a lung fungus. What a thought of any possible health problem arising. As our days were all messed up and jet lag had a bearing on how lousy a person can feel, your butt was dragging on the ground, but life does go on.

We had to continue processing in for our year stay that we were going to have to endure. Our embassy handled visas for our "Red" official passports expeditiously stamping them so we would not be held up, but be on our assigned positions as soon as possible. All of us with "Red" official passports were advised that if the Viet Cong caught or captured us they had an automatic $35,000.00 ransom on our heads, with less than two days being in Saigon that was one big problem, to handle and to make up our minds to be extra careful. You wonder as you look around, who might do you bodily harm as the area was fairly peaceful, at least it seemed like it. What a change, to begin seeing barbed wire fencing for our protection. That would shake you up to reality, and then you remember you're in Vietnam, a declared war zone. But who out there is the enemy? They would all look like normal Vietnam citizens, very friendly, always willing to assist or help you. The children would always be hanging around, like the type found in World War II, waiting for candy or gum.

With all our processing completed on 20 December 1966, arrangements were finally made for transportation to Vung Tau, where the United States Army Aircraft schools, Army Aviation Maintenance Technical Assistance Program (AAMTAP) were located. We were lucky a CH-47 (Chinook) helicopter was delivering supplies to Vung Tau the next morning, and we were on the passenger manifest. Early the next day we were at the Air Force/Army Airport at Tan Son Nhut. We all looked like we needed porters or red hats to assist in carrying our heavy baggage.

Little did I know that my first helicopter ride in the Republic of Vietnam would be in the CH-47 (Chinook). The Cadillac of all helicopters it had tandem engines (T-55's) and rotor blades which operated as smooth as silk because of its size, and weight, in addition the horsepower was sufficient for any required functions, and its carrying of cargo abilities was beyond belief, tanks, rubber fuel bladder and rubber water bladder, tanks, aircraft, etc.

An U.S. Army Major Schwartz from the 765th Transportation Company stationed at Vung Tau was the CH-47 (Chinook) pilot. He briefed us and advised us on all types of emergency procedures. When the pilot applied power for lift-off the CH-47 (Chinook), came out of the revetment area, straight up to 500 feet. This prevented any Viet Cong from sniper shots and to prevent aircraft damages. When he began gaining forward speed we were really getting into our mission. About twenty minutes later we began a descent toward a rice paddy where we landed on a narrow path or trail and picked up three U.S. army patrol personnel that were being shot at by the Viet Cong. A call provided overhead air coverage and again we went straight up and began a forward transition toward Vung Tau.

A short time later we arrived at Vung Tau's 765th Transportation Company parking ramp. What a sight. It looked like the sand in Texas had invaded Vietnam. The China Sea was at our doorstep, so to speak. French man's beach was a gorgeous swim area, beautiful green-blue water. But remember it could be a dangerous place. Where people gather, you're not safe.

The members on my United States Army orders reported into the AAMTAP School for initial procedures on when we would begin teaching classes. There were several offices that we had to report into to coordinate our instructor efforts. We were advised that our assistance could be utilized in addition to the school by the 765th Transportation Battalion (AM&S), to instruct the T-53/55 engine propulsion aviation mechanics of the various Vung Tau companies for maintaining their engines in tip-top shape.

Whenever we were working with units outside of the AAMTAP School we had to fill out AMC Form 1478—R (5 October 1966) and submit it to headquarters, United States Army Aviation Material Command, ATTN: AMSAV-FTT St. Louis, Missouri. This maintenance performance report is an example of what I sent to AVSCOM on a monthly basis. We did not always have the assigned maintenance officer available to sign the form and we did not have secretaries to type and send to higher headquarters.

We used what we had at hand. There were lots of things not available to accomplish your job. [Copy of AMC Form 1478-R 3-3]

After our T-53—L-13 Gas Turbine Engine Team arrived at Vung Tau AAMTAP School more requirements for our monthly accomplishments were required by AVSCOM. So we all sharpened our pencils and began filling out daily diaries, there were several flaws in accurately recording all the completed assignments. Our propulsion teams were required to visit the various organizations and assist their flying personnel on the latest information to correctly maintain the helicopters in flyable status.

Since my forms were sent to AVSCOM Technical Assistance Office I was careless in saving all copies for my personnel files, so please forgive me on the 1478-R forms Maintenance Performance Reports that I lost in my travels and could not be used for my illustrations in my "All or Nothing" book.

The importance of these forms was to inform headquarters of all types of discrepancies encountered in servicing and finding out field problems and of any other remarks, discussions and/or recommendations. In turn, the AVSCOM engineering office could alert worldwide commands of any pending problems.

After visiting the AAMTAP school area and signing in, we were transported by bus to the Pacific Hotel in Vung Tau where we acquired a room (temporarily) until we could make up our minds on where we would rent rooms. It's best staying close to our crowd because of transportation and dining requirements. For me it was safer to dine at the Officers Club than at civilian places. There were all sorts of problems in the Vung Tau area, service personnel had to be especially alert on walking about, there were unknown people carrying knives, machetes and guns of all descriptions. The end result was death.

To go back and mention our school bus, it was a 1965 Ford, 2 ½ ton, commercial flat bed. Then a cage was installed with one inch square mesh screen wire. This wire was placed around us so the Viet Cong could not toss hand grenades or any explosives into the passenger area. The wire would deflect grenades to allow them to hit the ground area and explode. This bus was a clumsy looking, hard to maneuver school bus, but it was suitable for our purpose of transportation. On one trip early in the morning our driver, Charles Gerau was having a hard time getting around other cars, bikes and motorcycles. He drove near a motorcycle and the right rear side hit the bike, throwing the man into a brush pile damaging his right shoulder. The first thing the Republic of Vietnam government did was began proceedings to sue someone. I heard that the United States Government settled for $10-15,000.00.

Bernie Reece and I were called immediately to begin the class on T-53-L-11 turbine engines used on a large number of UH-1 (Huey) helicopters. We had a full class, or complement of Army personnel, Officers, Warrant Officers and enlisted men. There were approximately twelve personnel assigned to our first class. The units sent their maintenance personnel to get them away from the war front and more or less on Rest and Recuperation away from combat. In addition, they learn the latest engine configuration and troubleshooting techniques for air worthiness of the helicopters in the field. I do know that the personnel attending these classes had a downright high technical background for the mechanical functions of the T-53 gas turbine engine. At least the personnel would be able to maintain the helicopter in an air worthiness status capable of going into any scrimmage with the Viet Cong. [Photo of T-53—L13 Army Personnel 3-4]

We had some well deserving soldiers that put lots of their efforts into our course on gas turbine engines. It was not an easy course; we had several tests and lots of oral testing to enable us to know who needed help in the course, as a grade of seventy was the minimum for passing, and up to one hundred to maximize the course. Most of the young soldiers attained a high score in testing and their diplomas indicated so. We also had an honor student from each class that would receive a three day pass and stayed on at the school for that period.

Since I was to be the team coordinator I could not get Mr. Russell to submit the necessary or required correspondence to AVSCOM which was spelled out in my instructions. I wrote a letter 10 February 1967 to Emmett Knight, my contact at the AVSCOM, pointing out the problem. There was no point in me trying to keep up with Preston S. Russell's school assignments. I had enough work combining all the reports to AVSCOM. My feeling was that he was a slacker in getting things accomplished. [My letter to Emmett Knight 3-5]

At Vung Tau, when any building was being built the mom-a-sons did the carpentry work. They were only about five feet tall and capable of carrying tremendous weight on their backs, shoulders or heads. It was incredible to watch their progress. Don't know what the papa-a-sons did, guess they stayed home and cared for the little ones or did Viet Cong duty. [Mom-a-son's the builders 3-6]

Our home office told Bernie and I to begin inventory of all the equipment used on the new T-53-L-13 gas turbine engines. Lycoming personnel put up a battle and would not relinquish any item, saying everything belonged to Lycoming which was a big fib, so we had to wait until the Army cleared it up. Finally the word came through for Lycoming to inventory all equipment and let the Army sign for it. On a given day our AAMTAP personnel began instructing the old T-53-L-11 turbine engine, in place of the T-53-L-13 engine.

Talk about trouble, in establishing an ongoing class for the United States Army personnel, the 765th Transportation Battalion supplied a T-53-L-11 gas turbine engine. We had to use a wooden crate in place of an engine stand to tear the hot end down to enable the personnel to get the latest method of measurements and necessary repairs.

Regardless, I feel that the 765th Transportation Battalion was giving us excellent support within their capabilities. Our first T-53-L-13 class was supposed to start on 27 December 1966. Lycoming personnel could not find a current packing list. It was missing so we had to delay the inventory. Lycoming personnel finally did find an outdated list to adequately begin the inventory of special tools.

Mr. Hubbs at AVSCOM was contacted by me and told of the problems we were having taking over all equipment, which we finally signed at 1200 hours 27 December 1966, and the scheduled class started under Department Army Civilian AAMTAP at 1230, 27 December 1966.

On Saturday we devoted all of our instructors entirely for the pilot ground school. The requirements were based on two experience levels. As of that date, overtime would be required to facilitate all instruction phases. Our worries were never over with, getting the new T-53-L-13 engine course going because of all kinds of roadblocks put down by the Lycoming Company's hesitation on assisting the United States Army to close out the Lycoming contract. Reason being, three Lycoming personnel went to Singapore during the second and third week of January 1967 for seven days leave which necessitated a delay of their own signing over tools and engine equipment for T-53-L-13 #2 team. Another delay resulted when the tool box keys could not be located, nor could a current packing list of available equipment stored in containers be located.

It appeared to me that all efforts to hamper our tasks were being taken by the Lycoming supervisors. They didn't want to lose their jobs and return to the United States. Mr. Fairfield, the T-55 Lycoming instructor, advised me that Mr. Dulley, Lycoming Team Chief, told him not to cooperate or assist the Department of Army Civilian teams in any way or method, to stall the takeover. When I asked Mr. Larry Dulworth if there were any keys available for the tool boxes, Mr. Dulworth stated there were none, also the containers had no packing list. I contacted Lt. Rex Hansen, AAMTAP

Officer in charge, and asked him to try and acquire the keys from the Lycoming personnel. Mr. Dulworth advised Lt. Hansen that the keys were in his desk. The keys were found and Lt. Hansen assisted in the inventory of tools and containers. Classes were scheduled to start 30 January 1967, which required us to work Saturday, 21 January 1967, and Sunday, 22 January 1967, to enable us to begin class instruction on the due date.

Then to jump another road block we sent a requirement to AVSCOM requesting special tools not available but required for completion of any T-53-L-13 engine course tear down. These tools were not physically in Lycoming's possession or in the boxes inventoried. But our work was two-fold, especially when one team was building up one engine and the other team was tearing down the other engine for hot end instructional purposes. It was a working team effort to accomplish two tasks simultaneously with no problems occurring.

Early January 1967, Mr. Fairfield with Lycoming company, was offered a position as a T-55 AAMTAP instructor at Vung Tau. AVSCOM approved of him, so a bunch of our instructors used long knives to cut Lycoming's patch off his shirt. Then Mr. Fairfield was sworn into civil service. He was an asset to the AAMTAP program and to the United States Army Aviation System Command as a highly qualified instructor.

During the period 24 December 1966 through 20 January 1967 we submitted for overtime for setting up classes, inventory of tools, preparing lesson plans and guides, class schedule, cleaning training aids, acquiring engine stands, adapters and engine maintenance technical manuals, and preparing lecture plans to fit the individual classes. AVSCOM replied overtime approved, but keep classes on time that were scheduled for United States Army Aviation personnel. From the above, I don't see what method Lycoming instructed the United States Army personnel. Of course, Lycoming's cooperation was null and void, and yet our classes were on schedule.

In addition to all the instructing, we were looking for new quarters, so one of other civilians, a GS-11 named Fredrick "Rocky" Demarest said there was a new hotel being built by Pacific, Architect & Engineering (PA&E), on the south side of Vung Tau and the owner wanted "Rocky" Demarest to be an assistant manager in exchange for part of his hotel bill, and that he would take care of all managerial items. He got into protecting us and he said there was no fear of any Viet Cong attacks because of the abundance of police. Guess what? That night there were sirens sounding that indicated a Viet Cong attack. So everyone took shelter in the best areas or shelters possible, mine was a cement wall and you could hear bullets hitting the outside of our quarters.

On 1 July 1967, I was called into the Commander's office of the 765th Transportation Battalion. What a surprise! I received a letter of appreciation dated 11 March 1967 from the President of the United States, Lyndon B. Johnson, forwarded through all the necessary channels for our logistics support of aviation units. [Letter of appreciation 3-7]

AMSAV-FTT

SUBJECT: Appointment of AAMTAP Team Leader

TO: Mr. Wayne A. Kuschel
        4175 Adams Street
        Riverside, California 92504

1. Mr. Wayne A. Kuschel is appointed as Team Leader of the T-53 AAMTAP Team in Vietnam.

2. As Team Leader, you will be responsible for coordination of all T-53 AAMTAP activities; insure prompt reporting, verifying and signing of all Time and Attendance Cards of other T-53 team members; and supervision of team military duties.

3. Your Time and Attendance Card must be verified and signed by your immediate supervisor.

4. Any problems which cannot be resolved at your level of supervision should be brought to the attention of Mr. H. Hobbs at the Customer Assistance Office in Saigon until the arrival of Mr. Bassett Turner on or about 15 Jan 67, who will be on duty as the Senior DAC Maintenance Specialist Coordinator at Hq, 34th General Support Group, Saigon.

Copies furnished:
    Mr. Bernard Reece   LEONARD E. BARTLEY, Chief
    Mr. Preston Russell   Technical Support Branch
    Mr. George Dixon   Technical Assistance Division
    AMC Cust Asst Ofc, Vietnam Directorate of Maintenance

3-1
Letter Appointment of AAMTAP team leader

DEPARTMENT OF THE ARMY
U.S. ARMY AVIATION MATERIEL COMMAND
12TH AND SPRUCE STREETS
ST. LOUIS, MISSOURI

MAILING ADDRESS
P.O. BOX 209
ST. LOUIS, MO 63166

IN REPLY REFER TO

AMSAV-ARE 201

LETTER ORDER 11-62   23 November 1966

SUBJECT: Travel Orders - PCS to Tan Son Nhut, Vietnam

TO: Commander
          Western Area, MTMTS
          Passenger Division, Building 1, Wing 3
          Oakland Army Terminal, California 94626

    1. On call of the port commander, the individuals listed below, members
of the T-53 Army Aviation Mobile Technical Assistance Program Team (AAMTAP)
will proceed as indicated to the port of embarkation designated in port call
to Tan Son Nhut, Vietnam pursuant to Vol 2, JTR. Individuals will report to
the AMC Customer Assistance Office for assignment to the 34th General Support
Group (AM&S) and subsequent reassignment as required. Employee will be available
for travel on or after 15 December 1966. The travel to be performed is necessary
in the public service. Travel is authorized by commercial air within United
States and by military surface or air transportation outside the United States.

Name, Grade, Title	Proceed From
Wayne A. Kuschel, GS-11, Team Coordinator Equipment Specialist	St. Louis, Mo.
George Dikun, GS-11 Equipment Specialist	St. Louis, Mo.
Preston S. Russell, GS-11 Equipment Specialist	St. Louis, Mo.
Bernard D. Reece, GS-11 Equipment Specialist	Ft. Lewis, Washington

    2. Transportation Agreements signed:

       Mr. Kuschel: 23 September 1966
       Mr. Dikun: 9 November 1966
       Mr. Russell: 16 November 1966
       Mr. Reece: 28 September 1966

3-2 Travel Orders

expeditious means, the following information: The name of the traveler, travel order shipment identifier, statement that the traveler will not report in accordance with the port call as directed in this order, and statement as to when the traveler will be available for embarkation.

10. The appropriate chargeable for travel:

Mr. Kuschel: 2172020 64-8040 P2300-21 oc 14 S23-204 cc 23LO.10223.A011MA UMA; P2300-25 cc 23LO.10223.A016MA FMA

Mr. Dikum: 2172020 64-8040 P2300-21 oc 14 S23-204 cc 23LO.10223.A011GB UGB; P2300-25 cc 23LO.10223.A016GB FGB

Mr. Russell: 2172020 64-8040 P2300-21 oc 14 S23-204 cc 23LO.10223.A011GD UGD; P2300-25 cc 23LO.10223.A016GD FGD

Mr. Reece: 2172020 64-8040 P2300-21 oc 14 S23-204 cc 23LO.10223.A011LB ULB; P2300-25 cc 23LO.10223.A016LB FLB

11. Entrance to and purchase of items at Army and Air Force Post Exchanges is authorized in accordance with local command policies.

FOR THE COMMANDER:

OFFICIAL:

MILFRED J. PETERS
Colonel, GS
Chief of Staff

P. JANUARY
Asst to Chief
Admin Svc Ofc

DISTRIBUTION:
50 - Employee
10 - Comdr, Western Area, MTMTS
 1 - Official Personnel Folder
 1 - IG
 1 - CINCUSARPAC
 1 - CG, USARV, ATTN: AVHGD-CA
 2 - F&A Div
 3 - Central Files
 1 - Editorial Br
 1 - CO, 34th, Gen Spt Gp, APO SF 96307

SPECIAL DISTRIBUTION:
 2 - DCSPER-OCP, Empl Mgt Div, Wash DC
 5 - DCSPER, OCP, I&RC Br, Wash DC W/cy SF 50
 2 - USAMC Wash DC

3-2 Travel Orders page 2

MAINTENANCE PERFORMANCE REPORT	1. REPORTING PERIOD

	FROM 3 Apr 67	TO 30 Apr 67

2. TO Headquarters US Army Aviation Materiel Command ATTN: AMSAV-FS	2. TYPE OF REPORT	
	MONTHLY	DA CIVILIAN
	SPECIAL	MILITARY
	OTHER	

4. FROM (Name, Grade-Rank-Title, Address, and Signature)

Wayne A. Kuschel, GS-11 Equipment Specialist
HHD, 765th Trans. Bn. (AM&S) AMTBF
APO San Francisco 96291

DATE 5 May 67

Wayne A. Kuschel

PART I

5. UNIT(S) OR ACTIVITY SUPPORTED

330th Transportation Company and subordinate units.

6. BASIC WEAPON (OR EQUIPMENT) SYSTEM ON WHICH ASSISTANCE WAS RENDERED

U-6 L-7, L-11
U-6 L-7

7. WERE PROBLEMS ENCOUNTERED THAT COULD NOT BE RESOLVED?
(If Yes Explain in Item 13)   ☐ YES   ☒ NO

8. INDICATE PROBLEMS ENCOUNTERED IN AREAS a THRU g BY LISTING NUMBER OF REPORTS SUBMITTED FOR EACH

a. TOOLS AND TEST EQUIPMENT		e. TAERS	
b. TECHNICAL PUBLICATIONS	3	f. MALFUNCTION	1
c. SUPPLY AND REPAIR PARTS		g. OTHER (Specify)	
d. CHECKS AND ADJUSTMENTS			

9. MANPOWER AND TRAINING DATA

a. DAYS WORKED THIS REPORTING PERIOD	25	b. ANNUAL LEAVE HRS	0	c. SICK LEAVE HRS	0	d. OVERTIME HRS	COMP	PAID 60
e. TOTAL HOURS SPENT W/UNITS IN ITEM 5	250	f. HOURS OF FORMAL TRAINING CONDUCTED		g. NUMBER OF PERSONS TRAINED (Formal)				
h. HOURS TRAVEL TIME	20	i. HOURS OF OJT	90	j. NUMBER OF PERSONS TRAINED (O/T)	10			
k. HOURS SPENT PERFORMING ACTUAL MAINTENANCE FUNCTIONS (Explain in Item 13)								
l. OTHER (See Instructions)								

10. WERE PROBLEMS AND VISITS DISCUSSED WITH THE COMMAND G4/S4
AND OR HIS MAINTENANCE OR MATERIEL READINESS OFFICER?   ☒ YES   ☐ NO

11. NAME, TITLE AND ADDRESS OF PERSONNEL CONTACTED OTHER THAN ROUTINE

Staff Officers for Gen. G. P. Seneff Jr., 1st Avn Bde, APO 96307

PART II

12. THE SERVICES REPORTED ABOVE WERE PERFORMED IN A (SATISFACTORY) (UNSATISFACTORY) MANNER
(If Unsatisfactory, Attach Explanation)

DATE	NAME, TITLE AND GRADE OF DESIGNATED SUPERVISOR	SIGNATURE
9 May 1967	JAMES L. STEWART, Major, TC	*James Stewart*

ORGANIZATION AND ADDRESS

330th Transportation Company
765th Transportation Battalion (AM&S)
APO 96291

AMC Form
5 Oct 66   1478-R

3-3 Copy of Maintenance Performance Report 1478-R

61

Item 11. Briefed Staff Officers on T-53 L-13 operation, maintenance of fuel
control and fuel system.
Assisted personnel in analyzing pilots EGT Overtemp. System. This
unit arrived from Ft. Rucker without sufficient instructions.

FOR HWP USE

DATE RECEIVED | FOLLOW UP REQUIRED | SUSPENSE DATE
☐ YES ☐ NO

ACTION ASSIGNED TO | DATE REPLY MAILED

REMARKS

3-3 Copy of Maintenance Performance Report 1478—R page 2

Photo 3-4
T-53-L13 Army Personnel

10 Feb '67

Dear Emmett:

In very sorry that I have to resort to writing this letter, but in this situation I believe you, as my supervisor should know what is actually happening here in Vung Tau. After my telephone Conversation with you several events took place.

When my team arrived in Vung Tau 20 Dec 66, Lt Hansen AAMTAP OIC, advised me, at the end of each class, the students were to fill out Critique Sheets.

Today 10 Feb 67, I asked Mr Russell where the Critique sheets were for his class that graduated on 3 Feb 67. Mr. Russell stated that there were no blank forms in the filing Cabinet. I asked him why he didn't give out plain sheets of paper, in lieu of the regular ones. Mr Russell stated that he didn't have to do this, that the AAMTAP school was to support him in this respect, In not denying this, but

3-5 My letter to Emmett Knight

64

we must be able to bend with the
wind and use anything at our disposal.
Mr Russell further stated that we
weren't receiving proper support from the
765th, so far he gotten anything required
in our course. Mr Russell supported
his statement by saying, he purchased
color pencils and one ac receptacle plug
on the local market. If the school
wanted to support him, then they could
supply these items to him. For myself,
I hand carried a lot of goodies, it added
extra weight and hindered myself by making
extra baggage trips. But I was using
foresight instead of hind sight.

I further stated to Mr. Russell as
Team Coordinator, it was my responsibility
of putting the required paperwork into the
proper channels.

Mr Russell stated, in front of Mr Reece
that I wasn't his supervisor. That he wasn't
going to follow any orders, I give to him,
and that "your not my boss".

3-5 My letter to Emmett Knight page 2

3.

I asked him if he read the letter from Mr. Bartley on what my responsibilities were. Mr. Russell stated "to hell with that letter", nothing in it gave me the authority to direct him to do anything. (Attached is copy - please let me know what my responsibilities are?; if I'm in error in accomplishing my assigned duties, I apologies)

Mr. Russell also stated that I wasn't qualified to judge anything involving the T-53 engine, but that I was fully qualified on the T-55. I answered by saying I'm equally qualified on both engines. One reason, I adhere strictly to schedules, lesson plans and cover all phases. That I'm no dunce, I've completed T-53-L13, and am happy when I have a challenge in front of me. I do believe my past performance will speak for itself.

This morning 11 Feb '67, Mr. Parker at Vung Tau Officer Open Mess, told me once again, that the brown stuff was going to

3-5 My letter to Emmett Knight page 3

hit the fan. That Mr. Mac Elveney, a Lt. in their class, a Specialist 6 (both of these were monitoring classes) and himself were drinking, and these students advised them how lousey some of the T-53 and Huey classes were. These students told Mac Elveney and Parker they could not afford to let any personnel attend these schools, because of personnel shortage and pulling various missions. So to prevent any students from attending, their own organizations would put in a report through channels of our school deficiencies, to the 34th General Support Grp. This would alleviate the Company of sending personnel TDY. All I can say is this is one hell of a way to win this war.

Then, Mr. Russell joined us at our table and he started to object to how I was handling my team "he stated "of all the DAC personnel, I was the only one F_____ up. I retorted by

3-5 My letter to Emmett Knight page 4

saying, as long as I'm Team Coordinator, we would obey any requirements or regulations set down for us, or words to that effect.

Emmett at this time, I'd like to say this, you know of my conversation with Harlyn Hubbs and yourself about the trouble I was having with Mr. Russell. I want to recommend that he be relieved of duty and returned to St. Louis before other factors catch up to him. But here are a few reasons.

Mr. Russell has a tendency of deviating from all schedules (Mr. Reece and I have used these schedule all the way through class instruction, and they are perfect in the presentation).

On another occasion, Mr. Russell started to argue with me in front of a class. One student witnessed it and wrote him up on a critique sheet. This arguement was caused, because he got all fouled up on his lectures. He

3-5 My letter to Emmett Knight page 5

asked me "What do I have to cover and what am I supposed to do?"
I replied have you followed the schedule?, Mr Russell said that the schedule was all screwed up. I again advised him, this schedule was the one Mr Birch and himself was using in the states. It was the most current item that he had and was supposed to met the Curriculum II Course of instruction. I asked why can't you follow your own guide, Mr Russell admitted that it was not organized. At this time Mr Reece and myself sat down and came up with the one we are presently using. In the event you would like to monitor either T-53 class, I'll furnish you with one of these schedules outlining the day and hour by hour of subjects to be taught.

Mr Russell will not adapt to policies sent to me from St Louis, such

3-5 My letter to Emmett Knight page 6

As using standard forms, that St. Louis request to be filled in and returned.

Mr. Russell has a habitual sore throat, on 30 Jan. to 3 Feb '67, Mr. Reece substituted for Mr. Russell. Again today, 11 Feb '67 Mr. Russell can't speak. The Doctor told him not to talk, drink or smoke for one week, this was on 30 Jan 67, two days was all that he could take, so he started to talk and smoke, consequent it has prolonged his illness. It appears to me that Mr. Russell cannot adequately give 80 hrs of instruction. He can go for 40 hrs, but on the next 40 hours he has this sore throat. If this pattern persists what would be a good solution? As my friend, and my supervisor can you assist me in solving this problem?

After arriving at AAMTAP office this morning 11 Feb '67 (The 765th Trans Bn had us scheduled to instruct Pilots in Ground school Saturdays). Mr. Mac Elveny

3-5 My letter to Emmett Knight page 7

really climbed all over me verbally, he stated that Parker and himself, were out drinking with a Lt. in a Huey Class, and a Spec-6 in my class, after getting them drunk they both told Mac Elveny and Parker they were monitoring the classes. Mr Parker and Mac Elveny, over heard these students, say they were to report back to their Maintenance Officer and recommending no more personnel attend these classes.

It so happened this Spec 6. Had 10 years experience in CH-21, H-13, H23, 3 months in UH-1, no gas turbine engine experience. On 10 Feb 67, this Spec 6 made 95 on the test and took "Top Honor" student. I have his test paper, background paper and critique sheets in my possession for my own protection.

If my course was so lousey, how could this man with no gas turbine experience, score so high. And no one can say I review or give "test"

3-5 My letter to Emmett Knight page 8

9

reviews, all I can say, Reece and myself did a good job of instructing.

Now to go back to Mac Elveney, he stated a letter was in Channels to 34th General Support Group, indicating the T-53 team #1 and team #2, also Mr Wood and Mr Grimes was doing an unsatisfactory job. Further, that the letter is recommending our being relieved and returned to states for inefficiency.

Mr Mac Elveney sat down and was writing direct to St. Louis advising him of this situation and letting them know first hand. I told him he should coordinate with you, he said to hell with you, he wasn't going to do that, St Louis should know about it now.

I tried all day to give you the poop, but phone was out.

I don't get it, why Mac Elveney and Parker think they are authorities on our jobs, why do they think they are

3-5 My letter to Emmett Knight page 9

so efficient on their jobs? dont ask me., unless fraternizing with students and buying them drinks is setting a high standard for them, and this gives them the authority to criticise others.

In doing everything in my power to stay out of their way and not cause any trouble. But Emmett I feel if this keeps going and not stopped our whole DAC program will suffer and in the end you and the rest of us will be hurt.

Along these lines one more thing Reece, Grimes and myself are the only ones over here with authorized clothing while the other team members wear civilian clothes, civilian khakis and any thing of their own liking. This sets a pretty poor picture, when St Louis directed me to have U.S. Army issue before leaving the states. This letter was also given to all members of DAC.

3-5 My letter to Emmett Knight page 10

11

At this time, by removing Mr Russell, this may make the rest of the DAC personnel wake up to the fact that they are still on trial period too, and that this could happen to them.

In writing this in strict confidence I'll do nothing or say nothing until you contact me personally.

Today Mr Russell informed me that a position in St Louis was open to him or offered to him. My own personal views - not another Cox, or riding a gravy train for a GS-12. But I do believe our Maintenance Assistance Team would be better off by letting him accept this position. He can always acquire a better instructor that can adapt to AMSAV's policies.

I'll do my best in this position, I'll never let St Louis down if in my earthly powers to prevent it.

3-5 My letter to Emmett Knight page 11

12.

I feel that I'm giving you as much first hand info afforded me, that these may be serious accusations but they are as true as can be stated, and accurate as possible.

Its true, relieving one member of the team would hamper our over all coverage, but Reece, I know, will or would assume his fair share load, and I'm willing to assume my duties.

So until I hear from you, or you can come down, I will sit tight and hold the reigns as Team Coordinator.

Sincerely,

Wayne A. Kuschel

3-5 My letter to Emmett Knight page 12

3-6 Mom-a-son's the builders

3-6
Mom-a-son's the builders

AMSAV-F(NMP) (11 Mar 67)   3d Ind
SUBJECT: Letter of Appreciation

Directorate of Maintenance, Headquarters, US Army Aviation Materiel Command,
P. O. Box 209, St. Louis, Missouri 63166   23 June 1967

TO: Mr. Wayne Kuschel, Technical Assistance Division, Directorate of
    Maintenance

   1. The attached letter from the President of the United States,
together with related correspondence, is forwarded with sincere appreciation
for your outstanding efforts in connection with the preparation of units for
movement to Vietnam.

   2. It goes without saying that it takes every member of the team, working together, to accomplish the desired objective. Your excellent contribution to the success of this endeavor is commendable and reflects creditably
on you, this directorate and the command.

   3. A copy of this correspondence will be placed in your official 201
file.

1 Incl   ALBERT NEWTON
   as   Colonel, GS
                                      Director of Maintenance (NMP)

3-7 Letter of Appreciation

AMSAV-G(RCS) (11 Mar 67)   2d Ind
SUBJECT: Letter of Appreciation

Headquarters, U. S. Army Aviation Materiel Command, P. O. Box 209, Main
Office, St. Louis, Missouri 63166 27 APR 1967

TO: Colonel Albert Newton, Director of Maintenance

1. It goes without saying that to have received a letter of appreciation from the President of the United States fills me with deep emotion
and personal pride. However, I immediately become humbly proud when I
realize that the credit for any praise belongs, not to me, but to those
members of my staff who have given so unstintingly of their time, know-how
and personal energy to assure the accomplishment of our mission.

2. Seldom is a Commander happier than when he is able to take stock
and find himself associated with and supported by such a capable and
efficient staff. My happiness is compounded when I find that I am the
recipient of letters such as the ones attached. Recognition of our capabilities and contribution, not only by President Johnson but also by members
of our Congress and the Secretary of the Army, helps to lighten our seem-
ingly insurmountable burden of logistics support in the current conflict.

3. I realize that there are many people on your staff who are to
receive a portion of this accolade and that without their assistance our
logistics program would not be recognized as an efficient operation.
Please extend my appreciation to other members of your organization.

4. A copy of this correspondence will be placed in your 201 file.

1 Incl
nc
                              HOWARD F. SCHILTZ
                              Brigadier General, USA
                              Commanding

3-7 Letter of Appreciation page 2

AMCPT-MP (11 Mar 67)   1st Ind
SUBJECT: Letter of Appreciation

HQ, U. S. Army Materiel Command, Washington, D. C. 20315   3 0 MAR 1967

TO: Brigadier General Howard F. Schiltz, Commanding General, U. S. Army
    Aviation Materiel Command, Post Office Box 209, St. Louis, Missouri
    63166

1. It is with great pleasure and pride that I forward the attached
correspondence concerning the logistical support of our forces in Vietnam
provided by you and members of your command.

2. To these commendatory expressions I add my personal thanks and
appreciation to you and each member of your command responsible for the
service which merited this recognition and which reflects such outstanding credit upon the participants, the U. S. Army Materiel Command and the
United States Army. I extend my congratulations on a job well done.

3. Copies of this correspondence should be placed in the official
files of all personnel concerned. Copies have been made a part of your
official personnel files.

1 Incl   F. S. BESSON, JR.
nc   General, USA
                                    Commanding

3-7 Letter of Appreciation page 3

80

UNITED STATES ARMY

THE CHIEF OF STAFF

11 March 1967

SUBJECT: Letter of Appreciation

THRU: Commanding General
          United States Army Materiel Command
          Washington, D. C. 20315

TO: Brigadier General Howard F. Schiltz
          Commanding General
          United States Army Aviation Materiel Command
          St. Louis, Missouri 63102

1. I am most pleased to forward the attached correspondence
from the Honorable Stanley R. Resor and the Honorable John Young
who commend you and the members of your command for the job
you are doing in support of our forces in Vietnam.

2. Copies of this correspondence have been placed in your
official files.

                              HAROLD K. JOHNSON
1 Incl   General, United States Army
  as   Chief of Staff

3-7 Letter of Appreciation page 4

SECRETARY OF THE ARMY
WASHINGTON

7 MAR 1967

MEMORANDUM FOR THE CHIEF OF STAFF, U. S. ARMY

SUBJECT: Letters of Appreciation

It is a pleasure to forward the attached letter from Representative John Young transmitting a copy of a letter President Johnson wrote to Brigadier General Howard F. Schiltz. A copy of my reply is attached for your information.

I want to add my appreciation for the support which General Schiltz and his men are giving our forces in Vietnam.

Stanley R. Resor

Stanley R. Resor

Incl
as

3-7 Letter of Appreciation page 5

JOHN YOUNG
14th District, Texas

Congress of the United States
House of Representatives
Washington, D.C.

February 27, 1967

Honorable Stanley R. Resor
Secretary of the Army
Department of the Army
Washington, D. C.

Dear Mr. Secretary:

Americans can be justly proud of the United States Army for many reasons. Of the highest order is the valor of our fighting men and the wisdom of leaders like yourself who exercise superb judgment in placing the right men in the right places at the right time. Our soldiers could not be the greatest fighting men in the world without the logistic support to keep them fully supplied at all times. The people you have placed in charge of this logistic effort are performing miracles heretofore unknown to the annals of military science. I commend you for your judgment.

The President has been most outspoken in his praise of our present logistic effort and the men behind it. From time to time, he has seen fit to express this admiration in writing; and, because he knows of my interest and support of the Army Materiel Command, he often favors me with copies of letters he has addressed to AMC personnel performing these modern-day miracles of supply and logistics.

In this connection, the President has sent me a copy of his letter of February 18 in which he pays the highest tribute to Brigadier General Howard F. Schiltz, U. S. Army Aviation Materiel Command, for the great and incomparable work he has done and is doing in the field of Army Aviation logistics. I have never met General Schiltz, but I know of him and I know that in him you have "the right man in the right place at the right time." The President has described General Schiltz' work "as important as any field commander's." I would go a step further and add that, by the very nature of things, there are few if any field commanders who could do the job General Schiltz is doing in the field of aviation logistics.

3-7 Letter of Appreciation page 6

83

I want to commend you for your effort in seeing that the right people are in the right jobs and to ask that you see that the copy of the President's letter which I am enclosing herewith is placed in Brigadier General Howard F. Schiltz' official file.

With kind best wishes for your continued success in heading the best supplied fighting force the world has ever seen, I remain

Sincerely yours,

John Young
United States Congress

Encl.

3-7 Letter of Appreciation page 7

February 18, 1967

Dear General Schilt:

I am sure that military history will record
the movement of American troops to Vietnam
as the high-water mark in logistics planning.
An Army is unable to fight unless it has the
materials with which to fight. I catalogue
your job as important as any field commander's,
and I share with you the pride that you and your
men must feel on this magnificent accomplishment.

I just want you to know that the work that you
and your men are doing is greatly appreciated
by me.

                    Sincerely,

              s/ Lyndon B. Johnson

Brigadier General Howard F. Schilts
Commanding General
U. S. Army Aviation Materiel Command
P.O. Box 209, Main Post Office
St. Louis, Missouri 63166

JJ:fs

3-7 Letter of Appreciation page 8

CHAPTER 4-
THREATS, SWEATS AND
TRANSFER TO CU CHI

Anyhow, Mr. Russell and I crossed swords at Vung Tau, so to speak, disagreeing on many things that AVSCOM stated were required by the head office. (You have to realize that I had never been a supervisor of other United States Army civil service employees before, and I had no knowledge of not being an actual supervisor on AVSCOM official orders). You're supposed to have orders indicating supervisor on civilian personnel orders to give any personnel instructions. Mr. Russell was a hot-headed character and would drag his feet whenever you needed correspondence for input, information, or reports on any AAMTAP requirement, especially for higher command's needs, to keep everyone on the same sheet of paper (so to say).

The letter Mr. Bartley gave me December 1966 stated "Supervision of team military duties", so I assumed, and you never assume, that was wrong. Mr. Russell quoted a line "You're not my supervisor" so I backed off from his lousy disposition. I had a job to do, so I went through military channels and accomplished the necessary correspondence for AVSCOM. I finally realized after I returned to AVSCOM that all official orders had to have a supervisor(s) on your assigned position. (But I'll say one thing, when I was assigned a permanent position on my return to AVSCOM and was made a supervisor, never had any more problems with the guys in the black hats and never overstepped my duties in accomplishing same).

The next chance we got to talk with our friend "Rocky" Demarest was when he showed Bernie and me a Thompson .45 Caliber machine gun that he said would be sufficient fire power to thwart or defeat any Viet Cong attack on the hotel. I mentioned before, no civil service personnel were to have any firearms and if caught that the Viet Cong would kill the person, so what do you do when no one listens to any command instructions? We got around to talking over spare time activity. Mr. "Rocky" Demarest said he was into a part-time gambling position working as a card dealer (gambler) and bouncer when needed. He volunteered more information that there was some sort of mafia type operation within a United States Sponsored Barge Company where the supervisors were responsible for the area gambling operations.

A couple of days later at our AAMTAP Vung Tau school instructors room, two other civil service employees "Mac" McElvaney and "Joe" Parker were talking about their taking over a house for gambling and other items. We put it out of our mind, and went on with our instructing of the T-53-L-13 gas turbine engine. I believe in the ethics codes, when you work for the Federal Government you work for the establishment, be honest and don't stab anyone in the back. Especially don't stab the one that is paying your way, or do anything to discredit the government. Eight hours work for eight hours pay, that's my motto. [Picture time at Vung Tau Officer Club 4-1]

My time spent in Republic of Vietnam was more business than anything else, of course you had party bums around you who thought of nothing but drinking and driving in that condition. My limit to drinking was very limited one or two beers period. Time off we used to go to the

French beach and admire the blue-green waters rolling up on the shores of the beach and talking about airplanes, combat situations plus the good old United States of America.

Once in a while if you had extra time on your hands, you would go visiting the other AVSCOM personnel. There were lots of buddy's that drank, guess to make time go by faster and some of their furniture was in bad shape-they could care less if any furniture broke, say a leg, all they would do is use a case or two of Pearl beer to prop under the furniture for use. Don't recall any deposit required when you rented the place.

As time went by, our "two Civil Service black hat bad boys" had a large helicopter fly in to Vung Tau a 10K watt gas powered generator to be used for lighting the gambling facilities. Who provided the fuel, oil, and maintenance, God only knows, probably the P.A.&E Barge Company, where in turn the United States tax paying people or by a big government contract. Since everyone was supposed to be on the job, the two pecks bad boys in black hats were set up differently, where one was on the job instructing the AAMTAP U-H1 (Huey) airframe daily, the other was running the gambling house, then next day the other instructor would swap out. Only one UH-1 (Huey) instructor was on duty at Vung Tau airbase at a time, this was a proven point in the ensuing United States Army CID investigation.

When I went to Vietnam I purchased $4,500.00 in Dallas, Texas, Republic National Bank traveler's checks. Four of these checks were given to our civil service friend, Captain R.D. Brown or Mr. "Rocky" Demarest at the hotel for rent thru 31 May 1967, as per my receipt which stated or showed for "Pete's Place #00109, date was 17 March 1967". [Rent Paid in Full 4-2]

I was being very careful with counting of my traveler's checks, but somehow I lost track of one. I wrote to the Republic National Bank of Dallas address and asked them for an accounting of what check numbers

I had used up. The bank did better than that they sent me an envelope dated 3 May 1967 copies of each check that I had used. This was real good material, so I began comparing numbers with the ones I had spent. Low and behold, four of the checks I gave to Captain R.D. Brown or "Rocky" Demarest for my quarters allowance turned up with "Hong Kong" stamped on them. Where I didn't write in the hotel name in the "pay to the order of" line, it had another company name on it (what are friends for, if you can't trust them?), so these checks were put on the black market for a profit of four to one or $400.00 for each $100.00. How many times would anyone write for verification of their used traveler's checks and find out they were illegally diverted to gain a monetary gain?

Time went by and the two fellows with black hats or Peck's bad boys were bragging about the large amount of cash they were accumulating in gambling funds. Mail was used to send it to the states. Some of us were abiding by all the rules set down by the United States Army the best way we could, and here were two fellows that could care less, all they wanted was the "green" cash or money over everything else, and would risk their Department of Army Civil Service Career Status in accomplishing their greedy money wants. Taking their daily duty pay without working for it, this in my book is fraud or the perversion of truth for their money gains.

On another occasion the two fellows in "black hats" stole a round drum of heavy duty electrical wire from the AAMTAP supply room. They simply rolled it out to a 3/4 ton truck and made off with it. They were rewiring the gambling house for their personal benefit. [Copy of Maintenance Performance Report 1478-R 4-3]

This one evening Bernie and I rode into the marketplace to see the sights on this market street, and take some camera shots of local businesses and various sights. There was a mom-a-son behind a shed holding a small duck and she was pulling the feathers off the little fellow. Well, Bernie went behind the shed and told the mom-a-son to dunk the duck in boiling water after the duck was killed then the feathers could be pulled off easy. She argued with Bernie, "No! No! Pull the feathers this way." We didn't make any points so we went to the Pacific Hotel to eat. The owner asked us to come up to the top floor and celebrate the "Grand Opening" of the restaurant that night. A shower was in order, and the proper clothing put on, then we proceeded to the roof. The hotel owner said he had a special meal for us tonight. Guess what turned up on the seven course meal? You guessed it, "DUCK"! I could hardly eat anything but the tea was good.

While on the roof that night the Viet Cong were attacking all sides of Vung Tau and the helicopters were dropping continuous flares to show where the Viet Cong were. No warning or sirens were blaring so we didn't go to any shelter. The United States Army helicopters kept dropping flares until the early morning. You could read a newspaper by the light of the flares.

The checks with Hong Kong stamped on them shocked the heck out of me, so Bernie and I on 8 May 1967 went to the United States Army CID Headquarters and reported the problems. After reporting into the CID the investigator kept questioning about the background and what was said and were we sure of passing the traveler's checks to the P.A.&E hotel manager. The involved "Hong Kong" traveler's checks were given to the CID 8 May 1967. The CID then gave me a receipt showing each check number. [Copy of military police receipt for property 4-4]

They even questioned us about the gambling situation, they were advised about the rumors of mafia organized gambling and everything that was going on with the current status. By all indications the CID started an in-depth investigation into all facets of the illegal gambling activities.

Leaving the CID area, we returned to Vung Tau Airbase to continue the T-53-L-13 engine course. After the class, we departed the AAMTAP school area. We returned to Vung Tau and were advised the white mice (Vietnam police) shut down all prostitution rings, gambling and the police were raiding homes where numerous United States Government items taken or stolen from the airbase were returned to the United States authorities. Gee! Whiz, guess I stirred up a bee hive or hornets' nest because when one's life is threatened it must be a serious matter to the persons wearing black hats (Peck's bad boys). Regardless, I did the best that I could do under the circumstances even though it took a change of climate and area to accomplish and elimination of the "Hong Kong" check episode. My brain was trying to tell me more things than I could comprehend, one being my safety. What would be a good method of describing to the authorities, who may be the unknown guilty parties if I'm killed for any reason?

That afternoon the base commanding officer, LTC Colonel Kincaid, called all civilians into a large room at Vung Tau Army Airbase and pulled no punches on what was taking place and what the end results would be if anyone was caught. Pecks bad boys continued their gambling venture as though no one had mentioned the speech by Colonel Kincaid, regarding not doing one's instructor duty to the United States government. The words went in one ear and out the other, like their brains were not engaged and they heard nothing.

A date requirement came through channels for me to select a site in the United States of America for a specific assignment. I considered a CH-47 (Chinook) Army post, the closest one was Fort Sill, Oklahoma and AVSCOM tentatively approved it (for now). [Rotation to the U.S.A. 4-5], [Copy of Maintenance Performance Report 1478 R 4-6]

Bernie and I had to play it cool and not discuss anything. It was hard to do with lots of your buddies around. I didn't believe Bernie or I was at fault. We were innocent victims of the Peck's bad boys get rich scheme. That night, Monday, 20 June 1967, Bernie and I were sitting in the Vung Tau Officers Open mess and Bernie pushed a small written note to me that read "Go home and pack, we will see LTC Kincaid at 0700 pm. The Vietnamese are going to get you." I was so shook up I couldn't even eat, but

I tried. So I cut short my eating and left for my hotel room. Shortly Bernie came over. He had the bus and I was all set, my suitcases were packed, so in the dark we put my things in the back of the bus. We were very careful and headed for the Vung Tau Army Airbase; we went through the gate and proceeded to LTC Kincaid office at 765th Transportation headquarters. [Bernie's warning at Officers Club 4-7], [LTC Kincaid's letter subject Mr. Wayne A. Kuschel DAC GS-12 4-8]

The Commanding Officer, LTC Kincaid, was in his office late that night, whereby Bernie and I repeated the whole sordid tale about what was happening and the cowboy threat against my life. To have a life snuffed out in Vietnam, the right people who had the correct mafia authority and connection to give the go ahead, would cost only $10.00. I had no protection against unknown participants; I was at the mercy of anyone that wanted to harm me. It was my understanding that a female employee of the Barge Company was, in reality in charge of ill-gotten money gains from personnel in the city of Vung Tau. She was that one person that had all the influential and crooked personnel working for her. When trouble arose she had specific people take necessary action to eliminate the problems, especially selecting the cowboys on motorbikes to wipe out their enemies for as little fee of $10.00. That is a small monetary amount to destroy one's life. My object was to stay ahead of these ruffians and be transferred to another area in Vietnam, which in my case happened.

LTC Kincaid made some phone calls to distant locations. He said that I would stay on Vung Tau Army Air Base until suitable accommodations could be found elsewhere. My thirty hours of waiting was torture enough, let alone the anxiety of what I was involved in, a United States Army investigation and that of saving my life. I tried to rest, thinking of what revenge the Pecks bad boys were up to, how they would prevent me from getting out of their reach where they could not do me bodily harm, such as paying the Viet Cong-type cowboys $10.00 to snuff out my life. What a payback that would be. I think that Pecks bad boys and all their buddies were the people wearing black hats and should have been taken care of, at least kicked out of Vietnam and lose their jobs. These were contractors or personnel working for the United States Government and should have been put in prison for their participation in ill gain money scheme of gambling.

After many miserable hours, I was escorted by the military police to a UH-1(Huey) helicopter and my bags put on board. I was really in the dark and scared to death where was I going. What was my destination? It was darker than I have ever seen it before. The only lights were search lights and little landing lights, the air inside the Huey was moist, hot, and very scary. What was I getting into, would I be in friendly territory? Time would tell.

You can say what you want to, but in my predicament a person's heart, such as mine, was pounding and beating away, waiting for the anxiety to end so that my heart would again smooth out and go back to normal. Of course, I mean my blood pressure.

As time went by, I began to feel more at ease in the helicopter and my heartbeat was settling or slowing down a little. It felt good to be in a secure area, away from Vung Tau. At least I didn't have really high blood pressure at this time and I began to breathe much easier than at any other time that I could remember as a result of my turning the traveler's checks in to the CID 8 May 1967.

Why did I, or should I feel guilty? For what transpired, I was protecting my career and personal being. I didn't do anything that any red-blooded person would not have done. When you know that you're involved, regardless of who was right or wrong, no one but me was going to take the blame on this black market incident because of Pecks bad boys and their involvement to receive ill-gained money. Just remember if you want to be a thief or crook, the wrong incident will come back and haunt you, if you have any type of a conscience, the likes of mine.

After I received the memorandum for record (MFR) from Headquarters 34th General Support Group (AM&S), dated 20 June 1967, SUBJECT: Mr. Wayne A. Kuschel, DAC, GS-12, the MFR became public knowledge. It pointed out that personnel thought I was an <u>informer.</u> My thinking on that matter was why didn't the guilty parties think of my rights as being violated, why did I have to take the extreme measures and turn my cancelled checks with "Hong Kong" stamped on them, over to the CID, and provide a sworn statement that I was <u>not</u> involved in black marketing? Why would I jeopardize my United States Army career for a gain of $1,200.00 from ill-gotten funds from "Hong Kong"?

Why should I have to defend my actions, as stated in a 20 June 1967 letter from HQ 34th General Support Group (AM&S) APO 96307? When you're a law-abiding citizen or a Department of the Army Civilian (DAC), I didn't do anything wrong, the bad black hat guys used my four traveler's checks for a gain in their monetary funds. Besides that, how come in another case, a check of mine given to the Vung Tau Officers Club for $12.50 went into an individual's personal checking account in San Francisco, California? So why would I be named as "Informer" or the culprit? Put the blame on the persons who did the wrong choice of their thinking, or their greedy desires. I didn't need money that bad to be on the other side of the law or cheat the service of my required on duty time.

The UH-1 (Huey) had gained altitude to be safe and we went towards a real orange glow in the distance, which was Saigon. We flew over Saigon and headed west into the dark. Again, it was nearly 0130 a.m. when the pilot called for landing instructions. I could not relate as to where I was. We started to drop down or descend in the UH-1 (Huey), which landed in an open field. My pilot (unknown) had personnel come to the UH-1 (Huey) for my luggage and I was taken to the Officer's Quarters of the 20th Transportation Company at Cu Chi located in the Iron Triangle, and given a place to relax and sleep for a couple of hours.

The next day after a restless night, I was greeted by the personnel of the 20th Transportation Company (ADS) commanded by Major John K. Clements. This organization was on the north edge of Cu Chi, a half block from what was known as "no man's land" through a barbed wire fence, and near the edge of a stream 1/4 mile north of us. There was no shrubbery or trees for about a mile out in front of this area, possibly Agent Orange was utilized first. It then looked like the "ball and chain" had rolled through the area, then bulldozers cleaned up the mess. This area was free of any hiding places for Viet Cong's to snipe or shoot at the camp area or carry satchel charges for destructive reasons, to blow up whatever type of aircraft or helicopters would be available to destroy or damage same.

Little did I know there was going to be a large scale United States Army investigation, not that I would have chickened out and withdrawn my paperwork from CID. The way I saw it, it was an established mark against my unblemished record. I paid my hotel rent for a month, with Republic National Bank of Dallas traveler's checks ($400.00 worth) and Peck's black hat bad boys had the gall, since they were involved with the hotel managers "who said they had a business stamp" in their office and would stamp them before depositing same. Well, they didn't fulfill their business obligation, and in doing so could have caused my career to go down the drain, plus their own careers. If the proper command and staff would have started to investigate the allegation of the black market or "Hong Kong" money being involved, I believe a lot of foot-dragging and cover-up was the reason nothing was accomplished.

Then all hell had broke loose on the T-53-L-13 gas turbine training because AAMTAP was again taking over Lycoming's contract and Lycoming didn't feel that the Army was capable and ready to begin instructing this new engine information to the United States Army Aircraft personnel. Mr. Gerau, AVSCOM current manager of gas turbine engines at Vung Tau, feels it would be unwise to bring me back with the CID black market investigation ongoing. This might put me on display or available for the Peck's bad boys to accomplish their threats against me or my life.

Things that were told about me were totally wrong, taken out of context and was said mainly to blemish my name, record or discredit me within United States Army channels. Rumors are hard to justify or suppress because many people believe in whatever lies or tales people spread, they like nasty things to hear and believe. Even if they think they are themselves above and beyond reproach.

Again all personnel were previously briefed by LTC Kincaid on the black market incident and knew it was a NO! NO! situation. If you went against existing regulations you were a dang fool or didn't want a sound job or a career. You know everyone took an oath of office and swore to do their duty, and uphold the position for which the oath was given. My oath meant everything to me. I gave 20 years in my military career with honorable results, and this position in Civil Service was a second career to do my best service for my government. I had no idea I was walking on very, very thin egg shells while in Vung Tau, Republic of Vietnam. I believe in giving eight hours of work for eight hours of pay, which is better than Pecks bad boys did. Two of them were returned 10 July 1967 to the AVSCOM in St. Louis. For their unforgettable performance of not performing their duties but they were paid $50.00 per diem per day for many months at AVSCOM for their involvement in the black market activities, their part in the United States Army criminal investigation. Why were Peck's bad boys allowed to stay on per diem, collecting the $50.00 per day when they should not have been assigned in PCS from Vietnam, the United States or even at AVSCOM? I truly believe there was hanky-panky going on or civilian personnel did not have knowledge of the correct regulations to get rid of the goof-balls. My thoughts were they should have been dismissed as undesirable personnel; we don't have to have that type of riff-raff in government service. There are more honorable persons available, let alone let them run the gauntlet of lawlessness and retire in the future for services rendered.

The letter from Alton H. Reel dated 23 June 1967, from St. Louis shows how far my friend would go to assist in dissolving the discrepancies or problems, and how much our own supervisor cared as to the real size of the problems that were being created in Vung Tau, Vietnam by unworthy civil servants. The third page where Alton stated "for your eyes only" meant just that, he felt that Mr. Bartley could care less about the problem, since it was in Vietnam, let those people or personnel take care of it. I don't blame Alton for cutting his visit short at Mr. Bartley's office. At least he tried to defend the problems we were having with a bunch of goof-balls that didn't give a crap about anything except making as much ill-gained money as they could. Instead, the Department of the Army should have dismissed them for their disloyal attitudes and behavior. [Alton Reed's letter from USA 4-9], [Copy of Maintenance Performance Report 1478 R 4-10]

4-1
(L To R, Keen, Kuschel, Parker Upper-r, McElvaney Lower-r)
Vung Tau Officer Club

PETE'S PLACE   No   00109

RECEIVED FROM___W. A. Kuschel___ ACCT No:___
FOR (Rent)___Rent thro 31 May 67___
DUES ___
MESS ___   17 Mar 67
CHITS ___   (DATE)
DEPOSIT___
     TOTAL REC'D___307 ⁰⁰___
                        R D Brown
                        (CASHIER)

4-2
Receipt rent paid in Full

MAINTENANCE PERFORMANCE REPORT

1. REPORTING PERIOD FROM *1 MAY '67* TO *31 MAY 67*

TYPE OF REPORT

X	MONTHLY	X	DA CIVILIAN
	SPECIAL		MILITARY
	OTHER		

3. TO *HEADQUARTERS*
US ARMY AVIATION MATERIEL COMMAND
ATTN: AMSAV-EFT

4. FROM (Name, Grade-Rank-Title, Address, and Signature)   **DATE** *1 JUNE '67*
WAYNE A. KUSCHEL GS-11 EQUIPMENT SPECIALIST
HHD 765 TRANS. BN (AM+S) ARMTAP
APO SAN FRANCISCO 96291

PART I

5. UNIT(S) OR ACTIVITY SUPPORTED
330 TRANSPORTATION COMPANY AND SUBORDINATE UNITS

6. BASIC WEAPON (OR EQUIPMENT) SYSTEM ON WHICH ASSISTANCE WAS RENDERED
T-53 L9, L11   UH-1C HELICOPTER
T-55 L7

7. WERE PROBLEMS ENCOUNTERED THAT COULD NOT BE RESOLVED?
(If Yes Explain in Item 13)   ☐ YES   ☒ NO

8. INDICATE PROBLEMS ENCOUNTERED IN AREAS a THRU g BY LISTING NUMBER OF REPORTS SUBMITTED FOR EACH (Assistance)

a. TOOLS AND TEST EQUIPMENT	3	e. TAERS		
b. TECHNICAL PUBLICATIONS	1	f. MALFUNCTION		1
c. SUPPLY AND REPAIR PARTS	2	g. OTHER (Specify)		
d. CHECKS AND ADJUSTMENTS				

9. MANPOWER AND TRAINING DATA

								COMP	PAID
a. DAYS WORKED THIS REPORTING PERIOD	27	b. ANNUAL LEAVE HRS	0	c. SICK LEAVE HRS	0	d. OVERTIME HRS			80
e. TOTAL HOURS SPENT W/UNITS IN ITEM 5	270	f. HOURS OF FORMAL TRAINING CONDUCTED				g. NUMBER OF PERSONS TRAINED (Formal)			
h. HOURS TRAVEL TIME	40	i. HOURS OF OJT			40	j. NUMBER OF PERSONS TRAINED (O/T)			8

k. HOURS SPENT PERFORMING ACTUAL MAINTENANCE FUNCTIONS (Explain in Item 13)
l. OTHER (See Instructions) *ASSISTED SUPERVISORS IN OPERATION OF EQUIPMENT*

10. WERE PROBLEMS AND VISITS DISCUSSED WITH THE COMMAND CM'S AND OR HIS MAINTENANCE OR MATERIEL READINESS OFFICER?   ☒ YES   ☐ NO

11. NAME, TITLE AND ADDRESS OF PERSONNEL CONTACTED OTHER THAN ROUTINE

PART II

12. THE SERVICES REPORTED ABOVE WERE PERFORMED IN A (SATISFACTORY) (UNSATISFACTORY) MANNER
(If Unsatisfactory, Attach Explanation)

DATE	NAME, TITLE AND GRADE OF DESIGNATED SUPERVISOR	SIGNATURE
1 JUNE 67	*JAMES L. SCHWARTZ, MAJOR, TC*	

ORGANIZATION AND ADDRESS
330TH TRANSPORTATION COMPANY
765TH TRANSPORTATION BATTALION (AM+S)
APO 96291

4-3 Maintenance Performance Report 1478-R

Item 13.

1. Assisted the 14Th Assult Support Helicopter Company in acquiring qualified personnel to inspect and troubleshoot #540 system on UH1-C 65-9555.

2. Instructed Dynaelectronic personnel on T-53 L11 engines assigned to 330th Engine Shop.

3. Assisted in research of parts and special tools utilized on T-53 L13 engine.

4. Assisted 330th Engine Shop personnel inspecting the following engines;

    T-53 L11 LE 10943. Number 2 bearing has oil leak. Repaired turn in as serviceable.

    T-55 L7 LE 01033A Power turbine package #4 & #5 bearing replaced Repaired turn in as serviceable

    T-63 Engine preserved in accordance with latest tech manuals.

    T-53 L11 LE 11469A Instructed personnel on removal and inspection of reduction gearing.

4-3
Maintenance Performance Report 1478-R page 2

T-53 L11B LE 12619 NRTS - 5th stage blades
worked to the rear.

T-53 L11 LE 11885A NRTS - Compressor hub
and damage to blades,
stator and centrifugal
compressor.

T-53 L11 LE 09196 Low power, dirty inlet
housing turned in as
serviceable.

T-53 L9A LE 03070 Foreign object damage
N R T S.

4-3
Maintenance Performance Report 1478-R page 3

101

MILITARY POLICE RECEIPT FOR PROPERTY (AR 190-22)	COMPLAINT OR CASE NR (If any) on (USARV-2524)-67-51

UNIT DESIGNATION OF RECEIVING HEADQUARTERS 252d MP Det (CI)	LOCATION APO San Francisco 96291

NAME OF PERSON FROM WHOM PROPERTY IS OBTAINED ☒ OWNER Mr Wayne A. KUSCHEL DAC ☐ OTHER	ADDRESS HHD 765th Trans Bn (AM&S) AAMTAP APO San Francisco 96291

LOCATION OF PROPERTY
252d MP Det (CI)

PURPOSE FOR WHICH OBTAINED
Evidence Evaluation

ITEM NR	QUAN-TITY	DESCRIPTION OF ARTICLES (Include model, serial Nr, identifying marks, condition, and value, when appropriate)
1	1	ENVELOPE, Air Mail sent from the Republic National Bank Of Dallas to Mr KUSCHEL Postmarked Dallas Texas May 3 67, initialed EDF, dated 8 May 67./////////
2	1	Letter from Republic National Bank to Mr KUSCHEL, dated May 3, 1967, initialed EDF, dated 8 May 1967./////////////////////////
3	6	CHECKS, Travelers, issued by the Republic National Bank of Dallas to Mr KUSCHEL numbered in sequence from C1230551 through C1230556, marked EDF, dated 8 May 67
4	6	CHECKS, Travelers, issued by the Republic National Bank of Dallas to Mr KUSCHEL numbered in sequence from C1230565 through C1230570, marked EDF, dated 8 May 67
////////////////////////////LAST ITEM////////////////////////////		

WITNESSED BY: *Clarence C Wallace* *Wayne A. Kuschel*
CLARENCE C. WALLACE   WAYNE A. KUSCHEL, DAC, GS 11
Criminal Investigator

I CERTIFY THAT I HAVE RECEIVED AND HOLD MYSELF RESPONSIBLE FOR THE ARTICLES LISTED ABOVE.

DATE 8 May 1967	TYPED NAME, GRADE AND BRANCH EUGENE D. FINNERAN, Criminal Investigator	SIGNATURE *Eugene D Finneran*

CHAIN OF CUSTODY

ITEM NR	DATE	RELINQUISHED BY	RECEIVED BY	PURPOSE OF CHANGE OF CUSTODY
		TYPED NAME, GRADE AND BRANCH	TYPED NAME, GRADE AND BRANCH	
		SIGNATURE	SIGNATURE	
		TYPED NAME, GRADE AND BRANCH	TYPED NAME, GRADE AND BRANCH	
		SIGNATURE	SIGNATURE	
		TYPED NAME, GRADE AND BRANCH	TYPED NAME, GRADE AND BRANCH	
		SIGNATURE	SIGNATURE	
		TYPED NAME, GRADE AND BRANCH	TYPED NAME, GRADE AND BRANCH	
		SIGNATURE	SIGNATURE	

DA. FORM 19-31

4-4
Copy of Military Police receipt for property

15 May 1967

Leonard E. Bartley
USAAVCOM Technical Assistance
Program Manager

SUBJECT: Rotational Program for Equipment
Specialists assigned to Technical
Assistance Division

1. The undersigned requests your permission to be returned to CONUS
15 December 1967 per Standing Operating Procedures Number SMOSM-FTT 65-5
dated 4 November 1965.

2. Request three weeks of leave be taken at my residence, 4175
Adams Street, Riverside, California 92504, before proceeding to my next
duty station. This leave will be used in selling my home, signing documents
and shipping household goods to my new duty station. I also would like
the latest information regarding PCS moves, what I can do, and what I
cannot do. This will eliminate any problem on my part.

3. Upon my return to CONUS, request that I be considered for a
geographical location on the west coast or mid-west area as a Technical
Representative on T-53 L-11, L-13 or T-55 L-7 gas turbine engines.

4. I would appreciate this consideration on geographic location
because of my wife's illness. Since 1957 she has been under doctors
care for bronical asthma and respiratory ailments. This requires her to
be in a relatively dry area.

5. I know that my position in AVCOM has no bearing on paragraph 4,
but this would give me the opportunity to be with my family after a long
period of separation.

6. In the future I would also like to be considered for another
overseas assignment, other than RVN.

Sincerely yours,

WAYNE A. KUSCHEL
DAC GS-11
Equipment Specialist

4-5 Rotation to the U.S.A.

MAINTENANCE PERFORMANCE REPORT	1. REPORTING PERIOD

FROM *1 JUNE '67* TO *15 JUNE '67*

TYPE OF REPORT

X	MONTHLY	X	DA CIVILIAN
	SPECIAL		MILITARY
	OTHER		

2. TO *HEADQUARTERS*
US. ARMY AVIATION MATERIEL COMMAND
ATTN: AMSAV-ETI

3. FROM *(Name, Grade-Rank-Title, Address, and Signature)*   DATE *15 JUNE 1967*

WAYNE A. KUSCHEL GS-11 EQUIPMENT SPECIALIST
HHD 765TH TRANS. BN. (AM+S) AAMTAP
APO SAN FRANCISCO 96241

PART I

4. UNIT(S) OR ACTIVITY SUPPORTED

330TH TRANSPORTATION COMPANY (GS) AND SUBORDINATE UNITS

5. BASIC WEAPON (OR EQUIPMENT) SYSTEM ON WHICH ASSISTANCE WAS RENDERED

T-53 L9, L11
T-55 L9

6. WERE PROBLEMS ENCOUNTERED THAT COULD NOT BE RESOLVED?
(If Yes Explain in Item 13)   ☐ YES   ☒ NO

7. INDICATE PROBLEMS ENCOUNTERED IN AREAS c THRU g BY LISTING NUMBER OF REPORTS SUBMITTED FOR EACH (*2331 TAMS*

a. TOOLS AND TEST EQUIPMENT	*5*	e. TAERS	*1*
b. TECHNICAL PUBLICATIONS	*2*	f. MALFUNCTION	*2*
c. SUPPLY AND REPAIR PARTS	*3*	g. OTHER (Specify)	
d. CHECKS AND ADJUSTMENTS	*2*		

9. MANPOWER AND TRAINING DATA

a. DAYS WORKED THIS REPORTING PERIOD	*13*	b. ANNUAL LEAVE HRS	*0*	c. SICK LEAVE HRS	*0*	d. OVERTIME HRS		COMP *0*	PAID *40*
e. TOTAL HOURS SPENT W/UNITS IN ITEM 3	*130*	f. HOURS OF FORMAL TRAINING CONDUCTED				g. NUMBER OF PERSONS TRAINED (Formal)			
h. HOURS TRAVEL TIME	*30*	i. HOURS OF OJT		*18*		j. NUMBER OF PERSONS TRAINED (O/T)			*5*

k. HOURS SPENT PERFORMING ACTUAL MAINTENANCE FUNCTIONS (Explain in Item 13)

l. OTHER (See Instructions) *ASSISTED SUPERVISORS ON OPERATION OF EQUIPMENT*

10. WERE PROBLEMS AND VISITS DISCUSSED WITH THE COMMAND *G & S*
AND OR HIS MAINTENANCE OR MATERIEL READINESS OFFICER?   ☒ YES   ☐ NO

11. NAME, TITLE AND ADDRESS OF PERSONNEL CONTACTED OTHER THAN ROUTINE

PART II

12. THE SERVICES REPORTED ABOVE WERE PERFORMED IN A (SATISFACTORY) (UNSATISFACTORY) MANNER
(If Unsatisfactory, Attach Explanation)

DATE	NAME, TITLE AND GRADE OF DESIGNATED SUPERVISOR	SIGNATURE

ORGANIZATION AND ADDRESS

AMC Form 1478-R
5 Oct 66

4-6
Maintenance Performance Report 1478-R

1. INSTRUCTED DYNAELECLTRONIC PERSONNEL ON T-55 L7 (OJT) IN 330TH ENGINE SHOP. (SYSTEMS AND PRESERVATION).

2. RESEARCHED FOR PARTS REQUIRED IN ENGINE SHOP.

3. ASSISTED 330TH ENGINE SHOP PERSONNEL INSPECTING THE FOLLOWING ENGINES:

T55 L7B LE 04626 COMPRESSOR DAMAGE (NRTS)

T55 L7B LE 04592 #1 SEAL LEAKING, INSTRUCTED ON PRESERVING, F/C. (NRTS)

T53 L11 LE 10301 #2 BEARING AND CARBON SEAL REPLACED - AWAITING ENGINE TEST STAND.

T-55 L7B LE 04328 ~~BORE~~ DAMAGE, (NRTS) REPAIR NOT AUTHORIZED

T-53 L11 LE 09150 COMPRESSOR ERROSION (NRTS)

T-53 L11 LE 11105 P.T. PACKAGE DAMAGED - #2 BEARING FAILURE (NRTS)

FOR NMP USE			
DATE RECEIVED	FOLLOW UP REQUIRED ☐ YES ☐ NO		SUSPENSE DATE
ACTION ASSIGNED TO		DATE REPLY MAILED	
REMARKS			

4-6
Maintenance Performance Report 1478-R page 2

4-7
Bernie's warning at Officers Club

DEPARTMENT OF THE ARMY
HEADQUARTERS, 34TH GENERAL SUPPORT GROUP (AM&S)
APO 96307

AVGF   20 June 1967

MEMORANDUM FOR RECORD

SUBJECT: Mr. Wayne A. Kuschel, DAC, GS-12

1. LTC Kincaid phoned, above date, and discussed problems in Vung Tau concerning Mr. Kuschel. This individual has had his life threatened by Vietnamese and is extremely frightened. The problem is primarily caused by a CID/Vietnamese Police investigation of a DAC operated gambling place. LTC Kincaid stated that Mr. Kuschel isn't involved other than there are individuals who think he has been an informer. Vietnamese homes have been raided by VN police, supposedly finding government equipment. In turn, the threats have been made.

2. Mr. Kuschel has been working in the engine test cell for the last couple of weeks but normally is a T-53 L-13 instructor.

3. The 520th is in need of an L-13 representative for the 20th DS Company. The 20th supports the 188th Assault Helicopter Company, equipped with UH-1H (L-13 engines). They have no L-13 engine representative. LTC Jersey would be happy to have Mr. Kuschel for this support. LTC Kincaid, was advised to move Mr. Kuschel to the 520th have him report to LTC Jersey. Mr. Al Sherman, 34th CAC Office fully concurred in this action. Mr. Kuschel is being moved for an indefinite period of time. LTC Kincaid stated the loss would not effect his mission performance.

GLENDON E. OLDEFENDT
LTC, TC
Deputy Commander

4-8
LTC Kincaid's letter subject Mr. Wayne A. Kuschel DAC GS-12

Dr. Wayne   23 June '67

Sorry about not writing sooner, but "Old Dad" had a sick spell.

I tried to call Mrs Kuschel twice from San Francisco and 4 times from St Louis and was unable to contact her. I do want you to know I tried.

There are strange things here. They have vehicles with glass instead of mice, it is called a sedan. People drink water out of pipes and use a thing called a toilet that has water instead of oil. When I say number one and number two they think I mean something else. The vehicle called a sedan, has springs that keeps my arse from getting sore. It also has a black box inside that blows cold air.

Is Bernie still on his "20 day" "don't rock the boat" kick. Tell him to be a good boy or he will be returned to the land of

4-9 Alton Reed's letter from U.S.A.

108

the 8 hour day.

Give my warmest regards to Col Kincaid and tell him to look me up when he visits Akron.

I passed your letter to F&A and perhaps you have received the results by now. If there is anything I can do let me know PDQ.

I bought a Mustang, V8, air cond. W/W etc. It is some car, but of course I am still riding the bus to work. The boy and wife now have a car each and I am still on foot.

Give my regards to everyone

Your Friend
Al Reed.

4-9 Alton Reed's letter from U.S.A. page 2

For Your Eyes Only

I made a short visit to Mr B and he made the statement. QUOTE – "It seem they think they have a problem over there"

With that statement hanging in the air I said goodby. For it would of been useless to try and put any points across to a closed mind.

I advised a highly placed Brother here at AVCON of my beliefs and he has a good memory that can be relied on that I am on the record.

I would like your reaction as to the capability of the three new AVCON supply instructors if you care to comment. You can write me at home

5745 Waterman Ave
St Louis, Mo 63112

4-9 Alton Reed's letter from U.S.A. page 3

	TYPE OF REPORT		
3. TO *HEADQUARTERS,* *U.S. ARMY AVIATION MATERIEL COMMAND* *ATTN: AMSAV-FTT*	MONTHLY	X	DA CIVILIAN
	SPECIAL		MILITARY
	X OTHER *(INEEKLY)*		

4. FROM (Name, Grade-Rank-Title, Address, and Signature)   DATE ___ 30 JUNE 67

WAYNE A. KUSCHEL GS-11 EQUIPMENT SPECIALIST
20TH TRANS. CO. (ADS)
APO SAN FRANCISCO 96353

PART I

5. UNIT(S) OR ACTIVITY SUPPORTED

330TH TRANS. CO (GS), AND SUBORDINATE UNITS (4 DAYS)
20TH TRANS. CO (ADS) " " " (11 DAYS)

6. BASIC WEAPON (OR EQUIPMENT) SYSTEM ON WHICH ASSISTANCE WAS RENDERED

T-53-L9, L11, L13
T-55L7

7. WERE PROBLEMS ENCOUNTERED THAT COULD NOT BE RESOLVED? (If Yes Explain in Item 13)   ☐ YES   ☒ NO

8. INDICATE PROBLEMS ENCOUNTERED IN AREAS 8 THRU 9 BY LISTING NUMBER OF REPORTS SUBMITTED FOR EACH *ASSISTANCE*

a. TOOLS AND TEST EQUIPMENT		e. TAERS	
b. TECHNICAL PUBLICATIONS	2	f. MALFUNCTION	2
c. SUPPLY AND REPAIR PARTS	1	g. OTHER (Specify)	
d. CHECKS AND ADJUSTMENTS			

9. MANPOWER AND TRAINING DATA

a. DAYS WORKED THIS REPORTING PERIOD	14	b. ANNUAL LEAVE HRS	0	c. SICK LEAVE HRS	0	d. OVERTIME HRS		COMP	PAID 48
e. TOTAL HOURS SPENT W/UNITS IN ITEM 5	148	f. HOURS OF FORMAL TRAINING CONDUCTED	0			g. NUMBER OF PERSONS TRAINED (Formal)			0
h. HOURS TRAVEL TIME	40	i. HOURS OF OJT	20			j. NUMBER OF PERSONS TRAINED (O/T)			10

k. HOURS SPENT PERFORMING ACTUAL MAINTENANCE FUNCTIONS (Explain in Item 13)

l. OTHER (See Instructions)   *4 PERSONNEL IN OPERATION & MAINTENANCE OF EQUIP*   8

10. WERE PROBLEMS AND VISITS DISCUSSED WITH THE COMMANDER AND OR HIS MAINTENANCE OR MATERIEL READINESS OFFICER?   ☒ YES   ☐ NO

11. NAME, TITLE AND ADDRESS OF PERSONNEL CONTACTED OTHER THAN ROUTINE

D.H. JERSEY LTC 590TH TRANS. BN   APO S.F. 96289

H.W. BYARS MAJ 269TH COMBAT AVN. BN. APO SF 96353

W.A. BEEDEN LTC HQ 25TH AVN. BN. APO S.F. 96353

PART II

12. THE SERVICES REPORTED ABOVE WERE PERFORMED IN A (SATISFACTORY) (UNSATISFACTORY) MANNER (If Unsatisfactory, Attach Explanation)

DATE	NAME, TITLE AND GRADE OF DESIGNATED SUPERVISOR	SIGNATURE
30 JUNE 67	*JOAN K. CLEMENTS*	

ORGANIZATION AND ADDRESS

4-10
Maintenance Performance Report 1478-R

1. Assisted inspecting T-55 L-7 Le04592 (APO 96291)
2. Assisted in acquiring T-53 L-13, Special tools on loan basis, flew to Dau Tieng (188th Trans. Co.) assisted Lycoming Rep on disassembly of combustor section. #2 carbon seal was glazed from carbon residue. No replacement #2 carbon seals available.
3. Assisted in troubleshooting engine and transmission oil pressures. UH-1C 3861.
4. Inspected UH-1H 66-16152, Mortar damage of T-53 L-13 engine LE 14237. Damage to comustion chamber, lines cut, shrapnel damage to compressor housing. Aircraft was evacuated to 539th Trans. Co. (GS).
5. Inspected UH-1H 66-16125, Mortar damage to fuselage, T-53 L-13 engine tailpipe had two dents. Scheduled for test hop.
6. Assigned to 20th Trans. Co. (ADS) by LTC Jersey, who briefed me on areas, where I could assist the organizations on T-53 L13 engines.
7. Had a meeting with LTC Bearden regarding preventative maintenance on T-53 engines, cleaning of engines, and EGT problems.
8. Assisted Maj. Byars, S-4 Officer on requisitioning correct T-53 L13, special engine tools.

4-10
Maintenance Performance Report 1478-R page 2

CHAPTER 5-
FIRST EQUIPMENT SPECIALIST
PROVIDED A UH-1 (HUEY)
FOR ENGINE MAINTENANCE

It seemed like I arrived at Cu Chi in time on 20 June 1967 for a full VC assault, because on my first Saturday at about 10:30 p.m., all hell broke loose at the Cu Chi base front gate. Perhaps they heard or found out that I arrived for duty, and were welcoming me! Ha, Ha, news does travel fast! [Map of Cu Chi 5-1]

I saw red tracer bullets streaking from the air to the ground by United States Army helicopter gunships and AH-1G (Cobra's) firing towards and outside the main gate of Cu Chi. All this time there were other helicopters dropping flares resulting in very bright descending lights surrounding the country-side. The iron fenced compound was completely encircled for battle and fully covered by security forces for any battle conditions that could come up regarding any penetration from the Viet Cong personnel.

However, when the Viet Cong stormed the concertina wire they were stopped because of the razor sharp points. When they realized the problem they would immediately began throwing their bodies on top of the wire for a path to gain passage inside of the base, or throw some sort of ladder on top of the wire to run over the rungs or boards to get inside the base to disperse and do damage to any item such as personnel, generators, vehicles, helicopters/aircraft, or housing.

Our base had a 155 Howitzer Company next door to our 20th Transportation Company. The Howitzers were always set up and ready for any type of unannounced intrusions. One specific night a convoy of vehicles was dispatched toward Tay Ninh on Highway #1. This included the 155th Howitzer Company. They all combined together for a show of force and our strength to the Viet Cong. It was our consensus of opinion that the convoy was too long for accommodating all the various units, and perhaps be in on some United States Army assault exercises. However, in this case the convoy was too lengthy. And because of this could have been easily attacked. So the 155th Howitzer Company was returned to their original site next to the 20th Transportation Company, which meant more protection for us from their location. The 155th Howitzer Company was always placed in battle position. Later that night the Viet Cong attacked toward and in front of the 155th Howitzer Company. After the alert was sounded and we were near our bunkers, the 155th Howitzers opened fire with the armament shells known as "bee hive" pins. The Viet Cong didn't have a chance to get over the fence, and the consequences were Viet Cong casualties were high with many of them killed.

On the barbed wire fence surrounding Cu Chi camp for our protection were attached anti-personnel Claymore mines, grenades and a few other surprises. So we felt very secure in our locations.

On my third day being at Cu Chi, the 20th Transportation Company Commander Major Clements called me into his office and stated the area commander Colonel Donald H. Jersey, 520th Transportation Battalion at Phu Loi would like for me to visit with him and he would outline any engine maintenance needs of the various companies located in the "Iron Triangle" area.

Colonel Jersey was an exceptionally experienced and well-adjusted individual when I met him. He was very fair and supported the men under his command. Our conversation evolved concerning where I would be best suited to serve the United States Army. The commander suggested that my experience in both T-55-L-11, Chinook helicopters and Huey, T-53-L-11, T-53-L-13, helicopter engines be served best assigned to the 20th Transportation Company and maintain aircraft in the Iron Triangle since that area had sufficient aircraft to utilize a professional gas turbine engine propulsion specialist, especially the 188th Assault Helicopter Company equipped with the new T-53-L-13 engines.

I was also advised to be careful and that news travels fast (regardless, there were people who knew where I was assigned and Pecks black hat bad boys knew this). Regardless of how bad it sounded I did my official duty with the 20th Transportation Company at Cu Chi and assigned areas, and received praise for accomplishing any assigned duties given to me.

Just a reminder of the good old days, I'll bet most of you young men remember how nice the barbers treat you when you receive a haircut. I know I will always remember about the good old barbers in the United States of America. However, it is a wee bit different in the Republic of Vietnam. They have Pop-a-son and Mom-a-son barbers. Take your pick, one is as good as the other but the equipment they use is the difference. It seemed like the barbers clippers, the hand job type were always real, real dull. Reason being, the Army troops would be in the field on patrol duty. Bathing was hard to come by so it could be a couple of weeks before they returned to civilization and the sand and dirt some of them were exposed to by chopper rotor blades picking up sand and dust and depositing it on soldiers heads, I know very well even with a long length of time under a shower did not remove the sandy deposit. So to a barber shop they would go, and the end results were when it was your turn in the chair their clippers were so dull that each time the barber would squeeze the handle on the clipper the clipper would yank a patch of hair out of your scalp and you would think "Gosh, I hope I survive this hair cut!"

Major Clements congratulated me on being assigned to his company; it would assist in getting the helicopter's turbine engines inspected and repaired for dispatching to assigned companies. Major Clements assigned Chief Warrant Officer (CWO-4) Bob Graves as my personal UH-1 (Huey) pilot. Bob Graves was the greatest helicopter pilot that I had anything to do with on a daily basis. He was very efficient and a well-qualified pilot and he knew all the Iron Triangle areas which was an A+ in my book in getting there in the shortest time and distance. Together we would inspect downed choppers, repair if possible and test fly them for safety, and ascertain if the repairs were accomplished, anything to return the helicopter to their bases or to a higher level qualified maintenance facility like the 20th Transportation Company (ADS) for necessary repair.

I advised Major John Clements the 20th Transportation Company Commander that I would use good judgment and common sense in my field trips and that I would never abuse my duties on accomplishing any work load scheduled in the Iron Triangle area. Of course as time went by and more maintenance personnel knew about this new service of traveling by UH-1 (Huey) helicopter to aviation maintenance units needing professional gas turbine experience. My qualifying factor was pushing 100% in resolving any and all propulsion problems. You can read my 1478—R reports and see the results.

I didn't know that my every move at Cu Chi was being scrutinized by our Command in St. Louis, Missouri. That there were personnel in RVN reporting very favorable on all my propulsion problems, and end results. Not a hint was ever revealed to me of what was transpiring and that I would be awarded a commendation and a step increase for the period 6 August 1967 to 5 August 1968.

This is a picture of me taken after returning from a sixteen hour day plus the flying time to return to Cu Chi. [Photo A Dirty Disposition of me 5-2]

In my civil service recorded time or work hours, how I spent my time was normally, 80 hours for a two-week period, and then I had a maximum of 81 hours of overtime for a total of 161.5 hours. I would usually stop at two or three Army Aviation posts for propulsion assistance. It would pay dividends for the young mechanics to receive my help in keeping the helicopters flying. They all needed a big pat on the back for a tremendous job they accomplished. Remember, the Viet Cong were communist and you could set your watch that they would attack when you least expected it. It seemed like the Viet Cong had their hand on the mechanic's pulse and knew when the helicopters required maintenance.

Major Clements even gave me his jeep to get around Cu Chi. I never misused the gift, especially when I had to assist repairing the gas turbine engines on General Senoff's, Commander of the 25th Infantry Division's, helicopter. The young Warrant Officer that worked in the 25th Infantry Division Maintenance always had a direct line to me in the 20th Transportation Company for immediate action to keep the General's helicopter flyable.

This young pilot would scare the pee-waddlers out of me on his test hops or take-offs, with the engine control's set for take-off he would pull the power for lift off immediately the tail boom would be real high and the nose was very low with the skids laying the grass down. I was afraid that if a Viet Cong would have gotten on to Cu Chi illegally and planted a circle or loop of wire in the grassy ground and be anchored by a large rock or rod, that we could have been in an accident upside down, but my flying imagination played heck with my brain. Nothing like that ever happened.

After arriving at Cu Chi and until I went state side Christmas time, I found out how bad the telephone system was, the United States Government spent millions of dollars in the latest pressurized phone system and along comes the Viet Cong (VC) and they tap into the pressurized system to gain access to a phone line or connection for his illegal gains and Uncle Sam's phone service or usage was deteriorated where you couldn't get the unit next door.

I had received United States Army personnel orders on 12 October 1967, Letter order 646 which assigned me to military region #3 which covered Da Ling, Tay Ninh, Loc Ninh, An Loc, Bien Lang, Bien Hon, Binh Tuy, Phi Loi, Cu Chi, Vinh Cu, Dau Tieng, Tri Tam, Phu and Saigon which were all within the "Iron Triangle" area. In addition to all of these areas my duties were also to work with the ship USS Corpus Christi, which had an engine test cell for T-55 and T-53s, the only ship in Vietnam to have this capability. Bob and I flew a UH-1 (Huey) to the Corpus Christi whenever necessary to assist in eliminating an engine problem that the test cell personnel could not solve. This was approved wholeheartedly by Col. Jersey, Commander 520th Transportation Battalion at Phu Loi. He gave me the go-ahead and I did exactly that, all the flying aviation companies enjoyed the end results. In return we saved time and money in the maintenance area. [My Duty Stations 5-3]

When I had my initial talk with Major Clements on 17 July 1967, he seemed like a real friend. He was the one person who was thinking ahead to gain the most value of knowledge from my experience and apply it to his maintenance requirements and keep the fleet flying. Since, I was a qualified triple threat by being trained on the T-55, T-53-L13 and T-53-L-11 gas turbine engines at least I should surpass everyone's expectations on gas turbine engines. I tried to go beyond my duty calls to help and assist any of the personnel requirements any hour of the day, even if it was for a 24 hour day. My time was theirs whenever needed, and then being assigned a specific area, the Iron Triangle, which was a very dangerous area to be involved in. There was a larger than normal concentration of Viet Cong in that specific area, so the greater percentage of flyable helicopters in the air the better survivor rate, for the United States Army personnel.

When Major Clements commented on my being assigned a UH-1 (Huey) helicopter to visit the various companies in the boondocks (out in never ending places), he was hoping that I would give him the maintenance engine support required by the United States Army Aviation companies so that the aircraft stay on their assigned location and not be delivered to the 20th Transportation Company for specialized maintenance.

Don't ask me to pronounce the names of the cities where the bases were located, but anyway I gave my ideas and views about that statement, that a fast way to expedite my services was by helicopter. I could do more good in keeping the aircraft in the air and ready for any emergency or usage that the officials required, or any altercations with the Viet Cong.

Then it was discussed how well CWO-4 Graves was doing as my personal pilot, and that's when I told him the plan was perfect and the helicopters were being repaired on site. That saved time and money with the chopper being available for flight purposes all the time. Bob had a special know-how to do things and fit into the situation exceptionally for a perfect match. I really believe that the reality of how fast Bob and myself traveled to the location of aircraft requiring maintenance was a determining factor of assigning a Department of the Army civilian for the expeditious remedy of required maintenance at Cu Chi and assigned areas.

The more you think of this idea it's no wonder the personnel involved with maintenance (high officials) enjoyed the benefits or end results. Why couldn't this system be utilized in future endeavors to recover aircraft faster and keep them flying? Perhaps Mr. Smith my replacement was not the type that knew the propulsion systems and instruct adequately to United States Army Personnel!

I believe my career was a rewarding one. I accomplished my maintenance schedule in the shortest period time frame and kept all personnel satisfied and the aircraft flyable.

In the 20th Transportation Company we had a large, tall African-American Major that I flew a few test hops with and he did things that would knock your britches off. For instance, we took off one afternoon testing an engine replaced for Foreign Object Damage (FOD) and while I was on the rear seat setting up the vibration tester, he had very carefully pulled the Huey up in a fairly steep climb, and then dropped the nose into a dive. When I looked at the panel it was a red colored glob of all the red bulbs, looking as if danger was the name of that flight. Scared the heck out of me that was what I got for not paying attention. Of course, look at it this way, it was a smooth transition that I'll know better the next time I fly a test hop with him. He was one sharp and experienced pilot that I respected. I learned lots of things by flying with these young helicopter pilots. One day Bob Graves said go ahead and fly it, in my mind I would give up on helicopters. I did not qualify as a helicopter pilot even though I held a United States Air Force pilot's instructors license. Helicopters and fixed wings are like cats and dogs; they don't mix unless you train as a helicopter or fixed wing pilot. So I skipped the chance to fly helicopters.

Perhaps if I would have had more time to be instructed on handling rotary blades and what the controls had to do with the functions of the helicopter I would have been able to land it in an emergency. Oh, I think I could get it back on the ground, but I don't know what condition we would be in or the helicopter itself.

Of course I love flying, mostly in fixed wing aircraft it's different than flying helicopters, in the good old days I did fly sometime in the OH-13 and H-5 as an observer writing down readings as required.

But my next episode was when I was accepted into pilot training 1947 and 1948 era that was the world I wanted to be a full fledge pilot which meant the pinnacle of success. You had to be mature and intellectual to withstand all aspects of regal's of flying

Then it was graduation time and the Pilot's Wings were pinned on your chest. Your feelings were you could jump over the moon.

But now here it was 1967 and my home was in Cu Chi, and guess where I was at this time in a UH-1 (Huey) helicopter flying at 5000 feet into no man's land to service a few helicopters with gas turbine engines problems. It was real peaceful no shooting at this altitude and with all the space ahead we had it made.

Next it was time to wake up to reality land and cure the problem then wait for further orders or return to our home base. Sometimes we had two, three, or four aviation bases to service the propulsion systems and return them to flyable condition.

I was in the 20th Transportation Company area one day checking with the mechanics about specific engine problems and remedies and this young mechanic wet behind the ears type, said, "You know when you're flying, do you ever pay attention to the transmission and the rotor blades?" I said, "No." Anyway this mechanic said, "Have you ever seen a Jesus wire?" and I thought he was kidding me. So he took me top side and showed me. It looked like a round piece of wire with a snap on it for a recess lock on the inside of the unit. All I could think and say was, "Well, I learn something new every day." But I will pay attention to that area for all future flights.

Shortly after being assigned to the 20th Transportation Company, my company commander Major Clements and I got into a conversation on what exactly happened in Vung Tau and me being assigned to his company. I told him the whole story. So to ensure the proper personnel were notified in case the cowboys did carry out their threat, I had only one (1) recourse. I told Major Clements about 20 June 1967 that I had already written a letter at Vung Tau 16 April 1967 to myself, sealed it in another envelope, and wrote on the envelope (instructions to follow) "For

Mrs. Wayne A. Kuschel, to be opened in the event of my death other than from hostile actions. Do not open after 16 December 1967, then please burn. Shortly I would be returning to California at Christmas time (I did not destroy the letter and envelope, I kept it for a souvenir). I wrote my wife, Marie a letter dated 12 May 1967 on envelope detailing the whole story in what happened and gave the steps to take in case the threat was carried out. [Copy of Wife's letter 5-4], [Maintenance Performance Report 1478-R 5-5]

Major Clements asked me to write the story down documenting the complete event, then to forward it to Mr. Leonard Bartley in AVSCOM to make it officially on record. This correspondence would relate my side of the story to anyone who would be associated or wanted knowledge into this web of entanglement.

Basically it goes back to whom was wearing the black hat (Pecks bad boys), not me. I was an innocent bystander who was taken advantage of for the greed of money.

Below is my copy of the letter dated 9 July 1967, sent to Mr. Leonard Bartley, my Directorate of Maintenance Technical Assistance supervisor at AVSCOM. [My famous letter to Mr. Bartley 5-6]

I got rather fond of my flying buddy Bob Graves. He was truly a loyal and trustworthy individual. I found out Bob came from Stillwater, Oklahoma and was a level-headed type, special individual. I can thank him for being an excellent pilot with special skills (helicopter) and for getting us out of some tight scrapes without any injuries or casualties.

Bob and I flew numerous missions, at least 500 hours in the seven months while I was attached to the 20th Transportation Company traveling to various camps, bases or isolated areas so we could quality check the maintenance of the turbine engine and fuel controls, plus the established power limits. My concern was with the limits of the fuel control when the crew chief felt that he could not maintain 100% top limits, for the pilot to maneuver the helicopter in tight areas. With a small wrench or tool and a screwdriver he could change or tweak the power setting to what they thought would help provide more power. In reality what these crew chiefs didn't know or realize was that for every 1% over the high limit they operated the engine, serviceability of the engine was eroded by the hot end losing the metal coating or metal content, which compromised or was drastically reducing the engine life and efficiency because of metal erosion, which could result in a power failure causing a possible crash with loss of life and/or the aircraft. After we ran up all the UH-1 (Hueys) in the unit, we took corrective action by resetting the power settings according to the maintenance specifications and then to ascertain the reliability of the overall fleet, I provided the crew chiefs the latest updated information on the new T-53-L-13 turbine engines on how to maintain them in the peak performance zone.

Upon returning to Cu Chi I reported into Major Clement. He requested that my findings be given to the 520th Transportation Battalion Commander, Colonel Jersey for his determination and correction. We didn't know if the fleet of UH-1 (Hueys) was in danger of engine failure or to expect any extra maintenance load to be performed by our transportation unit to keep the units flying safely. That was my main goal in working with the army aviation units, was to assist in keeping the choppers flyable and in the air.

I received a letter from Bernie Reece on 10 July 1967 saying that Mac and Joe (Pecks bad boys) were still in Vung Tau and that the CID and Mr. Sherman, Saigon AVSCOM Technical Assistance Manager called AVSCOM on 7 July 1967 to ascertain that they be returned 10 July 1967 to St. Louis for court action. The official orders since it involved two personnel to leave Vietnam was not received quickly, and because of them being registered with the embassies, the necessary correspondence or orders from Saigon would take time to accomplish. [Bernie's letter to me 5-7]

My knowledge and skills were called on many times to assist in accident boards and evaluating the propulsion systems for determining operational factors, and provide positive input for problems to AVSCOM for engineers to improve the performance of the gas turbine engine.

Working with the 20th Transportation Company, Major Clements called me early one morning to depart for Tay Ninh near the Cambodia border to assist the maintenance personnel on several different engine problems. One problem was the UH-1 (Hueys) did not have effective lifting capabilities. Since there were several aviation companies with T-53-L-13 engines, those units had been doing a lot of lift-offs in heavy clay, dusty areas, and I suspected dirt built up near the high velocity inlet air flow. I requested some ground up walnut shells for cleaning material, which had recently been put in to the Army supply system and was not known by many aviation maintenance personnel. We had a CH-47 (Chinook) go to the supply group in Saigon and pick up a load for the Iron Triangle area. We began working on the Huey helicopters and it took about fourteen hours to clean up the airflow problems. Had I not known about these specific problems and corrected the problem with a sound resolution, portions of the Tay Ninh fleet would have been at the mercy of the Viet Cong. [Copy of Maintenance Performance Report 1478-R 5-8]

I received official word 6 August 1967 that my promotion to GS-1670-12 had been received at Saigon civilian personnel office and my records were updated. In other words, my reputation was cleared effective that date because of my promotion. [AVSCOM orders for my GS-12 5-9], [Saigon CPO Promotion GS-12 5-10]

For my year in Vietnam, 1966-1967, I can say I was fired upon by small arms, endured mortar attacks, and with the enemy attacking the security fencing averaging about ten times a month. I can truthfully say our personnel involved in these staving or ward offs of these attacks were well disciplined, organized, and all of us utilized the established bunkers in an orderly fashion. This prevented casualties so they would be on duty when required, with no loss of production time to repair aircraft.

Several personnel searches, for drugs were scheduled during my stay at the 20th Transportation Company. I was never involved in that area. However from my observation of the Armed Forces personnel during my year in Republic of Vietnam, December 1966 to December 1967. I witnessed no one on drugs or addictions of any type. I saw socialized drinking of beer, when the party was over they returned to their sleeping quarters in an orderly fashion.

In my life time of eighty six years I have not used any type of drugs (except by my Doctor's prescription for pain i.e. earache, bone pain, headache, surgery and such).

I traveled in the Iron Triangle area on numerous missions and never came in contact with any person under the influence of drugs. This would be one area that would be suspicious of drug users, being on constant contact with fighting the Viet Cong (VC). But my meeting or memories of these fine intellectual armed force personnel was outstanding.

My folks ran a night club for some thirty eight years, since I was sixteen years old and there I saw people drunk with alcoholic drinks. Those drunks were addicted people and could not stand or sit in booths or bar stools without a drink in their hands or in front of them on the table.

I never heard about drug addictions until I was in my late forties, of course the Far East—China had opium addicts, that China official's supplied them with. This was the time marijuana 1940-1950 came into existence.

Why aren't the Senators and Congressman this day and age eradicated the Poppy fields in Afghanistan, why don't they fly over with the ingredients "Agent Orange" to kill the fields, and forget the big chiefs and agents holding the possible annihilating effect over our Washington, D.C. official's heads. It's better than allowing 400 million dollars to fall into their hands to buy guns, ammo, and armament for the Taliban or Al-Qaeda personnel from opium funds, to kill or maim our personnel.

One thing that I never understood was why someone in the Armed Services who has everything going for them would cross the line and mess with drugs of any type, whether by injection, snort or smoke. But there are some personnel that would venture down the one way street and with no escape route takes the chance to beat the system and accepts the drugs that can ruin his (or her) life and career. One thing the service person does not understand going against the rules and regulations is a court martial offense with a bad conduct discharge, time in prison and the remains of this. He will have a hard time finding a job, no more VA assistance, no government jobs; it's a hell of a mess to be in. It's easier to stay on the good side and have friends and neighbors and perhaps a wife and family to enjoy the rest of their life.

Now to change the subject, perhaps someone has had my experience of taking a shower after a hard day's work flying in a UH-1 (Huey) helicopter. After returning to Cu Chi and before bed time you feel real grungy, sweaty, greasy and felt like the last heat day of summer is here. So you get your shower gear and head into the shower area. Above the shower area you will find a water tank and some water heaters there for a reason. The water is really cold, even though the temperature outside is over 100 degrees. You start the shower, then soap up, when all of sudden a green slimy string of wild vegetation wraps itself around your neck, then down your chest, legs and is sucked down the drain. Regardless, you wait for another one of those green monsters to come down out of the shower head and try to again warp your brain. It won't happen now, but when will it happen again, you wait and do the endless thing. Keep guessing, play the guessing game. The event of showering in the Republic of Vietnam was an episode to remember, when you make it back to the good old United States of America.

I received a letter from Emmett Turner, our AVSCOM representative in Saigon, shortly after he wrote it on 18 July 1967. My performance appraisal was due in St. Louis, which was more or less required in my records as a progress report. Emmett was down in the dumps for the problem caused by Peck's bad boys (black hats) and like everything else the AVSCOM personnel had to have someone to blame in place of putting the problem where it belonged. In this case an innocent bystander was blamed for the complete cause for the CID investigation and could have possibly lost his civilian position. [Emmett's letter to me 5-11], [My appraisal DA Form 1052 5-12]

I heard through the grapevine that the 20th Transportation Company was to ferry some UH-1 (Hueys) to Pleikeu up north, so I talked to the Commanding Officer and requested that I be assigned in case any propulsion problems might arise. It would take about a week for a round trip and to return three (3) UH-1 (Hueys) to be put through a maintenance refurbishing at the 20th Transportation Company. Major Clements said it was a good idea and approved my TDY trip. That way the UH-1 (Hueys) would be cleared of any discrepancies and arrive at Pleikeu in a minimum amount of time. [Letter from Don Pittman 20 July 1967 Promotion to GS-12 5-13]

That evening after dinner before leaving for Pleikeu, a Technical Manual box from AVSCOM in St. Louis arrived. My heart felt like it was in my throat, when I opened up my package, early part of July 1967, containing technical manuals, to update my management files, I found that our Pecks bad boys (McElvaney and Parker) had included threats toward me. So I immediately sent a letter to Don Pittman on 25 July 1967. [Letter to Don Pittman 5-14] [Reference pictures "of Threat Labels" from AVSCOM Manual Box 5-15 Label, 5-16 1st Threat, 5-17 2nd Threat] Our travel orders to Pleikeu were given to all of us for official use, in case of any incidents and to be safe while en-route. I never carried my red official passport, it was in the CO's safe for numerous reasons, and for safety factors, i.e. VC ransom.

When we first processed into MAC-V in Saigon, in December 1966, we were advised that under the Geneva Convention no civilians were authorized to carry or have guns in their possession. If we had any weapons on us, the VC would shoot us, if we were captured, and that's how they handled problems, and they cared less about human life to eliminate the enemy by the rules from the communist regime.

There were four of us in the UH-1 (Huey) and upon pulling power we headed out northeast to Bon Son, en-route we had to refuel, we were supposed to sit down in a designated spot, arriving at the correct latitude and longitude there was a small tarmac and an old iron shipping crate but nothing else. There was lots of movement in the distant trees about a half mile away. There sure was no chow, or relief there, and not wanting to be ambushed by the Viet Cong we all elected to get on the road again. We had to go over or through the Dien Bien Phu pass where the French lost 5,000 troops. They were laid to rest on the hill top, near the pass. The four of us voiced our opinions that if there was to be an ambush this pass would be an ideal spot. The pilot approached the pass very high in altitude and then he came in straight between the pass, ready for anything to happen. Our one gunner with an assault weapon was in position in the door for anything that might occur. We were supposedly in friendly territory up the east coast of Vietnam, but it didn't appear that way to me. The refueling area was located in no man's land and no one was around to give information, period.

I would bet if the wrong colored clothes or uniform would appear, meaning VC, close to the fuel dump while refueling all heck would have taken place. As our gunner was ready for any problem to arise, Bob Graves after refueling put the power to the UH-1 (Huey) and we were airborne towards Pleikeu.

Our overnight stop was up the coast inside a three-sided barbed wire Army camp. It wasn't too large but well maintained in and around the site. All the personnel were happy to see us and shook our hands after we landed. The Army Captain with infantry insignias on his collar told us the camp was ours, however, the Viet Cong on the high ground overlooking the site would be unhappy, and we needed to be ready and available for any incidents that might take place. It wasn't two hours after we had landed that there was round after round of mortar fire coming in to the camp. The camp returned fire for a while. The captain advised our pilot, Bob Graves, it would be best if we flew out to the next Army or Air Force station a few miles north. So about 10:00 p.m. our crew boarded the chopper and was airborne heading north. It was a real dark night with no visible means of orientation except for the choppers illuminated instrument panel. Of course the Huey had a distinct whoop, whoop sound given off by the main rotor blades that would wake the people in the cemetery, let alone friendly or unfriendly forces.

After a short time we landed at An Khe and were provided quarters for sleeping the few remaining hours. So far, so good, and today we would deliver the chopper's to the designated unit. We arrived about 1430 at Pleikeu and we were well received by the maintenance personnel. The chopper that we were to ferry back to Cu Chi for maintenance was not ready, so we had time to look the camp over. There were UH-1 (Hueys) making auto rotation landings to maintain pilots' proficiency in the event of engine, transmission or tail rotor failure or other problems. At least the crew was up on the latest techniques of saving the helicopter and crew. We were scheduled to depart the next day when I had to visit the rest room or latrine. I was near the wash basins when an Army soldier came in with a boa constrictor wrapped around his body. The head of the snake was kind of dropping down in front of the soldier. The head of that snake was a good six inches across. Well, anyhow, he had a friend in one of the stalls, so the soldier pointed the head of the snake under the stall door and whoever the soldier was sitting on the throne came up over the stall in one fast leap yelling. If it would have been me I would have collapsed in a heap on the throne. At least the soldiers were buddies and were talking over old times when I left the area.

The next day all paperwork on the UH-1 (Huey) was finished so we gathered up our gear and headed for the UH-1 (Huey) on the ramp. The maintenance officer shook hands with all of us, as there was nothing to do but depart company and head south. This time we decided to head out over the South China Sea and avoid the ground terrain to prevent any ambushes. The decision was to go over the water as far as we could, then go inland to refuel; accordingly the course was set for Cu Chi. When we were close to the refueling point there was lots of activity with people going toward Bon Son. They were not on the road but on paths parallel and away from the roads. As we agreed to stay only a minimum of time to refuel, we could not attest to what might transpire if we stayed on the ground too long. There was no town or village nearby, so where these people went only God knows. It was spooky going into the fuel dump. Nothing was visible on top of the ground so you had to have prior training as to where the pumps were. These pilots knew all the secrets. We fueled up and hit the road toward Saigon. When we got near Saigon we were at 4,500 feet. We must have hit a nerve on the ground because red tracers began coming up towards our UH-1 (Huey). The red tracers lost their power or speed on the way up because they slowly disappeared into the night, thank our lucky stars. The landing at Cu Chi was a dark, rainy night and a perfect walk away landing.

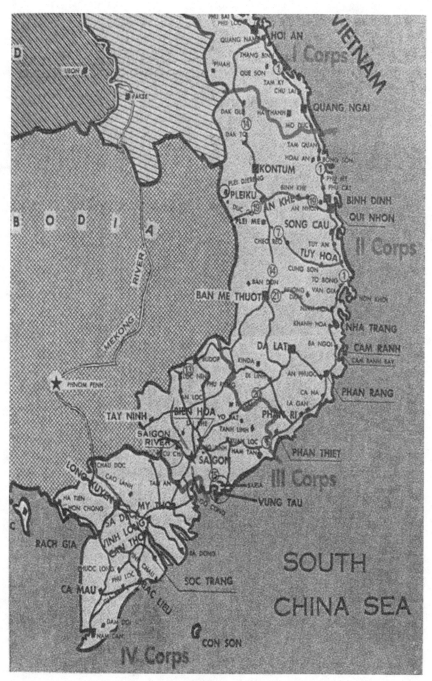

5-1
Map of Chu Chi

131

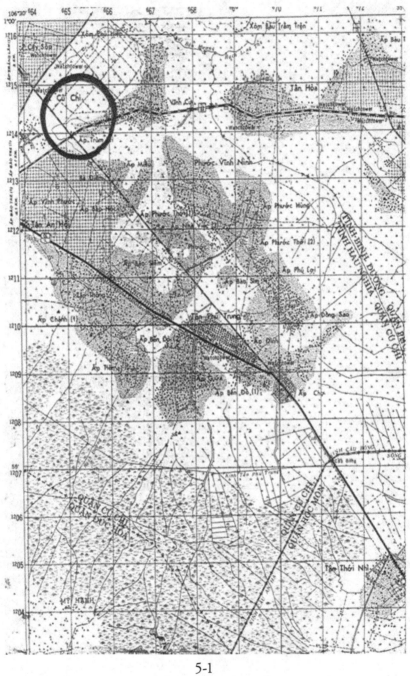

5-1
Map of Chu Chi page 2

5-2 Photo
A Dirty Disposition of me

LETTER ORDERS   12 October 1967
NUMBER   646

SUBJECT: REPEATED TRAVEL (TDY)

TO: Individual Concerned

    TC 202. REPEATED TRAVEL (TDY) btwn home sta and pl shown below dir as indic.
RFSCTDY. TDN.

KUSCHEL, WAYNE A. DAC GS-12 Equip Spec, HQ 34th Gen Spt Gp (AM&S) APO SF 96307
    WP to: Cu Chi, Phu Loi, Vung Tau, Can Tho, Vinh Long, Bien Hoa, Saigon, CIPAP
    WP date: 12 Oct 67
    Scty clnc: S
    No days: 60 days
    Purpose: Tech asst on US Army acft
    Acct clas: 2182020 6 B-8054 P2300-211 S33031 VS
    Sp instr: Exc bag alw 150 lbs auth. Priority: II

        FOR THE COMMANDER:

                               CHARLES B ROEDER
                               CPT, TC
                               Asst Adjutant

DISTRIBUTION:
    1 - File (1-02)
    25 - Indiv
    5 - 10th Fin
    1 - S1, 34th Gp
    1 - Msg Ctr, 34th Gp

5-3 My Duty Stations

For Mrs. W. A. Kuschel
to be opened in the event of my death
other than by hostile action. Do not
open after 16 Dec '67. Please burn

Wayne A. Kuschel

5-4
Copy of Wife's letter

To whom it may concern, I, Wayne A. Kuschel on the above date, Am writing this letter to my wife Gussie M. Kuschel in the event my life is threatened or taken by ~~this~~ means other than hostile action.

On Thursday 13 Apr '67, Mr Emmett Turner and I disclosed to Major Wedin Black marketing activities in the Vung Tau area and personnel suspected of taking part. (Mr Reece was appraised of all this.) Mr. MacElvaney - Mr Parker - Mr Russell Mr Fairfield - Mr Geran - Mr Mahaffey Mr Demarest and Mr Blalock (Saigon) During early Jan 67 Mr Parker parked in front of Botany Clothing Store stated Mr MacElvaney was inside transacting a money deal.

On numerous occasions I told Mr Russell to change checks in proper on base channels meaning Officers Club Base finance and Post Exchange. He stated he would change money where ever

5-4 Copy of Wife's letter page 2

he disered to. During Dec 66 - Jan 66 -
Feb 66 - Mar 66 - Apr 66 none of the
above named individuals were ever
seen buying piasters. Yet their
outlandish spending of piasters
on motor Bikes (Mac had 2 or 3) housing,
liquor, parties, women and maids
would acquire a great deal of money.
Russell bought furniture - bike (Honda 50)
Watches - Camera - Vietnamese wife and
household expenses plus upkeep of RVN's
wife two children - Electricity - gas
   On the night of 13 April 67 Mr
Turner showed me a check that he
repaid a $100 bill to Mr Russell on
the front it was stamped * CASH *
On back indorsed by P.S. Russell
Cancelled by Security Nat'l in S.F. and
One other Cancelling stamp round
oval ＿＿＿ of Hong Kong. This has
all the appearance of a trade for
money on the open or local market.

5-4 Copy of Wife's letter page 3

137

③

On 14 April 67 we (Mr Turner + I) talked more on this activity with Maj Weden. At this time he asked me to talk to Lt. Col. Kincaid of 765th Trans. Bn. As he was being brought to Saigon on a pretense of looking over and signing his O.E.R. I told Maj. Weden I'd gladly talk to him.

On 15 Apr '67 I flew back to Vung Tau on his Huey acft. after landing I reported to him in his office. I told him of all the persons involved. Also of Mac + Parker carrying .25 Cal. pistols and the possibility of having the local Cowboys snuff out our lives for a $10 fee. I again gave him the location of the Botany Clothing, and also more background info on Mac and Parker dealing Poker at our PA+E Villa (or American Villa) this could be a cover up on acquiring piasters and M.P.C. monies.

5-4 Copy of Wife's letter page 4

④

On 16 Apr '67 Mr Geo. Mains DAC
stated Glen Perry did not change
all U.S. green currency in, but
held approx half. Later on, he gave
Mr Geran and Mahaffey $200 of it
in exchange for a Chuck. He also
has in his possession a .32 or .38
revolver and a large quantity of
silver dollars. Mr Reece was
present when this statement was told.
    This statement is as true as the
time permits in putting in black and
white form and made to the best
of my knowledge on 16 April '67

                    Grayne A. Knochel

Wayne A. Kuschel DAC
HHD 765th Trans. Bn. (AMTS) AAMTAP
Apo San Francisco 96291

Mrs. Wayne A. Kuschel
4175 Adams St.
Riverside, Calif
92504

5-4
Copy of Wife's letter page 6

MAINTENANCE PERFORMANCE REPORT

1. REPORTING PERIOD FROM *1 July 67* TO *15 July '67*	

TYPE OF REPORT

2. TO *HEADQUARTERS U.S. ARMY AVIATION MATERIEL COMMAND ATTN: AMSAV-FTT*

MONTHLY		X	DA CIVILIAN
SPECIAL			MILITARY
X	OTHER *BIWEEK*		

4. FROM (Name, Grade-Rank-Title, Address, and Signature)
WAYNE A. KUSCHEL GS-11 Equipment Specialist
20TH TRANS. CO. (ADS)
APO SAN FRANCISCO 96353

DATE *15 July 1967*

PART I

5. UNIT(S) OR ACTIVITY SUPPORTED
20TH TRANS. CO. AND SUBORDINATE UNITS
725TH TRANS CO (ADS)

6. BASIC WEAPON (OR EQUIPMENT) SYSTEM ON WHICH ASSISTANCE WAS RENDERED
T53 L9, L11, L13

7. WERE PROBLEMS ENCOUNTERED THAT COULD NOT BE RESOLVED? (If Yes Explain in Item 13) ☐ YES   ☒ NO

8. INDICATE PROBLEMS ENCOUNTERED IN AREAS a THRU g BY LISTING NUMBER OF REPORTS SUBMITTED FOR EACH *ASSISTANCE*

a. TOOLS AND TEST EQUIPMENT	3	e. TAERS		
b. TECHNICAL PUBLICATIONS		f. MALFUNCTION		1
c. SUPPLY AND REPAIR PARTS	1	g. OTHER (Specify)		
d. CHECKS AND ADJUSTMENTS	1			

9. MANPOWER AND TRAINING DATA

a. DAYS WORKED THIS REPORTING PERIOD	13	b. ANNUAL LEAVE HRS	0	c. SICK LEAVE HRS	0	d. OVERTIME HRS COMP PAID 48
e. TOTAL HOURS SPENT W/UNITS IN ITEM 5	130	f. HOURS OF FORMAL TRAINING CONDUCTED		g. NUMBER OF PERSONS TRAINED (Formal)		
h. HOURS TRAVEL TIME	30	i. HOURS OF OJT	10	j. NUMBER OF PERSONS TRAINED (O/T)		5
k. HOURS SPENT PERFORMING ACTUAL MAINTENANCE FUNCTIONS (Explain in Item 13)						80
l. OTHER (See Instructions)						

10. WERE PROBLEMS AND VISITS DISCUSSED WITH THE COMMAND G4/S4 AND OR HIS MAINTENANCE OR MATERIEL READINESS OFFICER? ☐ YES ☒ NO

11. NAME, TITLE AND ADDRESS OF PERSONNEL CONTACTED OTHER THAN ROUTINE

PART II

12. THE SERVICES REPORTED ABOVE WERE PERFORMED IN A (SATISFACTORY) (UNSATISFACTORY) MANNER (If Unsatisfactory, Attach Explanation)

DATE	NAME, TITLE AND GRADE OF DESIGNATED SUPERVISOR	SIGNATURE

ORGANIZATION AND ADDRESS

AMC Form 1478-R
5 Oct 66

5-5
Maintenance Performance Report 1478-R

141

1. Assisted organizations on correct Special tool nomenclature requisition
2. 725th T.C. 269th Comb. Avn. Bn. 20th T.C 20th Trans. Co. requested my assistance on inspecting helicopters assigned to 116th Assualt Helicopter Co. (2 July 67)
3. Assisted and advised 20th Engine shop personnel on inspecting T-53 L-11 LE10433 Had metal filings in and around bleed band, also a few particals in actuator filter. This engine had a compressor rub between 4th and 5th stage. 98:00 hr shipped to depot as repair not authorized this level.
4. Inspected and assisted on UH-BD 66-16114, T-53-L113 LE14199. Fuzz on chip detector plug. Flushed system, flew test hop. Re-checked system, found O.K.
5. Assisted Co. B. 25th Avn. Bn. in troubleshooting systems on UH-1B 66-603 T-53 L-11 LE12156A. Could not start. Required new start fuel nozzles.
6. Inspected UH-1C 65-13952 T-53 L-11 engine LE09590 79:00. Had five rounds of .45 cal hits in and around engine compartment. One bullet dented rear part near V-band. Pilot wrote up "suspected engine seizure". Oil cooler had one hole through it. Aircraft had flown approx. 5 minutes or 7 mileathis way. Forced down, evacuated to 20th T.C. area for repairs. Engine shipped with oil samples.
7. Assisted 725th Trans Co. on proper procedure for flushing oil system because of contamination.
8. Assisted Co. B. 25th Avn. Bn. on acquiring tools for helicoil installation.
9. Inspected engine on UH-1D 65-9663.
10. Assisted Co. B. 25th Avn. Bn. Maintenance personnel on UH-1D 65-9435 T-53 L-11 #LE 10988 154:00 adjusted military trim, and part power trim. Flew test hop with Maintenance Officer

FOR HMP USE		
DATE RECEIVED	FOLLOW UP REQUIRED ☐ YES ☐ NO	SUSPENSE DATE
ACTION ASSIGNED TO		DATE REPLY MAILED
REMARKS		

5-5
Maintenance Performance Report 1478-R page 2

WAYNE A. KUOSHEL WAC
20th TRANS CO (ADS)
APO SAN FRANCISCO, 96353

9 July '67

Dear Mr. Bartley:

In writing this letter, on the advice of maj. Clements, C.O. of the 20th Transportation Company, where I am presently assigned.

This letter will indicate a problem area, in which I feel only you can give me advice and guidance. I have no one else to make a sound decision on this matter. My main concern is my physical well being.

Last night I received a letter from Mr. Reece at Vung Tau. Itho indicated all sorts of things were happening. That the AAMTAP instructors were taking over the T53 L13 engine course in August. At this time, Mr. Geran is very reluctant to return me to Vung Tau under the existing conditions to instruct the T-53 L13 course. Because of the following circumstances.

In March 1967, I acquired billeting at the Pacific Architect and Engineering Hotel (P.A+E) now called

5-6
My famous letter to Mr. Bartley

American Villa. I gave Capt Brown the treasurer, six traveler checks in the amount of $300 for advance payment of rent. I asked Capt Brown, if he had a stamp for "pay to the order of" on the check front. He replied that he had a stamp. About five weeks later, I wrote to the bank who handled these checks, asking them to verify numbers versus indorsers. The bank returned to me photostat copies of the checks. Which revealed three checks that were questionable. One was cashed at a government concern, that had been diverted by an individual and deposited in his personal account in the U.S. Two fifty dollar checks were made out to * CASH * and had Hong Kong stamped on them.

This perturbed me, because of the black market activities in Vung Tau area, and I wanted no part of it. I contacted the CID and showed them the photostat checks. They took down a brief statement, and asked me if they could keep the checks. In return, I accepted a receipt,

5-6
My famous letter to Mr. Bartley page 2

Which I have in my possession.

A short time later, the CID called several of us, living at the P.A. + E. to their headquarters, where they took sworn statements, involving the operation of the P.A. + E. Hotel. There were 20 or more questions made out on a format regarding all phases of their operation, such as, who is the manager, the owners, gambling the use of military pay certificates, checks, liquor, cigarettes and private and army weapons.

At this meeting with CID, the names of Mr. Mac Elvany and Mr. Lonnie Barker was brought out because of their running of the poker game and cutting the pot. Also, Mr. Demarest being associated with Mr. Rockdaschal, PA+E manager and Capt Brown, treasurer. The CID was still investigating this situation when I left Vung Tau.

Sometime in the early part of May 1967, Col Kincaid, Commander of the 765th Trans. Bn. Called a meeting of all civilians. At this

5-6
My famous letter to Mr. Bartley page 3

145

meeting, he stated facts, that the CID was investigating rackets, such as black market, civilian business, cashing of checks on local market, which were going to Hong Kong. That if anyone was involved in any illegal operation, to cease, right now. That if they didn't heed his warning that serious consequence would result.

That same afternoon, lumber was seen taken from the AAMTAP school, and unloaded at a civilian Club, along with several cases of beer and ten to twelve bottles of whiskey. At this time the Club was operated by Mr. Mac Elvany and Mr. Parker.

Most of the personnel on the truck were called to CID headquarters and questioned, their statements taken. The CID also questioned me on a roll of wire supposed to have been taken by Mr. Mac Elvany and Mr. Parker from AAMTAP Supply Room. Also about a large power generator, that was flown

5-6
My famous letter to Mr. Bartley page 4

into Vung Tau Airfield for their use in the Club. Of private fire arms and several other items.

On 18 June 1967, around noon, Capt Brown approached me in the Officers Club. He questioned me on why the CID Called me in. He stated "Was it over those checks?" I replied "yes" He said had he known about it, that he could have prevented all this investigation from happening. Upon departing he stated that his whole career and ~~commission~~ commission was at stake, and he didn't like it one damn bit. Why as a friend I didn't tell him. I told him that the CID had classified the whole package. He said I had constitutional rights and could do anything I wanted to, regarding this investigation. I replied I wasn't going to jeopardize my position

On 19 June '67 at 1815 pm. arriving at the Pacific Hotel from the airfield Mr. Warren, DAC

5-6

My famous letter to Mr. Bartley page 5

6.

Mr Reece, DAC and myself were in the dining area. Mr Reece wrote on a piece of paper " Go home + pack I will see Col Kincaid at 0700 pm. The Vietnamese are going to get you". Outside and in the truck Mr Reece stated that Mr Gerou received the above message from Mr Mac Elvany and Mr Parker. It came about from this circumstance. Two women who were associated with Mr Mac Elvany and Mr Parker at the Civilian Club, had relatives and friends in influential positions within the National Police (white mice), Quan Canh (local police) and Army of Republic Vietnam (ARVN's) That these two women vowed vengeance to anyone who was responsible with closing down the Civilian Club, or of the investigation of both Mr Mac Elvany and Parker. Regardless of how minor the incident. It was mentioned that there was a tremendous loss of money,

5-6 My famous letter to Mr. Bartley page 6

because of rent, equipment, local nationals working and payoff / protection

Living at the P.U.+E. was a National Police Sergeant, I heard that he was in the protection racket, he was always on duty from 1830 to 2230 every evening. This one individual made it a point to know everyone.

Early in March '67 a conversation took place in my presence, there was another DAC present, that for $10⁰⁰ a cowboy type individual would exterminate the life of a human being. This also swayed my judgment and desires to leave Vung Tau.

I'm in no position to know what extremes these people would go to revenge this situation, or if they are bluffing. If you look at the whole picture of what they are about to give up I believe that anyone would be capable of violence. But to me, I don't want the opportunities of kindness

5-6 My famous letter to Mr. Bartley page 7

I've sent word to my wife to contact you personally, in the event anyone calls and/or threatens her in anyway.

Vung Tau has to many civilian populous to know who is friendly, or who is the enemy. At 1900, 19 June '67, I reported to Col Kincaid, told him the complete story. He provided Security guards in and around the compound I stayed in his headquarters this one night. On 20 June '67 34th Group, approved me going to 520th Trans. Bn. and subsequent assignment to 20th Trans Co (ADS) in support of T53 L13 engines.

There's more info available at CID headquarters. This is a brief explanation of the problem surrounding me, and reasons for not returning to Vung Tau to instruct.

In view of the above, and of keeping my sanity. I'll Wait for an answer to alleviate this situation.

5-6 My famous letter to Mr. Bartley page 8

9.

In the best interest of this program, would it be possible to have someone designated by you, come over here and find out why so many of our personnel are unhappy with their assignment?

If I can be of any assistance please, let me know.

Sincerely yours

Frayne C Kuschel SAC
20ᵗʰ Trans. Co. (ADS)
Apo San Francisco 96353

P.S I hope that Im not stepping out of line in writing this letter to you personally. But with Turner gone and maj. Heddon on R + R theres no one to contact in Saigon.

5-6 My famous letter to Mr. Bartley page 9

5-6
My famous letter to Mr. Bartley page 10

July 10 1965

Hi Wayne,

Received your letter and will try to bring you up to date. Mac & Joe are leaving this morning for St. Louis. Two more instructors are due in this week. The folder you gave Sgt. Reed was given to Mr. Sherman, he said he would get it to you. I picked up your T-55 Lesson Plans and will send it out today. Your shoes are a problem, I can't seem to catch the ole Mama San there, but will keep trying, keep your fingers crossed. Sing came in to see me again crying for the 1,100 piastres for your laundry, so I paid her. Must close before the rest of the gang gets here, drop a line when you can. Hope you like your assignment. Bye for Now

your friend, Bernie

5-7 Bernie's letter to me

1. REPORTING PERIOD		
FROM 16 July 1967 TO 31 July 1967		

TYPE OF REPORT

MONTHLY	XX	DA CIVILIAN
SPECIAL		MILITARY
XX OTHER Biweek		

3. TO Headquarters
U.S.Army Aviation Materiel Command
Attn: AMSAV-FTT

4. FROM *(Name, Grade-Rank-Title, Address, and Signature)*
Wayne A. Kuschel GS-11 Equipment Specialist
20th Trans. Co. (ADS)
APO San Francisco 96353

DATE 1 Aug 1967

Wayne A. Kuschel

PART I

5. UNIT(S) OR ACTIVITY SUPPORTED
20th Trans. Co.
725th Trans. Co. (DS) and subordinate units.

6. BASIC WEAPON (OR EQUIPMENT) SYSTEM ON WHICH ASSISTANCE WAS RENDERED
T-53 L9, L11, L13

7. WERE PROBLEMS ENCOUNTERED THAT COULD NOT BE RESOLVED?
(If Yes Explain in Item 13)   ☐ YES   ☒ NO

8. INDICATE PROBLEMS ENCOUNTERED IN AREAS a THRU g BY LISTING NUMBER OF REPORTS SUBMITTED FOR EACH Assistance

a. TOOLS AND TEST EQUIPMENT	4	e. TAERS	
b. TECHNICAL PUBLICATIONS	2	f. MALFUNCTION	1
c. SUPPLY AND REPAIR PARTS	3	g. OTHER *(Specify)*	
d. CHECKS AND ADJUSTMENTS	1		

9. MANPOWER AND TRAINING DATA

a. DAYS WORKED THIS REPORTING PERIOD	14	b. ANNUAL LEAVE HRS	0	c. SICK LEAVE HRS	0	d. OVERTIME HRS — COMP / PAID 57
e. TOTAL HOURS SPENT W/UNITS IN ITEM 5	137	f. HOURS OF FORMAL TRAINING CONDUCTED	0			g. NUMBER OF PERSONS TRAINED (Formal) 0
h. HOURS TRAVEL TIME	25	i. HOURS OF OJT	32			j. NUMBER OF PERSONS TRAINED (O/T) 3 45
k. HOURS SPENT PERFORMING ACTUAL MAINTENANCE FUNCTIONS *(Explain in Item 13)*						112
l. OTHER *(See Instructions)* 3 maint personnel 3hr 45 pilots for 2 hour lecture						

10. WERE PROBLEMS AND VISITS DISCUSSED WITH THE COMMAND G4/S4 AND OR HIS MAINTENANCE OR MATERIEL READINESS OFFICER?   ☐ YES   ☒ NO

11. NAME, TITLE AND ADDRESS OF PERSONNEL CONTACTED OTHER THAN ROUTINE

J. Stewart   Maj.   Maint. Off.   602d Trans. Det.   Tay Ninh, RVN

C. Fleming   Maj.   Maint. Off.   3/4 Cav.   Cu Chi, RVN

E. Campbell   Maj.   Commanding Officer   604th Trans. Co. Pleiku, RVN

PART II

12. THE SERVICES REPORTED ABOVE WERE PERFORMED IN A (SATISFACTORY) (UNSATISFACTORY) MANNER
(If Unsatisfactory, Attach Explanation)

DATE	NAME, TITLE AND GRADE OF DESIGNATED SUPERVISOR	SIGNATURE
1 Aug 1967	John K. Clements Maj. TC Commanding Officer	*John K. Clements*

ORGANIZATION AND ADDRESS
20th Trans. Co. (ADS)
APO San Francisco 96353

5-8 Maintenance Performance Report 1478—R

1. Assisted in troubleshooting T-53 L11 engine on UH-1B 64-13952. Electric and fuel.
2. TDY to assist 602d Trans. Det. on T-53 engine problems. Two hot-ends on UH-1D 66-829, LE12308 737:15hr and 66-817 LE10544 776:00hr (49:00 since O/H Aradmac). Showed signs of overtemp condition. Both HI nozzles had erosion, bulging, and holes burned in trailing edges of blades. In addition these areas had the appearance of turquoise to green in color. I turned one of these HI nozzles into Mr. TWA at 34th Group for analysis or evaluation. (Today, 1Aug67, Mr. TWA stated Lycoming had confirmed that fuel contamination was the cause of the HI nozzle problem). EIR submitted by 602d Trans. Det. Samples of fuel taken from tanks of the aircraft above, were sent to POL lab by 34th Group. (Fuel report or analysis were returned to me indicating that the samples were within limits of JP-4 specifications.) The Maint. Off. was advised of methods and procedures to alleviate or minimize further problems.
3. Lycoming special tool/ LTCT 2075, FSN 4920-923-2773 Fixture Holding. Has been received without center portion in which to engage the sun gear on T-53 L13 engines.
4. Assisted 116th Assault Helicopter Co. on removing studs in #2 bearing housing area.
5. Assisted and instructed 725th Engine Shop personnel on operation and adjustment of T-53 bleed band.
6. Assisted 20th Engine Shop on determining FOD on UH-1H 66-16150, T-53 L13, LE14227, 85:00hr. This engine is awaiting blades and stator vanes to return to operational status. New engine T-53 L13 LE14479, arrived tagged "engine dropped" Can showed no evidence of any dents or scratches. Inside the can, the engine showed no physical signs of external damage. We visually checked all mounts, seals, drive box, hose lines. Engine was installed on aircraft. A run-up at these intervals 5 min, 10 min, 15 min, 30 min and shut-down after each time, indicated no contamination in any of the screens or filters, last chance strainers. Called Mr. TWA at 34th Group, stated the circumstances, requested that we be allowed a one hour flight to check for vibration then inspect engine. If no trouble developes, release it as OK. Mr. TWA approved this method. ~~With the shortage of T-53 L13 engines, and considering all costs, it would assist all units if same approved method be implemented and sent to the field.~~ *JWA*
7. Inspected T-53 L13 engine LE14133 on UH-1H, 66-16115 for FOD. Engine EDP, engine is awaiting parts to return to supply.
8. Assisted in inspecting "float" aircraft: UH-1D, 64-13837 LE10416
    UH-1D, 6413603 LE11020
    UH-1D, 64-13546 LE09677 721:00hr (49:00 hr since O/H) Hot end 506:00 hr.

FOR HMP USE			
DATE RECEIVED	**FOLLOW UP REQUIRED** ☐ YES ☐ NO	**SUSPENSE DATE**	
ACTION ASSIGNED TO		**DATE REPLY MAILED**	
REMARKS			

5-8 Maintenance Performance Report 1478—R page 2

KISCHEL, WAYNE A.   MR.

                                         F-340-67   20 Jul 67
PROMOTION

                                         6 Jun 67   Sensitive

Equipment Specialist (Aircraft Propulsion
System)
JN 9561   GS-1670   11

USAAVCOM, Directorate of Maintenance
Technical Assistance Division
Technical Support Branch, Field Section

Equipment Specialist (Aircraft Propulsion
System)
JN 9202   GS-1670   12

USAAVCOM, Directorate of Maintenance
Technical Assistance Division
Technical Support Branch, Field Section

Vietnam

23L0.10223.A011GD - Permanent position
30 Apr 67 TD - Para 92C line 04

        Employee EOD 6 Jun 66 at GS-11 level. I have determined the incumbent is
well qualified and performing fully the higher graded Equipment Specialist duties of the
position and I desire the incumbent to be advanced with the position.

LEONARD E. BARTLEY, Actg C, Tech Asst Div

                                         ALBERT NEWTON, Colonel, GS
Marge Naas, Ext 2281   Director of Maintenance (DRP)

5-9 AVSCOM orders for my GS-12

156

NOTIFICATION OF PERSONNEL ACTION

(EMPLOYEE - See General Information on Reverse)

8 Aug 67

50-114-09

1. NAME (CAPS) LAST - FIRST - MIDDLE	MR. - MISS - MRS.	2. (FOR AGENCY USE)	3. BIRTH DATE (Mo., Day, Year)	4. SOCIAL SECURITY NO.
KUSCHEL, WAYNE A.	MR.		12-06-23	

5. VETERAN PREFERENCE	6. TENURE GROUP	7. SERVICE COMP. DATE	8. PHYS HAND CODE
2 1. - NO 3. - 10 PT. DISAB. 5. - 10 PT. OTHER 2. - 5 PT. 4. - 10 PT. COMP.	2	02-01-56	00

9. FEGLI	10. RETIREMENT	11. (FOR CSC USE)
1 1. - COVERED 2. - INELIGIBLE 3. - WAIVED	1 1. - CS 2. - FICA 3. - FS 4. - NONE 5. - OTHER	

12. NATURE OF ACTION	13. EFFECTIVE DATE (Mo., Day, Year)	14. CIVIL SERVICE OR OTHER LEGAL AUTHORITY
702 CODE Promotion	08-06-67	Reg. 335.102

15. FROM: POSITION TITLE AND NUMBER	16. PAY PLAN AND OCCUPATION CODE	17. GRADE OR LEVEL	18. SALARY
#9561		11/2	Pa $9536

19. NAME AND LOCATION OF EMPLOYING OFFICE

20. TO: POSITION TITLE AND NUMBER	21. PAY PLAN AND OCCUPATION CODE	22. GRADE OR LEVEL	23. SALARY
Equipment Specialist (Aircraft Propulsion Equipment) #9202	GS-1670	12/1	Pa $10,927

24. NAME AND LOCATION OF EMPLOYING OFFICE
U. S. Army Aviation Command
Directorate of Maintenance
Technical Assistance Division, Technical Support Branch, Field Section

25. DUTY STATION (City - State)	26. LOCATION CODE
Saigon, Republic of Vietnam	95-7000-945

27. APPROPRIATION	28. POSITION OCCUPIED	29. APPORTIONED POSITION
	1 1-COMPETITIVE SERVICE 2-EXCEPTED SERVICE	(FROM) 1-PROVED (TO) 2-WAIVED STATE

30. REMARKS: _____ A. SUBJECT TO COMPLETION OF 1 _____ YEAR PROBATIONARY (OR TRIAL) PERIOD COMMENCING _____
_____ B. SERVICE COUNTING TOWARD CAREER (OR PERM) TENURE FROM _____
SEPARATIONS: SHOW REASONS BELOW, AS REQUIRED. CHECK IF APPLICABLE: _____ C. DURING PROBATION _____ D. FROM APPOINTMENT OF 1 MONTHS OR LESS

Action effected under provisions of CPR CP1, par 1.4-2b(3)(c).

ENTRANCE PERFORMANCE RATING: Satisfactory

31. DATE OF APPOINTMENT AFFIDAVIT (Accessions only)	34. SIGNATURE (Or other authorization) AND TITLE
	FOR THE APPOINTING OFFICER
32. OFFICE MAINTAINING PERSONNEL FOLDER (If different from employing office) Saigon Area CPO, USARV, APO 96243	William a. Methvin
	WILLIAM A. METHVIN
33. CODE AR 41 EMPLOYING DEPARTMENT OR AGENCY DEPARTMENT OF THE ARMY	Civilian Personnel Officer
	35. DATE 08-06-67 3222

1. EMPLOYEE COPY

5-10 Saigon CPO Promotion GS-12

157

3. CITATION TO APPLICABLE STANDARD AND ITS DATE OF ISSUANCE	4. TITLE Equipment Specialist (Aircraft Propulsion Equipment)		
CSC, GS-1670, Jun 64	5. PAY SCHEDULE	6. OCC. CODE	7. GRADE
	GS	1670	12

8. EVALUATION APPROVAL	SIGNATURE	DATE
Title, pay schedule, code and grade of this job have been fixed in accordance with Department of the Army official policy and grade level standards.	*Anton Imhof, Jr.* ANTON IMHOF, JR.	20 Aug 65

9. SUPERVISORY CONTROLS, DUTIES, AND WORKING CONDITIONS *(Indicate percent of time for each duty, where pertinent.) (Continue statement of duties, etc., on reverse side if necessary.)*

SUPERVISORY CONTROLS

Work is performed in an assigned area overseas or within CONUS under the general direction and administrative supervision of a supervisor located in St. Louis, Missouri. Detached duty station results in incumbent's receiving broad policy guidance outlines on objectives to be accomplished at time of assignment. Has full responsibility for work activities while on assignments and has wide latitude in exercising independent judgment in the interpretation and implementation of applicable maintenance policies and procedures. Adequacy of performance is judged through analysis of written reports, oral reports, and personal visitation.

MAJOR DUTIES

As a representative of the command with duty station located overseas or within CONUS, incumbent serves as a topmost technical expert and advisor in the maintenance of a specific series of reciprocating or turbine propulsion equipment used in the make-up of Army aircraft. As such, he furnishes expert and specialized advice, assistance, and instructions to Department of the Army personnel in maintenance, adjustment, repair, servicing, testing, processing, packaging, preservation, assembly, in-storage maintenance, and modification of his assigned aircraft propulsion equipment.

1. Maintains continuing contact with the command and close liaison with the U. S. Air Force, the U. S. Navy, and aircraft manufacturers to assure constant cognizance of the latest maintenance engineering data, such as engineering change proposals, blueprint changes, microfilm, factory bulletins, and other data pertinent to his assigned type of aircraft propulsion equipment. Develops and submits proposed changes to DA maintenance publication, maintenance procedures, and practices. Investigates, analyzes, and corrects diverse and complicated operational and mechanical problems requiring intensive knowledge covering maintenance and construction of his

10.	JOB CONTENT APPROVAL *(Complete on organization file copy only.)*
ORGANIZATION LOCATION	
Directorate of Maintenance, Technical Assistance Division, Technical Support Branch	

THIS STATEMENT ACCURATELY DESCRIBES THE WORK REQUIRED IN ONE POSITION OR IN EACH OF A GROUP OF POSITIONS IN THE ABOVE ORGANIZATION.	THE ABOVE DESCRIPTION, WITH SUPPLEMENTAL MATERIAL, IS ADEQUATE FOR PURPOSES OF EVALUATION.
SIGNATURE OF APPROVING SUPERVISOR	SIGNATURE OF ANALYST
Howard Broch	*Anton Imhof, Jr.*

11.		REAUDIT APPROVAL						
DATE								
SUPERVISOR'S APPROVAL								
ANALYST'S SIGNATURE								

DA FORM 374 1 JUN 61   PREVIOUS EDITIONS OF THIS FORM ARE OBSOLETE.

5-10 Saigon CPO Promotion GS-12 page 2

assigned type of Army aircraft propulsion equipment. Investigates deficiencies for the purpose of establishing areas that should be reported for equipment improvement. Makes occasional flights as technical observer to determine causes of malfunctions, such as improper fuel adjustment or flow, improper ignition system operation, origin of unusual noises, unusual vibrations, improper valve train adjustment or functioning, abnormal rpm indications, etc.

2. Researches and assembles information for classroom training purposes and based on practical experience and ingenuity, conducts classes (including lectures and demonstrations) for maintenance and operational (military and civil service) personnel in the maintenance and operation of assigned type of aircraft propulsion equipment. Further, effects training required by instructing all Department of the Army personnel or by training of maintenance personnel and overseeing their subsequent training of other troops. Conducts on-the-job training by demonstration and/or overseeing troops conducting maintenance at actual site to insure proper methods and techniques are used. Slants training toward preventive maintenance to avert engine breakdown and deadline of equipment. Also, assembles and prepares on request of installation commanders, direction from higher authority, or observation in the field, a wide variety of information from technical and administrative publications (including TO's, TM's SB's, TAB's, AR's, SR's, etc.).

3. Represents the command at Army supply and maintenance conferences National Guard conferences, and other top level meetings and conferences to discuss maintenance and operating procedures and is empowered to make commitments which obligate the command to a course of action. Renders technical advice and assistance to accident investigation boards in determining cause or probable cause of accidents, corrective and/or preventive action to be taken, and recommends applicable product changes and modifications. As required, inspects and furnishes analysis of engine damage and recommends repair methods, repair levels, and/or engine salvage. Makes periodic trips to manufacturers or training agencies to maintain current knowledge of assigned propulsion equipment and to keep abreast of the latest maintenance and operating procedures.

4. Prepares and submits written reports at predetermined intervals to the command, indicating clearly and factually the nature of tasks accomplished, trouble encountered, corrective measures taken or adopted, recommendations made and to whom made, and any other pertinent information related to the general adequacy of maintenance facilities, parts supply, tools, and publications.

Performs other duties as assigned.

NOTE: Travel for TDY will be made by commercial or military aircraft as directed by superiors. Involves temporary assignments requiring world-wide travel.

(Title and grade are established in accordance with position classification standards and guides referenced in Item 3. These referenced materials are available for your review in the Civilian Personnel Office.)

5-10 Saigon CPO Promotion GS-12 page 3

18 July 67

Wayne,

Here's your performance appraisal and we completed all I can without your help. Check section 11 Part A Plans on what your goals and training requirements are. When you complete this you can send the whole bundle to St Louis for typing or if you have the typist leave it completed. Id like to get up to see you before I leave here however I doubt it very much as I depart here on 30 July for St Louis. I guess the mess at Vung Tau created quite a lot of excitement with the wheels. Riker & McElwain departed here a week ago today and should be on the carpet by now. The letter from here recommends immediate removal. Ill probably get the same treatment from Black Bart when I get back. At least Im expecting the worst and have made a move to get out of this phony set up. I may have to resign I don't know. I've at least made contact with LTC George Martin at Sharpe Army Depot for a transfere. I hope I get it. Only time will tell. Joe Braugh is due back here this friday so I may

5-11 Emmett's letter

160

got an idea of whats going on.

Wayne if you get a chance drop down and see me. I can possibly clue you in on a few things. As you know Cantu is to be my replacement.

I may need some help from you after I get back to St Louis. If so I'll drop you a line OK?

As ever

Emmett

EMPLOYEE PERFORMANCE APPRAISAL *(Civilian Personnel Re_ _on P4)*	1. TYPE OF APPRAISAL		PROBATIONARY OR TRIAL PERIOD
	OFFICIAL	UNOFFICIAL X	

PART A

2. NAME (Caps) LAST - FIRST - MIDDLE MR. - MISS - MRS.	3. POSITION TITLE, NUMBER AND GRADE
KUSCHEL, WAYNE A.	GS-1670-11 Equipment Spec (Acft Prop Equip) JN 9561

4. NAME AND LOCATION OF EMPLOYING OFFICE

USAAVCOM, Dir/Maintenance,
Tech Asst Div, Tech Supt Branch

5. APPRAISAL PERIOD	FROM 0766	TO 0367

6a. SUPERVISOR'S NARRATIVE EVALUATION OF PERFORMANCE ON THE ABOVE JOB *(Cover all aspects of performance as outlined in "Performance Appraisal a Reference Manual for Supervisors". As appropriate, indicate trend toward better or worse performance, identifying favorable aspects of performance and aspects which may warrant further improvement.) (If more space is needed, use separate sheets and attach).*

The performance of Mr. Kuschel has been outstanding in all areas. The leadership and initiative he has displayed were instrumental in the development of a superior engine AAMTAP team in the Technical Assistance Program. His technical competence is unquestionable, and his work is always of the highest quality. Mr. Kuschel is very stable under pressure, and his planning and organizing are always with sound judgment. His appearance and personality are always above average.

6b. FOR PROBATIONARY OR TRIAL PERIOD APPRAISALS, CHECK APPROPRIATE BOX IN THE FOLLOWING STATEMENT: ABILITY, CONDUCT, AND GENERAL CHARACTER TRAITS ARE SUCH THAT IT IS RECOMMENDED THE EMPLOYEE BE XX RETAINED IN) I SEPARATED FROM) THE FEDERAL SERVICE.

7. PERFORMANCE RATING (Check one)	8. SUPERVISOR'S SIGNATURE Emmett A. Turner	9. DATE 20 Feb 67
XX SATISFACTORY RATING ASSIGNED	10. RECOMMENDED RATING APPROVED BY Leonard Bailey	11. DATE 28 Feb 67
OUTSTANDING RATING RECOMMENDED	12. THIS APPRAISAL WAS DISCUSSED WITH ME. MY COMMENTS (if any) ARE ON THE REVERSE.	
UNSATISFACTORY RATING RECOMMENDED	Wayne A. Kuschel (Employee's Signature)	20 Feb 67 (Date)

NOTE: The official adjective rating assigned may be appealed. Information on the appeal procedure may be obtained from your supervisor, or if you prefer, from the Civilian Personnel Office.

DA FORM 1 NOV 63 1052   Replaces DA Form 1052, 1 Nov 56, and DA Form 1052 (Test), 1 Dec 61, which will be issued and used until 1 Nov 64, unless sooner exhausted.   OPERATING OFFICIAL'S COPY 2

5-12 My appraisal DA Form 1052

162

20 July 67.

Dear Wayne

Just a few lines in reply to your
letter. Will try to get the manuals
that you requested out to you.

~~The~~ ~~too~~ no one has been promoted
as yet. The original course of action
on this turned out to be a long drawn
out affair. We just completed action
today to get the following promoted,
effective on their anniversary date:

     Mr. W. Kaschell
     Mr B Reece
     Mr. B. Russell
     Mr. C. Reed.
     Mr. C. Grimes.

Now we just got into effect a cross-
servicing agreement with Saigon CPO
all the records for those pers assigned PCS to
Vietnam are being hand carried by Mr
Ray Carter, who is replacing Mr Turner,
to Saigon CPO. It will become
their responsibility to process the paperwork

5-13
Letter from Don Pittman 20 July 1967 Promotion to GS-12

The 52's for the promotion were processed and approved by this command today. It will just be a matter of Saigon CPO processing the additional required paper work. We are looking out for you Wayne. If you see any of the above pass the word on to them. For the others that will be coming due, Mr Buckley will review their records and performance and if they deserve being promoted, action will be taken.

There's not too much new from this end of the world, McElvany & Parker are currently in-house.

Take it easy Wayne & we'll see you upon your return to Corus

Don Pittman.

5-13
Letter from Don Pittman 20 July 1967 Promotion to GS-12 page 2

25 July 67

Dear Don:

Just received your most welcome letter, so will try and answer it.

I had to go into Saigon on fuel Contamination problems this morning, so I stopped by 34th Gp and saw Roy Cantu. Talked to him about a few small problems. He told me the records were turned over to CPO and everything looked good.

Don! What I'm writing in this paragraph, I regret to write, but, if something isn't done to stop Mac + Parker from intimidating me, there's going to be hell to pay. I'm trying to do my job and those people are sure harassing me. I opened up a large envelope and a shipping label from AVCO was on the papers "WE'LL SEE YOU LATER. MAC & JOE" Then I open up a box of TM's and on one label was written "LOOKING FORWARD TO YOUR RETURN"

5-14 Letter to Don Pittman

2.

I'm expecting a little bit of assistance in Correcting this problem, I Can take these items to the C.I.D. and make damn sure that this is put on record for future use. But would rather, you do something about it from there. I only hope that its in jest. Because if its for real someone is going to get hurt. Why are they (Mac + Parker) allowed "free" reign to get into mailing items.

I'd much rather have my business handled by personnel authorized to do so.

Thanks for all the help you've given to me. Hope you Can give me good news or something on above matters.

P.S. I didn't write to Mr Bartley because I think you Can help me! OK? If you want to verify these items I'll send them in.

Sincerely,

Wayne G. Kuschel SPc
90th Trans. Co. (ADS)
Apo San Francisco 96353

(WO-1 GRAVES WITNESSED THIS PROBLEM)

5-14 Letter to Don Pittman page 2

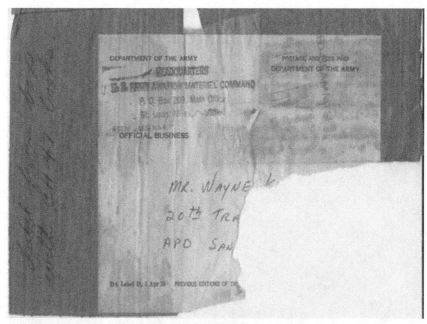

Chapter 5-15 Box Label

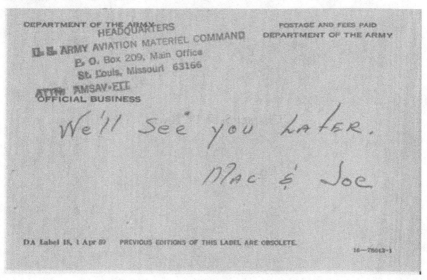

Chapter 5-16 1st Threat

Chapter 5-17 2nd Threat

CHAPTER 6-
KEEP TRAVELING,
WITH AMENDED TRAVEL ORDERS

Shortly after our return to Cu Chi, the rainy season was upon us, starting at 1630 each afternoon. For days it was the same "rain" diet. It was sickening. You could set your watch each and every day. The gullies filled up with water and would stay that way, then during the day the sun reflecting off the water would give a person a red tint with a slight sun burn on your face, especially with over 120 degrees in temperature. They were very humid sultry days, and then at night it cooled off a wee bit. They had a dangerous malaria mosquito that had a tendency of not buzzing and zapping you without any warning. To counter that enemy we all purchased fans from the Post Exchange. These were placed near our heads and blew the air toward the foot of the bed, not allowing the mosquitoes to land, so the theory goes. However, to be sure that no one could contact malaria we were also issued one orange and one white pill each week. The result of that was a good case of diarrhea weekly.

Each week, use of these pills spelled disaster. To many people the saying in the 20th Transportation Company was that you couldn't drive a ten cent piece in between your buttocks with a sledge hammer. You would see some personnel walking very slow, getting close or near to the outhouse or privy. It was critical that you didn't change the position of your tongue in cheek or you would lose it all and a change of clothes was in order. Another example is the person who is taking six inch steps, no longer, no shorter. He will get right up to the step and stub his toe, then he would lose that round, another change of clothes was in order.

From our hooch or quarters in Cu Chi we had a boardwalk to our 2 and 3 seater outhouse or privy. No special plumbing or septic tanks, just plain out houses. Each morning the refuse containers were taken out and mixed with a burnable liquid or substance such as JP-4 fuel, and then you could see the black smoke miles and miles away. You never knew if the Viet Cong were attacking, the time of day would tell you which it was. [Copy of Maintenance Performance Report 1478—R 6-1]

My time was getting more difficult to schedule as there were more responses to our fast flying maintenance requirements than time allowed. For example, sending this letter to Mr. Bartley at AVSCOM regarding my returning to Vung Tau to instruct T 53-L-13. [reference copy here], [My 15 August 1967 letter to Mr. Bartley 6-1a]

In the best interest and safety of my life I thought I could do more good working with the 20th Transportation Company, which I believe I could save time and money for the government by using the helicopter flying to the downed aircraft or maintenance in the unit. I felt it was as important as teaching and I also accomplished power plant instruction's to pilots, staff personnel and aviation mechanics or anyone interested. Since Mr. Bartley made me the AAMTAP team leader and pair of goof-balls were threatening me with paper labels from AVSCOM, you would think they could control the bad guys behavior or work assignment, or get rid of them as undesirables. [Copy of Maintenance Peformance Report 1478—R 6-2]

While at Vung Tau I met Merle Travis from Nashville, Tennessee, country western guitar player and singer at his USO meeting with the troops. Another entertainer I met was Wendell Corey from Hollywood, California. The 20th Transportation Company was responsible for flying him to various locations. Wendell was one nice actor and gentleman. He told jokes and was always curious about the flying characteristics of the helicopters. [Pictures of actor Wendell Corey, Wayne, MAJ Clements, CWO Graves 6-3]

I had to hitch rides to Tan Son Nhut (Saigon) to visit the United States Embassy and have my Republic of Vietnam Visa updated. We never accepted the use of assigned aircraft, our hitch-hiking was done on our own time with whatever method we wanted to use. I didn't like to go to Saigon because of the risks involved. There were too many variables. If you stood too close to a group of service people, someone might throw a hand grenade and who could say what person might have been injured or hurt?, on one of these six months visits to the USA embassy.

I kept running into old friends everywhere I went, so I proceeded with caution to Tan Son Nhut for one of our ferry flights to Cu Chi. My friends at Cu Chi always knew where I was, and continuously made sure I had a ride home.

A few days after my return to Cu Chi I was sitting in our trailer typing a report to AVSCOM when a Sergeant told a Private First Class (PFC) to get the big lawn mower and mow the weeds to the no man's fence. The young fellow fueled the lawn mower, started it up, leaving it to warm up while he put the gasoline away. He grabbed the handle and began mowing. He had about a hundred square feet done when he came to the trailer and got a drink of water. The PFC asked the Sarge if he could finish mowing after dinner. The Sarge said, "No!" It had to be done as soon as possible (ASAP). So the young fellow again began to push the mower into the higher grass which was about 15 inches tall. About five minutes later the PFC turned white as a sheet, left the lawn mower and ran out of the grass into our trailer. The Sarge asked him what was wrong. He said, "I'm not going to cut anymore grass out there, there are many cobra snakes out there!" We all ventured out in the grass area and the PFC had gotten into a whole family of cobras and had chopped several to pieces. There were several snakes with heads and/or tails missing. Some were still crawling around but dangerous. It wasn't a comfortable place to be. This pointed out that the grass had to be cut regularly and not allowed to get high enough to hide cobra snakes. So there was a company letter placed on the bulletin board to that effect.

In our quarters (20' x 60') one Sunday, I went out to our personnel wash room and returned, by chance looking up I saw where a very long large snake had shed its skin. The snakeskin was still draped over the rafters. It measured over twenty feet long. All of our personnel looked for the snake. There was no sight of it. Where it went no one knows, it was a terrible feeling not knowing if the snake was hiding or just a visitor. We all watched the rafters from then on, not taking a chance with a hungry snake.

One hot humid night around midnight I awoke with incoming mortar rounds hitting the runway. The sirens were alerting everyone to take cover. We had an ambitious warrant officer pilot that grabbed a folding chair and began to charge through a door when he found out that a chair can be detrimental, especially when it goes cross-wise and no one can get through the door. I immediately pulled on my flight suit and rubber overshoes with a special spurt of speed, when I ran into a bunch of fellow personnel bunched up at the door. Finally the Warrant Officer got the chair down and we got out of our quarters and toward our underground bunker. There were two dangers facing us, the VC and the cobras, which would sit on the sand bags. Without flashlights you never know what lay ahead of you. When we turned a corner into the bunker this evening, there were two cobras sitting curled up ready to strike, which were short lived by one of our expert weapons men.

A quote from the magazine "Disabled American Veterans" March-April 2010 (page 5 and 31) Titled "King Cobras and a Purple Heart" by RVN Robert McBride as a young army specialist McBride served with C Company of the 544ᵗʰ Engineers in Cu Chi, South Vietnam, during the Vietnam war, his company seemed to come under mortar attacks nearly every night.

(I can attest to this statement my tour of Cu Chi was 10 July 1967 to 19 December 1967 that the Cobras were very plentiful plus the mortar and VC attacks on Cu Chi.)

Army Specialist McBride also stated that he was exposed to Agent Orange 2-4-D the same as myself you never knew where you would be exposed to this material in the field.

I spoke with DAV personnel 19 March 2010 for approval on using this article (they ok'd the use).

There was an African-American Second Lieutenant, new on the job that did us a beneficial service. He slipped back into our quarters to answer the telephone and received an "all clear". He came back to the bunker and told all of us to hit the sack, the work day was coming earlier than expected. We got back to the quarters when another VC attack began. It came in spurts with mortar shells hitting various locations close by. We all cheered the Lieutenant for the warning. You had to be ready for any type of attack that could occur day or night. Aimed at specific targets, they tried to destroy aircraft or helicopters, and if personnel were available the VC would delight in destroying them also.

We flew regularly to the 520th Transportation Battalion at Phu Loi to attend meetings with the Aviation Commanders involving all assigned Iron Triangle aircraft, regardless of type. Fixed or rotary aircraft, it didn't matter, just so nothing would fall through the crack, so to speak. There were units outside the Cu Chi telephone system where we periodically had to fly into their units because of a lack of communication to assist in maintenance scheduling and acquiring assistance in logistics support from their headquarters in Saigon. On our way back to Cu Chi from a meeting at about 2,500 feet altitude, Bob Graves and I witnessed over 300 hardcore VC regulars heading toward Cu Chi. We called in to our Headquarters the location and their direction, so no one would be surprised. When we landed at 20th Transportation Company we were questioned on the VC details. It looked like Cu Chi was going to be hit in the next day or two, because of other VC sightings on the other sides of Cu Chi. No army personnel could visualize where all the VC were going to what location, or how they disappeared so conveniently. (While I was in Fairfax, Virginia in 1999-2001. the Washington Post Foreign Services Writer Rajiu Chandrasekaran put an article "Vietnam's Tours of Duty" in their paper. It started out, "Cu Chi, Vietnam had 125-mile maze of underground bunkers five stories deep and supply tunnels that snaked up to a United States military base at Cu Chi. The jungle here hosted some of the most intense fighting between American Soldiers and Viet Cong guerrillas during the Vietnam War and should be brought out to let the public know what the life in Republic of Vietnam (RVN) was really like".)

One night there were small skirmishes around the outside of Cu Chi camp perimeter. The towers had their hands full using the moonlight scopes. There were snipers trying to get to the CH-47 (Chinook) unit just north of us to blow up the aircraft using satchel (bomb) packs. However, the security guards with the moonlight scopes did a good job in pointing out the enemy; whereby, countermeasures were used to eliminate the Viet Cong.

On the 8th of September 1967 I received a letter from AVSCOM that read "appears that you can be assigned duty at Fort Sill, Oklahoma". The ink hadn't dried before I received another assignment in St. Louis, Missouri. [My Fort Sill, CONUS assignment 8 September 1967 6-4]

My buddy Bob Graves and I had to fly to Tay Ninh for propulsion problems. We flew past An Loc where the VC had mortared and shelled the United States Army troops in an acre or so of land. To me it looked like the place was plowed under by a tractor. I never saw such a devastating disaster area. It was beyond belief where so many young troops lost their lives. Both of us felt sad that nothing could be done about it. There was no way to retaliate. However, this was a war that hopefully could be won, and to keep the communists out of the Republic of Vietnam. But I felt there were too many regulations that we had to follow or comply with prior to any engagement with the enemy. I want to apologize right here if I have stepped on any toes on my comments regarding regulations. If you sighted the VC or enemy you called in the information to personnel who would get approval and advice the team to fire or hold your fire which was most of cases that involved me why be in a war if you can't destroy the enemy especially communism.

Upon arrival at Tay Ninh, we checked in with the maintenance officer and found out they had turbine airflow problems. We located some walnut shell cleaner and had the complete fleet back up to 100% operation within three hours. This Tay Ninh unit treated us like heroes, but we were only doing our jobs to assist the unit to ensure a fully operational flying unit was available 24/7.

On One (1) of my visit in August or September of 1967, my memory lapse the location (Tay Ninh or Dan Tieng) came under enemy attack mortar shells started falling near us. I immediately jumped off the engine platform and fell into a foot long hole, immediately I felt a terrific pain in my right chest area the pain was over in seconds. The pain came back after that day periodically, never to bad, until after I came back to the states, like it was a stomach pain.

Before we had a chance to take off and return to Cu Chi, we received an operational call to the location of a UH-1 (Huey) that went down with either engine or fuel problems. We were escorted to the location by two gunships. The UH-1 (Huey) was forced down in tall weeds or elephant grass. I proceeded to the downed UH-1 (Huey) and did several checks and tests and determined it was a fuel problem. The valve was not properly seated, allowing a minimum amount of fuel (JP-4) to reach the fuel control on the engine. The maintenance team and I in about thirty minutes had the UH-1 (Huey) ready to fly to its home base for further maintenance or inspection. Because of priorities for take-off procedures we had to wait. So I was seated in the rear seat of the Huey when a commotion occurred in the area. The gunships took off and we followed to their base. After checking in with the maintenance officer, we returned to Cu Chi for a restful night of sleep. [Copy of Maintenance Performance Report 1478 R 6-5], [Copy of Maintenance Performance Report 1478 R 6-6]

Time was getting short. My Travel Orders L.O. 267-67 dated 6 November 1967, Subject: Travel Orders—PCS to CONUS, arrived in Cu Chi at the 20th Transportation Company. AVSCOM assigned me to Fort Sill, Oklahoma, which was fine with me. [Staying in practice, receiving another travel order 6-7]

However, on 15 November 1967, I received another AVSCOM Technical Assistance Division letter from Mr. Bartley stating I was to be assigned at St. Louis, Missouri and selected to attend the Maintenance Management course at Fort Lee, Virginia from 7 January 1968 through 16 February 1968 for a mid-level management position within the United States Army Aviation Maintenance area. [Letter Assigning me to St. Louis, Missouri and school 6-8]

My mind couldn't comprehend what was going on. No Fort Sill? Going into AVSCOM? No black market problems? Then my next assignment would be a higher grade position because of my college degree and Maintenance Management course. So I obey and comply with all my new AVSCOM orders and I agree going to school, hurrah! That is a swell switch around, better than being placed at the low side of the totem pole.

Guess I wasn't through receiving more travel orders. L.O. 324-67 dated 30 November 1967 from the Saigon civilian personnel office for "required minimum period of service in the command which was curtailed by CG AVSCOM" which controlled all civilians in the Republic of Vietnam. [Amended letter orders 324-67 6-9]

Then before the ink was dry another travel order L.O. 339-67 was received dated 12 December 1967. It was issued to correct the other three travel orders assigning me to Fort Sill, Oklahoma and then to St. Louis, Missouri, in addition to my household goods and dependents. My feelings were that the AVSCOM personnel were awaiting my arrival so they can get me on their schedule for my future duties or use my abilities acquired up to this time period for solving unknown problems received from the field. I was game for any circumstance; my expertise could be used for AVSCOM's benefit. Inside the travel order packet were all kinds of information regarding money transactions between our civilian personnel returning to the United States of American, Land of Our Dreams. [My Individual Concerned Travel Orders 6-10]

A few days later we heard through the grapevine that one of our flying friends in Tay Ninh had been killed flying a routine test flight at night. There are no routine test flights supposedly flown at night. In this case he was trying to get the minor test flights out of the way because of a big push that was pending on early morning take-off time.[Copy of Maintenance Performance Report 1478 R 6-11]

Several days later I got woke up early one morning with a large number of UH-1 (Huey) landing. They began loading up troops and taking off over our west side area. I counted 150 UH-1 (Hueys) in this compliment. They went north to Song Saigon River where they cornered a large group of VC regulars. The United States troops forced them into a city about ten miles north of us, where they lost the VC regulars. My buddy came back and told me the VC just vanished so the United States Army troops kept searching and found doors in some building leading down into a concrete corridor or tunnels going under the river toward our base. After this discovery our United States Air Force B-52 bombers put those tunnels under the river out of commission. This action was really fast. I would bet my paycheck that the VC had begun to rebuild the corridors shortly after the bombing attack stopped.

The following morning we all went to the mess hall for a coffee break. As I went into the kitchen there was a Vietnamese gal peeling potatoes and had her foot on the rim of the kettle with her big toe holding down a potato. I thought what a delightful taste that big toe will bring into that pot of potatoes and to the troops eating them.

A week or so later one morning I heard lots of noise. The noise was getting louder. All of a sudden everything was shaking violently. My wall lockers with my luggage or suitcases on top was jumping around, rightfully so. Again the B-52's were dropping their bombs just north of Cu Chi. When I got outside all I saw was the big bombs bursting and a very red glow on the surface of the earth. That's the closest I have ever been to a bomb bursting scene such as this. The noise was terrifyingly loud. How any personnel could live through this type of actual combat catastrophe is beyond imagination.

At any time after dusk you had to be ready for loud noises from the roaming eight inch Howitzer mounted on tracks. When you least expected it, the big boom would ripple your hair or raise the sheets off of you while you were in bed. That wouldn't be so bad but the muzzle blast seemed to pick up rocks, pebbles, and debris that would fall on our metal roofing causing all types of noises. A person had to have no heart problems or a dang good heart because of oddball noises, plus the aircraft that would attack targets out in no man's land from slow flying type to almost sonic speeds; you got sleep whenever you could. There was one thing going for us. The big diesel electric generator's noise was lulling, in its continuous purring sound, you had a tendency of putting things or noises out of your mind, and drifting off to sleep. When a person wakes up in Cu Chi, the morning temperatures were really hot, since it's located near the equator. It's almost unbearable heat-wise; you're feeling filthy, dirty, greasy and sweaty. It makes no difference if you shower hour after hour you're still uncomfortable. Then you think boy it will be nice to get back to the good old United States of America and home, and have a milk shake or a properly made glass of iced tea. There are a lot of things lacking the American touch. However, we were in a war zone and everything is not like home which was 6,000 miles away.

Numerous times CH-47 (Chinooks) or UH-1 (Huey's) transported downed helicopters to the 20th Transportation Company at Cu Chi for investigation, repair or salvage. It's surprising the various conditions some of the helicopters were in. Unbelievable that personnel survived a crash such as some of them, nothing left except twisted metal and forms or stringers.

I knew of one UH-1 (Huey) that had been shot down three times by the VC. It had 27 hours on the airframe. In the last flight the pilot was killed by a Viet Cong bullet that entered the rear armored seat through a corner crevice or crack. It was a safe, secured area that would not appear that any type of projectile could enter and do any harm. On many flying days there were other helicopters that were flying close support missions near the ground in wooded areas when the VC would pop up from nowhere, cut a burst with a handheld Thompson machine gun or an AK-47 that got in a lucky shot and the chopper would go down. On several occasions the VC were acting alone or two or three in a group, then they would decide to take on the flying helicopters because of their own bravery aspect of nothing can happen to me. Once the chopper was downed the VC would disappear. We hoped that no ambush would take place around our assigned downed chopper. Of course, our gun ships were always ready for any action required.

(I was watching a special on the television in Henrietta, Texas in late 2001, when it was mentioned again and shown that close to Cu Chi base was the largest underground 120-mile tunnel network or complex that was not ever discovered, nor was it ever disclosed in correspondence. I was flabbergasted that we never had more personnel killed or wounded.) I reported this item several pages back. I could not believe that it was being exploited for the communist benefit and where I was assigned at Cu Chi there was no evidence of so many VC being in a place underground, with no fighting taking place.

There was a road on Cu Chi going east and west near our unit that choppers used to bring body bags to the hospital. We all hated to see the choppers proceeding down the road knowing that another buddy, friend or some dear one had been killed. (I was elated that the Vietnam War Memorial became a reality. I had the opportunity October 2006 for a Class 48-C Pilot reunion in Washington, D.C. to visit and touch the beautiful Vietnam Memorial panels, plus in addition all the Veterans Memorials. This would be the last Class 48-C Pilot's reunion because all of us veterans were getting too old).

On one Friday, December 1967, my buddy Bob Graves asked me if I would fly a test with him since I had nothing scheduled to do except type my monthly reports to AVSCOM. I told him okay. I got my flax-jacket and helmet and proceeded to the UH-1 (Huey). The maintenance crew had performed required maintenance including an engine change. I had installed the vibration analyzer instrument for final inspection requirements in the air. Bob Graves talked over some problems and on the pre-take off inspection we found a couple of Zuess fasteners not properly installed. These were called to the attention of the crew chief who corrected the problems. We got into the UH-1 (Huey) and started the gas turbine engine. All systems were in the green and ready for take-off. Bob Graves pulled power and began lift-off. When we were about 200 feet high the tower called and said we had a bunch of sparkling items coming out the combustion exhaust outlet. I turned around to see if I could see anything.

Nothing was visible so we continued to climb and went toward the east end of the road when we began to lose a small amount of power. Bob Graves hollered at me again that there was an emergency in the power section. We began to lose more power and also altitude. Bob began a fairly fast turn to the right to return to the 20th Transportation Company landing area. We were over a number of tents and billeting quarters and were still losing altitude when I looked ahead and saw that we were over a friendly mine field. I could see the mine's detonators, like quarter size, sitting amongst the rocks and gravel. Bob hollered and said he had full power on and the chopper was still sinking toward the mine field. Again I looked down and saw a barbed wire fence about 16 inches high. Our skid was below the top of the barbed wire. Bob said he did not have any more power remaining to lift the UH-1 (Huey). I told him, "Oh yes, go through the procedure once more!", and he again began manipulating controls causing the UH-1 (Huey) to inch up and slide the skid over the wire and as we inched forward somehow we got the UH-1 (Huey) far enough forward of the mine field and he allowed it to settle to the ground. What a relief to be safe and able to kiss the ground. They say when you get in a tight spot such as this incident that your butt stamps out washers from the aluminum seat. I truly believe both Bob and I had many thousands of washers from this incident. [Photo showing compressor blade damage 6-12]

After landing we inspected the T-53-L-13 engine for the Zuess fasteners, and one was missing. The collar was broken and had come apart allowing the loose Zuess to go into the intake and chew up the turbine compressor blades. When we took the top compressor housing off, the turbine blades were worn down about 3/4 inch, so it's no wonder we had a loss of power emergency. This was one close call that not one of us would ever want to do the second time around, especially with live mines in one's path or under the UH-1 (Huey).

Since I was doing my assigned responsible job working out of Cu Chi everyone was patting me on the back for accomplishing so many tasks of so many various functions in support of the United States Army Aviation Organizations. I tried to tell them that is what I'm supposed to do, eliminate maintenance problems. But I'm so glad I have, and that in such a short time had good friends in the Iron Triangle. It was a wonderful time in my life.

Since Christmas 1967 was nearing and I was anxious to get on my 6,000 mile trip (vacation) home, I was in the process of training as many of the 20th Transportation Company personnel as I could. My replacement, Mr. Smith, was processing in at Saigon civilian personnel office, so he would arrive shortly at Cu Chi. Then we could escort him around to the bases and acquaint him with the units that he would be working with.

Mr. Smith arrived on the weekend and I began getting him settled in. He was very reluctant about being assigned at Cu Chi. He said it was too dangerous because of the VC attacks on this camp. I didn't feel it was any more dangerous than any other Republic of Vietnam area. For myself I felt very secure and that it was the fact we had good infantry and security personnel on duty at Cu Chi to ward off any type of attack.

Saigon had a lot of individual personnel attacks, so what was so different from here or there? A thorough indoctrination of all facets of being a helicopter advisor in the field convinced Mr. Smith that he would be required in the Iron Triangle at Cu Chi, period.

I understand that Mr. Smith quit, before 30 days went by, again saying it was too dangerous at the 20th Transportation Company in the Cu Chi area. For me it was as safe a location as any place in the Republic of Vietnam. Even though my year-long tour we averaged at least ten mortar attacks monthly and several other types of intrusions such as trying to get into the interior of the base, satchel attacks on the helicopters, and all types of shelling. These attacks were always dangerous and the personnel knew of the extent of preventing casualties by utilizing the bunkers, slit trenches and heavy equipment. Don't stand in open areas but take cover. Protect yourself by lying down behind iron items, sand bags, etc.

Major Clements, the Commanding Officer gave me a going away dinner with the whole company being in attendance. The operations officer presented me with three scoops of ice cream (powdered at that) so I wouldn't forget the good old days at Cu Chi. The next day my buddy Bob Graves provided me with a ride to Tan Son Nhut Air Base, Saigon, to commence processing out at our Saigon civilian personnel office. We parted company as special friends. I asked him to come visit me at AVSCOM and I would help him find a job as a civilian or military member. I felt he was a great pilot to have kept us alive.

When I arrived at MACV, I was treated like I had a plague because of my supposedly turning in the black marketers, thieves or gamblers. I learned that Pecks black hat bad boys were still in St. Louis. My buddy Reece was and has always been very friendly. (I was happy for him since he married a very nice Vietnamese gal and had one child, a boy, prior to returning to the United States. They both joined him stateside when required paper work was approved. He and his family visited us in St. Louis, then he was assigned to another location and I lost track of him because of my promotion and changing offices.)

After four days of Saigon civilian personnel office processing, we were provided a ticket to Travis Air Force Base, California on "Overseas World Airways", my orders to be assigned at Fort Sill, Oklahoma were rescinded and I was reassigned to AVSCOM in St. Louis, with duty in the Technical Assistance program, Directorate of Maintenance, which suited me. One place was the same as another; duty was duty, wherever one is assigned.

I thought it was strange to assign me to Fort Sill, then immediately tell me they wanted me to attend United States Army Maintenance Management course at Ft. Lee, Virginia. My mind was telling me the problem I had in Vung Tau was catching up with me, that was in my thoughts at that time. This was before my flight to return to the United States occurred. However, time went by and I began thinking that Mr. Bartley, when I was first assigned to Directorate of Maintenance, Technical Assistance team, said he was glad I had a college degree because they would use me in another capacity. Maybe things were changing, to better my career, I could be wrong in my expectation of my future position, as being in a negative situation—Hopefully the Maintenance Management course would be in my favor and my life would improve.

Our trip via Tokyo was fine. The only thing is that I was sitting next to a Staff Sergeant that had malaria. He had more blankets on top of him to keep him warm that took up more space than what a person could imagine. The three seats felt like a vibrator had been installed, that's how bad he was shaking. In my view, if the SSGT would have taken his malaria medications, I doubt if he would have contacted malaria in Vietnam, nor that the United States taxpayers would have to support him through his life of difficulties. But I didn't know if malaria medication was available or if he was on a mission and ran out of it, or what the circumstance was, so I apologize. There were enough mosquitoes to go around, believe me.

That trip to the good old USA was the longest trip in the air. I felt like saying, "Are we there yet!" It was similar to my B-36 flying in SAC, long and boring and some up to 44 hours long. But that wasn't all, the airline played Christmas tunes, the tinkly bell type. It was very monotonous and seemed like we would never get there. Perhaps it was because of being away from Riverside, California and being in Vietnam for one Thanksgiving and two Christmases away from my family and home. We were scheduled into Tokyo to pick up passengers bound for the good old United States of America. Since I had lots of time to think and reminisce on my return to the United States, one thing I can't understand is why anyone wants to be a communist. I've fought or battled that brand for 68 years of my total life and to see people starving from lack of food and loss of freedom didn't make good sense. Why, there is always a large army of communists taking the majority of whatever you produce to give to their higher authority for their use and then everything left over belongs to that country and you don't have anything to say. Other than being tortured, thrown into prison or killed over nothing, doesn't make me want to ever live that life. The communist theory is the elimination of private property and the totalitarian system for the USSR with a minimum authoritarian party controlling all produce, material and economic goods, which are supposed to be distributed equally, or so they say, but we know the truth.

Myself, I don't want anything to do with this type of governing party. I don't want a person with a rifle or gun of any type behind me and work "free", and have nothing to show for your life's work.

I've carried this "what-ISMs-Do what you want"? around in my correspondence package for a long time. Maybe there are people who would like to know my feelings on these radical groups. It takes in lots of ground or territory.

SOCIAL-ISMS: You have two cows, give one cow to your neighbor.

COMMUN-ISMS: You have two cows, give both cows to the government and they might give you some milk!

FASC-ISMS: You have two cows you give all the milk to the government and the government sells it.

NAZ-ISM: You have two cows, the government shoots you, and takes the cows.

ANARCH-ISM: You have two cows, keep both cows, shoot the government agent and steal another cow.

CAPITAL-ISM You have two cows, sell one, then buy a bull.

But you can see and make up your mind what kind of government you would like to be associated with. Myself, I like our United States of America for our freedom and the Constitution. "We the people of the United States of America in order to form a more perfect union establish justice, insure domestic tranquility, provide for the common defense, promote the general welfare, and secure the Blessings of Liberty to ourselves and our posterity, do ordain and establish this Constitution for the United States of America." (It's the best country in the whole wide world.)

THE-ISM: I believe in the existence of a God. (To prove my point and feelings this was taken from Webster's Dictionary and should be accurate in our thinking and meanings)

MAINTENANCE PERFORMANCE REPORT	1. REPORTING PERIOD			
	FROM 1 Aug 67 TO 15 Aug 67			
	TYPE OF REPORT			

3. TO Headquarters U.S. Army Aviation Materiel Command Attn: AMSAV-MTT	MONTHLY	XX	DA CIVILIAN
	SPECIAL		MILITARY
	OTHER (Missouri)	XX	

4. FROM *(Name, Grade-Rank-Title, Address, and Signature)*
Wayne A. Kuschel GS-11 Equipment Specialist
20th Trans. Co. (ADS)
APO San Francisco 96353

DATE 15 August 1967

Wayne A. Kuschel

PART I

5. UNIT(S) OR ACTIVITY SUPPORTED
20th Trans. Co(ADS)
725th Trans. Co. (ADS)

6. BASIC WEAPON (OR EQUIPMENT) SYSTEM ON WHICH ASSISTANCE WAS RENDERED
T-53 L9, L11, L13

7. WERE PROBLEMS ENCOUNTERED THAT COULD NOT BE RESOLVED? *(If Yes Explain in Item 13)* ☐ YES ☑ NO

8. INDICATE PROBLEMS ENCOUNTERED IN AREAS 6 THRU 9 BY LISTING NUMBER OF REPORTS SUBMITTED FOR EACH

a. TOOLS AND TEST EQUIPMENT	5	e. TAERS	
b. TECHNICAL PUBLICATIONS	2	f. MALFUNCTION	1
c. SUPPLY AND REPAIR PARTS	6	g. OTHER *(Specify)*	
d. CHECKS AND ADJUSTMENTS	2		

9. MANPOWER AND TRAINING DATA

a. DAYS WORKED THIS REPORTING PERIOD	14	b. ANNUAL LEAVE HRS	0	c. SICK LEAVE HRS	0	d. OVERTIME HRS	COMP	PAID 98
e. TOTAL HOURS SPENT W/UNITS IN ITEM 5	146	f. HOURS OF FORMAL TRAINING CONDUCTED	0			g. NUMBER OF PERSONS TRAINED *(Formal)*		0
h. HOURS TRAVEL TIME	25	i. HOURS OF OJT			10	j. NUMBER OF PERSONS TRAINED *(O/T)*		5
k. HOURS SPENT PERFORMING ACTUAL MAINTENANCE FUNCTIONS *(Explain in Item 13)*								121

l. OTHER *(See Instructions)* 5 Maint. personnel lectured on disassembly of engine/components

10. WERE PROBLEMS AND VISITS DISCUSSED WITH THE COMMAND O's AND OR HIS MAINTENANCE OR MATERIEL READINESS OFFICER? ☑ YES ☐ NO

11. NAME, TITLE AND ADDRESS OF PERSONNEL CONTACTED OTHER THAN ROUTINE

A. Pitts, Maj Bub 269th Combat Avn Bn. APO 96225

PART II

12. THE SERVICES REPORTED ABOVE WERE PERFORMED IN A *(SATISFACTORY)* (UNSATISFACTORY) MANNER *(If Unsatisfactory, Attach Explanation)*

DATE	NAME, TITLE AND GRADE OF DESIGNATED SUPERVISOR	SIGNATURE
15 Aug 1967	John K. Clemente Maj. TC Commanding	*John K Clemente*

ORGANIZATION AND ADDRESS
20th Trans. Co. (ADS)
APO San Francisco 96353

AMC Form 1478-R
1 Oct 66

6-1 Maintenance Performance Report 1478-R

1. Assisted the 116th Assault Helicopter Company, troubleshooting low power on UH-1D, 65-10127.
2. Instructed pilots on accomplishing correct part power trim of T-53 L13 engines. Flew test hop to confirm power settings, and vibration test on UH-1D, 66-16150, T-53 L13 LE14479 (Engine dropped, reported on 1478-R, 1Aug67).
3. Inspected UH-1D, 64-13743, T-53 L11 engine LE 10756 for FOD. Repaired.
4. Assisted pilots and engine shop personnel on part power trim on new T-53 L13 engine, installed on UH-1D, 66-16115, engine number LE14449.
5. Researched for special tools, and assisted organizations in submitting requisitions. on T-53 and T-55 engines.
6. Assisted organizations on compliance with TB55-1500-207-20/1, defective fifth stage.
7. Assisted 20th Engine Shop on UH-1D, 65-9613, T-53 L11, LE10889 for compressor stall. Had slight FOD and erosion. Engine removed at 1071 hours.
8. Inspected for combat damage. UH-1D, 66-819, T-53 L11B, LE12206. Bullet/hit near exhaust diffuser and V clamp, then severed the fuel start manifold. Oil tank had one hole through it. Engine had oil starvation causing #3 & #4 bearing to fail.
9. Inspected for combat damage UH-1D, 66-934, T-53 L9A, LE06453. Bullet hole through oil tank. Engine had oil starvation causing #3 & #4 bearing to fail.
10. Inspected for combat damage UH-1D, 66-932, T-53 L11 LE11863A. Bullet hole through oil tank. Engine had oil starvation, causing #3 & #4 bearing to fail.
11. Visited 602nd Trans. Det. at Tay Ninh. Picked up #1 nozzle, which I sent to Steve Polinsky for analysis and information. Due to the number that are showing up as defective on hot end inspections. This one component could develope into a problem area. The 25th Division requires all units to pull hot ends at each 100 hours operation or at Periodic Inspections, Until some trend is developed or knowledge of what is causing engine failures, or components to fail.

FOR HMP USE		
DATE RECEIVED	FOLLOW UP REQUIRED ☐ YES ☐ NO	SUSPENSE DATE
ACTION ASSIGNED TO		DATE REPLY MAILED
REMARKS		

6-1 Maintenance Performance Report 1478-R page 2

15 Aug '67

Dear Mr. Bartley:
    Just a few lines to say hello,
hope that this letter finds you in
the best of health. So far my
nerves are a bit touchy, because
of all the artillery shooting, which
is a 24 hour affair.
    I just received Don. Pittmans
letter asking me to send in the
items I received in the box of
TM's. As you have already read
his letter, I'm not going to take
your time on reiterating.
    You will find the label from
the box, and two other pieces
that were inside of the box.
    Don asked me if I was
going to return to Vung Tau on
53 L/3 AAMTAP team. The last
letter I received from Bernard Reece

6-1a My 15 August 1967 letter to Mr. Bartley

189

2.

he stated, the other instructors (which were Mac Elvany and Parkers friends) are holding what happened to them, against me.

If what I did was wrong, then I'm 100% wrong, and will resign, if you so desire. Myself I can look at myself in a mirror without any guilty conscience. I've tried to be as loyal an employee to the U.S. Army as possible. I know I'm ignorant of some regulations, but my upbringing and service career can assist me in determining wrong from right.

When I return to St. Louis, I'll be willing to brief you on anything required by you. Including problems within our program. I wish I could put on paper my true feelings of past happenings. Maybe I can assist future prospective hiring through our office.

6-1a My 15 August 1967 letter to Mr. Bartley page 2

3.

I still say this is one wonderful program, but all of us must work as one team, not separate individuals. Afraid someone is going to get ahead, of the next person.
Guess I'd better close for now hoping to hear from you in the event you have the time.
Until later.

Sincerely yours,

Grayne A. Kuschel, DAC
20th Trans. Co. (ADS)
Apo San Francisco 96353

6-1a My 15 August 1967 letter to Mr. Bartley page 3

MAINTENANCE PERFORMANCE REPORT

1. REPORTING PERIOD		
FROM 15 Aug 67		TO 31 Aug 67
TYPE OF REPORT		

2. TO Headquarters
U.S. Army Aviation Materiel Command
Attn: AMSAV-TD

	MONTHLY	X	DA CIVILIAN
	SPECIAL		MILITARY
X	OTHER		

4. FROM *(Name, Grade-Rank-Title, Address, and Signature)*
Wayne A. Kuschel GS-12 Equipment Specialist
20th Trans. Co. (ADS)
APO San Francisco 96353

DATE 1 Sept 67

Wayne A. Kuschel (signature)

PART I

5. UNIT(S) OR ACTIVITY SUPPORTED
20th Trans. Co. (ADS)
725th Trans. Co. (ADS)

6. BASIC WEAPON (OR EQUIPMENT) SYSTEM ON WHICH ASSISTANCE WAS RENDERED
T-53 L9, L11, L13

7. WERE PROBLEMS ENCOUNTERED THAT COULD NOT BE RESOLVED?
(If Yes Explain in Item 13)   ☐ YES   ☒ NO

8. INDICATE PROBLEMS ENCOUNTERED IN AREAS a THRU g BY LISTING NUMBER OF REPORTS SUBMITTED FOR EACH

a. TOOLS AND TEST EQUIPMENT	5	e. TAERS	1
b. TECHNICAL PUBLICATIONS	2	f. MALFUNCTION	2
c. SUPPLY AND REPAIR PARTS	2	g. OTHER (Specify)	
d. CHECKS AND ADJUSTMENTS	6		

9. MANPOWER AND TRAINING DATA

						COMP	PAID
a. DAYS WORKED THIS REPORTING PERIOD	15	b. ANNUAL LEAVE HRS	0	c. SICK LEAVE HRS	0	d. OVERTIME HRS	0	69
e. TOTAL HOURS SPENT W/UNITS IN ITEM 5	149	f. HOURS OF FORMAL TRAINING CONDUCTED	0	g. NUMBER OF PERSONS TRAINED (Formal)	6
h. HOURS TRAVEL TIME	15	i. HOURS OF OJT	12	j. NUMBER OF PERSONS TRAINED (O/T)	6 37
k. HOURS SPENT PERFORMING ACTUAL MAINTENANCE FUNCTIONS *(Explain in Item 13)*							134

l. OTHER *(See Instructions)* 37 Maint. personnel lectured on T-53 engine systems.

10. WERE PROBLEMS AND VISITS DISCUSSED WITH THE COMMAND AND OR HIS MAINTENANCE OR MATERIEL READINESS OFFICER?   ☒ YES   ☐ NO

11. NAME, TITLE AND ADDRESS OF PERSONNEL CONTACTED OTHER THAN ROUTINE

James L. Mitchell Jr. 25th Div. Avn. Bn. Maint. Officer APO 96252

PART II

12. THE SERVICES REPORTED ABOVE WERE PERFORMED IN A (SATISFACTORY) (UNSATISFACTORY) MANNER
(If Unsatisfactory, Attach Explanation)

DATE	NAME, TITLE AND GRADE OF DESIGNATED SUPERVISOR	SIGNATURE
2 Sept 67	John K. Clements Maj. TC Commanding	*John K. Clements* (signature)

ORGANIZATION AND ADDRESS
20th Trans. Co. (ADS)
APO San Francisco 96353

ANC Form 1478-R
5 Oct 66

6-2 Maintenance Performance Report 1478-R

1. Assisted in hot end inspection on UH-1B 64-13650, T-53 L11 LS09990 and UH-1B 63-12 963, T-53 L11 L412986. Instructed personnel on bumper clearances.
2. Assisted in troubleshooting UH-1B 65-1027. Slow in starting. At 20% NI EGT was indicating 600 degrees. Normal troubleshooting procedure. Clean inlet area. Fuel control changed, start fuel nozzles changed, ignition exciter changed, start fuel solenoid changed. Could not correct. Engine removed, sent to test stand for evaluation.
3. Inspected UH-1B 64-13955, T-53 L11 LS09737. Engine installed 25 July 67. Failed on 16 Aug 67. NI system seized internally. Time since overhaul 18:00 hours.
4. Troubleshooting UH-1B 64-9433, T-53 L11 L410509 150:00 since overhaul. For low power. Normal troubleshooting procedure used. Found, after 15:00 hours of operation a fine layer of dust on filters in dust and sand separator. Recommend re-emphasis to all units in NVR the importance of performing a daily inspection as directed in TM 55-1520-211-20MTD and 210-20MTD. This one cleaning increased the engine performance.
5. Assisted in troubleshooting UH-1D 65-9857, T-53 L11 L410216. Problem in flight, any change of collective or RPM, the EGT would increase. Found, temperature sensing element installed wrong. Flew test hop, EGT reduced 10-15 degrees. Jet Cal used to check T/C harness, found a burned spot near cannon plug area, which caused a false reading on EGT.
6. Researched unit NIR files for NI nozzle failures in past 12 months, for 34th 08 Op.
7. Assisted in hot end inspection of UH-1D 65-9461, T-53 L11 L410385. Insp. NI nozzle.
8. Assisted in evaluating FOD on UH-1B 64-13954, T-53 L11 LS09319 (O/H 5-2-67). Minor damage to first through sixth stages, required blending of blades. Replaced NI nozzle, NI turbine wheel, NII turbine wheel. (These items were dented, small chunks missing, where FOD made contact) Engine repaired.
9. Engine shop personnel advised me that they were encountering a few internal failures caused by wires coming loose in the new type linear actuator manufactured by Barber Colman Co. Rockford, Illinois FSN 2995-990-3163 P/N 204-060-762-1.
10. Assisted troubleshooting UH-1C 66-513, T-53 L11 L410072 (O/H 1-14-67) for excessive smoking and rise in EGT when collective pulled. Engine was in temp. storage. Cleaned engine interior. Problem was resolved.
11. Inspected UH-1C 66-664, T-53 L11 L412379. Bullet went through air intake, striking top of reduction gearing, causing a 2X1 inch to dislodge and go into engine. This resulted in considerable damage to inlet guide vanes and 1st stage axial comp. blades. Engine removed and shipped to overhaul. New engine installed.
12. Recieved two special tools for T-53 engine, that were rusted and gouged on the bodies. No protective coating or waterproof paper used. Recommend more efficient handling and packaging of expensive tools.
13. Request that the wording "SUB-MAINTENANCE SIGNIFICANT" be spelled out for meaning or interpatation in NTOs and also be placed in th U.S.Army dictionary.
14. Inspected T-53 L11 L410003, oil coming out bleed band. Engine cleaned, ran-up, after shut down oil was still coming out bleed band. Engine removed for a defective #1 carbon seal.
15. Recommend that a change be made in TM 55-2800-200-30/1, T-53 Engine Inspection Guide, dated Aug 67. To include a requirement for vibration testing of replaced engines, or on removal/installation of hot end.

FOR HMP USE		
DATE RECEIVED	FOLLOW UP REQUIRED ☐ YES ☐ NO	SUSPENSE DATE
ACTION ASSIGNED TO		DATE REPLY MAILED
REMARKS		

6-2 Maintenance Performance Report 1478-R page 2

Continuation of AMC fc 1478-R

16. Assisted in evaluation an engine on UH-1D 64-13053, T-53 L11 LE12426.
Suspected of engine failure in flight, inspection revealed the following;
a. Engine oil tank "low".
b. Main oil filter had a small amount of carbon residue and four pieces of bright metallic filings (very small pieces).
c. Chip detector, had four small pieces of metal filings.
d. #2 last chance, no contamination.
e. #3 & #4 last chance, no contamination.
f. Through- bolt was in three pieces.
g. MII (#3 & #4 bearing package) gear spline twisted or snapped off, where it mated with MII power shaft.
h. Sample of oil was taken from tank and forwarded for analysis.

17. Troubleshooting peculiar problem on UH-1B 65-9433, T-53 L11 engine. Engine oil pressure at flight idle read 65 PSI, after approx. 2 minutes of operation the oil pressure would creep up to approx. 120 PSI on cockpit gage. Normal troubleshooting procedures used;
a. Filters cleaned.
b. Generator for instruments changed.
c. Oil pressure gage changed.
d. Filter by-pass checked.
e. Installed pressure gage at the filter, read 50 PSI.
f. Called electrical shop for their assistance.
g. With their test instrument indicating 20 PSI and installed to pressure input to instrument generator. The cockpit gage read 20 PSI, then slowly creep to 40 PSI.
h. Trouble was located in cannon plug on engine deck, where a slight leakage of voltage between pins was at fault. Per reference TM55-1520-210-35P, figure 403A, FSN 2925-758-9770, P/N 204-175-4153, Cable assembly.

6-2 Maintenance Performance Report 1478-R page 3

6-3 Picture of actor Wendell Corey, Wayne, MAJ Clements

6-3

Picture of actor Wendell Corey, Wayne, CWO Graves

8 September 1967

Mr. Wayne A. Kuschel, DAC
20th Transportation Company (ADS)
APO San Francisco 96353

Dear Mr. Kuschel,

Reference is made to your letter of 15 May 67, with regards to your rotation from RVN and reassignment in CONUS.

Your request for leave will be granted, and at the present time it appears that you can be assigned duty at Ft Sill, Oklahoma, as this is the only known requirement in the geographical location you are requesting.

As for information with regards to PCS moves, the Government authorizes movement of dependents, household effects, miscellaneous expenses of $200 or two weeks' pay when substantiated, a house hunting trip for spouse or reimbursement for temporary quarters, when authorized, and also certain expenses incurred in selling home at old duty station, and expenses incurred when buying home at new duty station. (See Incl 1, SAV-R Form 1085).

If you have further questions feel free to inquire, and we will endeavor to be more expeditious in the future.

Sincerely yours,

HARLYN H. HUBBS, Acting Chief
Technical Support Branch
Technical Assistance Division
Directorate of Maintenance (NMP)

1 Incl
SAV-R Form 1085

6-4 Fort Sill, CONUS assignment

MAINTENANCE PERFORMANCE REPORT	1. REPORTING PERIOD FROM 16 Sept 67 TO 30 Sept 67		
	TYPE OF REPORT		
2. TO	XX MONTHLY		XX DA CIVILIAN
	SPECIAL		MILITARY
	OTHER		

4. FROM (Name, Grade-Rank-Title, Address, and Signature)	DATE 1 Oct 67
Wayne A. Kuschel GS-12 Equipment Specialist 20th Trans Co (ADS) APO San Francisco 96353	*Wayne A. Kuschel*

PART I

5. UNIT(S) OR ACTIVITY SUPPORTED

20th Trans Co (ADS) and Subordinates.

6. BASIC WEAPON (OR EQUIPMENT) SYSTEM ON WHICH ASSISTANCE WAS RENDERED

T53 L-9, L-11, L-13 engines

7. WERE PROBLEMS ENCOUNTERED THAT COULD NOT BE RESOLVED? (If Yes Explain in Item 13)	X YES	☐ NO

8. INDICATE PROBLEMS ENCOUNTERED IN AREAS a THRU g BY LISTING NUMBER OF REPORTS SUBMITTED FOR EACH ASSISTANCE

a. TOOLS AND TEST EQUIPMENT	3	e. TAERS	1
b. TECHNICAL PUBLICATIONS	2	f. MALFUNCTION	0
c. SUPPLY AND REPAIR PARTS	5	g. OTHER (Specify)	0
d. CHECKS AND ADJUSTMENTS	2		

9. MANPOWER AND TRAINING DATA

a. DAYS WORKED THIS REPORTING PERIOD	15	b. ANNUAL LEAVE HRS		c. SICK LEAVE HRS	0	d. OVERTIME HRS	COMP	PAID 67+30
e. TOTAL HOURS SPENT W/UNITS IN ITEM 5	148	f. HOURS OF FORMAL TRAINING CONDUCTED			0	g. NUMBER OF PERSONS TRAINED (Formal)		0
h. HOURS TRAVEL TIME	10	i. HOURS OF OJT			20	j. NUMBER OF PERSONS TRAINED (OJT)		10
k. HOURS SPENT PERFORMING ACTUAL MAINTENANCE FUNCTIONS (Explain in Item 13)								138
l. OTHER (See Instructions) 10 Maint. personnel instructed on T53 Systems								

10. WERE PROBLEMS AND VISITS DISCUSSED WITH THE COMMAND G4/S4 AND OR HIS MAINTENANCE OR MATERIEL READINESS OFFICER?	☐ YES	X NO

11. NAME, TITLE AND ADDRESS OF PERSONNEL CONTACTED OTHER THAN ROUTINE

PART II

12. THE SERVICES REPORTED ABOVE WERE PERFORMED IN A (SATISFACTORY) (UNSATISFACTORY) MANNER (If Unsatisfactory, Attach Explanation)		
DATE 2 Oct 67	NAME, TITLE AND GRADE OF DESIGNATED SUPERVISOR JOHN D. ADAMS CPT, TC	SIGNATURE

ORGANIZATION AND ADDRESS
20th Trans Co (ADS)
APO San Francisco 96353

AMC Form 1478-R
1 Oct 66

6-5 Maintenance Performance Report 1478-R

1. After compliance of MWO 55-1520-211-30/16 Droop Compensator Installation Modification 17 Feb 67. Three UH-1C helicopters have experienced a loss of NII RPM. On test hop, the pilot would pull collective and NII RPM would bleed off 200 to 500 RPM. Personnel completely re-rigged this system, which did not alleviate the problem. In attempting to correct this situation the droop cam was reset, this caused more problems, when collective was pulled, the NII RPM would gain up to 100 RPM. As the pilot lowered the collective, NII loss of 50 RPM was experienced. Assistance from Bell Helicopter Company (Mr. Louis Jones and Clifford Nelson) found the trouble in rigging procedures. Nominal settings were not adhered to on tubes 204-061-703-19 and 204-061-716-13. Recommend that this and future, modification of similiar detail, be spelled out in workable language. This would assist in cutting costly manhours in troubleshooting systems.

2. Assisted in inventory and ordering T 53/55 engine special tools.

3. Inspected engine on UH-1C 65-9442, T53-L11 LE1C014 for foreign object damage. First stage through centrifugal compressor stage completely destroyed. Engine removed and forwarded to depot.

4. Numerous UH-1 helicopters are experiencing oil leaking, around #2 last chance strainer. The special preformed packing appears to be used more that one time. Recommend organizations replace this packing when ever #2 last chance strainer is removed. Reference TM 55-1520-210-35P, Figure 216, Index 38, PREFORMED PACKING.

5. Inspected engine on UH-1H 65-9118, T53-L13 LE14209 for foreign object damage. The compressor half was pulled. Twenty-eight of first stage transonic blades had minor damage. In addition signs of oil leaking out of the compressor halves, indicated #1 carbon seal leaking. The axiel compressor hub appeared to be coated by oil. Recommended engine change. (106:00 hrs.)

6. In TM 55-1520-210-35P1 the Droop Cam pictured in figure 113, index 92 P/N 204-060-780-1 (used on UH-1A), and figure 115 index 11A FSN 2915-980-1645 P/M204-061-709-1 (used on UH-1B, C, & D) is also shown as the droop cam presently used on T 53 L-13 engine.

7. Troubleshoot high EGT (590°C at flight idle) on UH-1D 65-9615, T 53-L11 LE14344, 302:00 hours since overhaul. Jet cal Tester read 590°C hot and pulled all items checked for condition, T canes checked, #2 carbon seal was leaking and replaced, changed asbestos seal and rechecked for proper bumper clearance. After installation, and first engine run, EGT indicated 580°C. Main fuel manifold removed, two orfices were plugged. I pulled the fuel dividers, engine shop personnel were instructed on proper cleaning of vaporizer tubes. I, re-installed the fuel dividers, On Engine run, EGT dropped to 525°C at flight idle. Engine developed a #1 carbon seal leak (oil came out bleed band) Recommended engine change. 302:00 hrs since overhaul.

FOR HMP USE		
DATE RECEIVED	**FOLLOW UP REQUIRED** ☐ YES ☐ NO	**SUSPENSE DATE**
ACTION ASSIGNED TO		**DATE REPLY MAILED**
REMARKS		

6-5 Maintenance Performance Report 1478-R page 2

8. Troubleshoot .. seizure on UH-1D 66-9652, T 53 .il LE12362. Gas producer turbine wheel (NI) had started to disenegrate, throwing small melted particles onto flange, this caused three or four long turbine blades to contact the high spots of melted particles. Could not determine cause, but recommend pilots be cautioned on low battery voltage, which could create "hot" starts, and using proper starting techniques.

9. Inspected battle damage to engine on UH-1B 65-9440, T 53 L11 LE10510. Bullet entered bottom rear door and proceeded up into engine cowling area. Fragments entered engine, causing damage to axiel compressor blades. Blades were blended and cleaned up. Engine was serviceable.

10. Recommend literature or information concerning lubrication oil MIL-L-23699 and MIL-L-7808 be researched. With higher headquarters stating types of oil to be use in T 53 and T 55 gas turbine engines. There are too many conflicting letters, TB's and TM's arriving in the field, which make it hard on organization to comply with higher headquarters request for proper usage of lubrication oils. Example TB AVN-2 states these oils can be mixed. A newsletter states to flush the systems, and use the specified oil. The TM 55-1520-210-20 and 211-20 speak only of MIL-L-7808.

11. In reply to your letter, subject: Request for information/monthly reports, dated 25 Aug 67.

Item I. I'm using a copy belonging to Quality Control this is only copy I can locate.

Item J. Yes I'm assisting a Tech Inspector on making sufficient display boards for various conditions and exampled.

Item K. By bringing the full requirement of this TB to the responsible personnel. ~~Sorry~~ Assist the company on the proper procedures of filling these tags/labels ~~out and~~ by spot checking for compliance, advise the maintenance officer of the progress.

6-5 Maintenance Performance Report 1478-R page 3

		1. REPORTING PERIOD
		FROM 1 October 67 TO 31 October 67

TYPE OF REPORT

2. TO		XX	MONTHLY	XX	DA CIVILIAN
Headquarters			SPECIAL		MILITARY
U.S. Army Aviation Materiel Command			OTHER		
Attn: AMSAV-FTT (SMP)					

4. FROM *(Name, Grade-Rank-Title, Address, and Signature)*

Wayne A. Kuschel GS-12 Equipment Specialist
20th Trans. Co. (ADS)
AFO San Francisco 96353

DATE 31 October 1967

Wayne A. Kuschel

PART I

5. UNIT(S) OR ACTIVITY SUPPORTED

20th Trans. Co. (ADS) and subordina te units.

6. BASIC WEAPON (OR EQUIPMENT) SYSTEM ON WHICH ASSISTANCE WAS RENDERED

T-53 L9/L11/L13
T-55 L7

7. WERE PROBLEMS ENCOUNTERED THAT COULD NOT BE RESOLVED?
(If Yes Explain in Item 13)   XX YES   ☐ NO

8. INDICATE PROBLEMS ENCOUNTERED IN AREAS a THRU g BY LISTING NUMBER OF REPORTS SUBMITTED FOR EACH Assistance

a. TOOLS AND TEST EQUIPMENT	6	e. TAERS	1
b. TECHNICAL PUBLICATIONS	1	f. MALFUNCTION	1
c. SUPPLY AND REPAIR PARTS	4	g. OTHER (Specify)	
d. CHECKS AND ADJUSTMENTS	2		

9. MANPOWER AND TRAINING DATA

a. DAYS WORKED THIS REPORTING PERIOD	28½	b. ANNUAL LEAVE HRS	0	c. SICK LEAVE HRS	0	d. OVERTIME HRS		COMP	PAID 138:30
e. TOTAL HOURS SPENT W/UNITS IN ITEM 5	298½	f. HOURS OF FORMAL TRAINING CONDUCTED		0		g. NUMBER OF PERSONS TRAINED (Formal)			0
h. HOURS TRAVEL TIME	20	i. HOURS OF OJT		60		j. NUMBER OF PERSONS TRAINED (O/T)			15
k. HOURS SPENT PERFORMING ACTUAL MAINTENANCE FUNCTIONS (Explain in Item 13)									278:30

l. OTHER (See Instructions) Maint. personnel instructed on gas turbine engine systems

10. WERE PROBLEMS AND VISITS DISCUSSED WITH THE COMMANDER AND ON HIS MAINTENANCE OR MATERIEL READINESS OFFICER?   XX YES   ☐ NO

11. NAME, TITLE AND ADDRESS OF PERSONNEL CONTACTED OTHER THAN ROUTINE

J. Comers, Major   269th Combat Avn. Bn. APO 96353

PART II

12. THE SERVICES REPORTED ABOVE WERE PERFORMED IN A (SATISFACTORY) (UNSATISFACTORY) MANNER
(If Unsatisfactory, Attach Explanation)

DATE	NAME, TITLE AND GRADE OF DESIGNATED SUPERVISOR	SIGNATURE
31 Oct 67	John D. Adams Cpt. TC Maint. Officer	*John D. Adams*

ORGANIZATION AND ADDRESS

20th Trans. Co. (ADS)
AFO San Francisco 96353

AMC Form 1478-R
1 Oct 66

6-6 Maintenance Performance Report 1478-R

1. Assisted inspecting engine on UH-1C 65-9558, T-53 L11 LE10608 of suspected power failure. Assisted accident investigating board. NII turbine blades were sheared off.

2. Instructed 20th Engine Shop personnel on proper procedure for part-power trim and related systems.

3. Inspected UH-1D 65-9667, T-53 L11 LE10372. Hot end inspection. EI nozzle had several burned areas and cracked, replaced it. Minor FOD, blended out blades. Engine made serviceable.

4. Troubleshooting no start on UH-1D 65-9607. Engine had both fuel and ignition. The battery was nicad, which had a low charge.

5. Inspected engine on UH-1D 65-9634, T-53 L11B LE12548. Minor FOD, T1 sensing element installed w rong, and #1 carbon seal leaking oil out of the bleed band. 1300:00 since new. Engine replaced.

6. Assisted in engine alignment on UH-1C 65-9466.

7. Instructed engine shop personnel on hot end inspection UH-1D 65-9628, T-53 L11 LE09604. 1287:00 since new, 914:00 hours since O/H.

8. Had a persistent fuel leak on UH-1D 65-9667. After many starts and stops and all corrective measures were used, the ma in fuel manifold wa s pulled, I found a fuel injector that had a crack around the collar, this half was replaced. Corrected the leak. Recommend that these injectors be made availa ble to DS and GS units. TM55-1520-210-35P, Figure 184, Index 5 & 11, FSN 2915-991-9145, P/N 12128, Injector, Fuel.

9. Inspected UH-1C 66-15210 for battle damage. Required a new electrical harness.

10. Troubleshooting hard to start engine on UH-1D 65-1183, T-53 L11 LE10177. A clicking and grinding noise was heard coming from the accessory gear drive box. After changing the accessory gear drive box we attempted another start. Sa me noise was heard. The starter was pulled and a rebuilt one re-installed, sa me thing happened. After installing a total of two engines and five starters, we pulled a starter from a flyable aircraft and installed it, this time the engine started and no grinding noise was heard. (Engine that was removed,was installed on another aircraft). Another aircraft UH-1C 65-9461 had a grinding noise in the same area as above. Upon inspecting this starter-genera tor we requistioned another one from supply. This was installed and it corrected the problem. Recommend that any hard to start engines accompanied by a grinding noise, that an inspection be performed to determine if a GE starter-generato Model 2CM63E1 is installed. If so, have the electrical shop check it out. Replace if defective. (The five starter-generators were all GE types).

FOR NMP USE		
DATE RECEIVED	FOLLOW UP REQUIRED ☐ YES ☐ NO	SUSPENSE DATE
ACTION ASSIGNED TO		DATE REPLY MAILED
REMARKS		

6-6 Maintenance Performance Report 1478-R page 2

11. Assisted 3/4 Cavalry on UH-1C 65-9433, T-53 L11. Crew Chief could not obtain proper maximum trim setting. I set up the maximum trim, pilot and I flew a test flight for correct topping. Aircraft cleared for its mission.

12. Troubleshooting high EGT on UH-1D 66-852. Inlet housing was cleaned, gaskets on air bleed adapter was replaced. Hot air valve in the "open" position, electrical shop repaired the valve. Engine was restored to EGT operational limits.

13. Assisted the 187th Assua lt Helicopter Company on UH-1D 66-926, for defective NI electrical system problem. Changed defective tachometer generator. Aircraft released for a high priority mission.

14. Instructed and assisted on Commander, 25th Division helicopter, UH-1D 66-852, T-53 L11 LE10501. Assisted at night to assure the powerplant checked out, pulled several part-power trim adjustments. Aircraft released for flight.

15. Inspected and assisted 20th Engine Shop personnel on determining condition of one NI nozzle, FSN 2840-839-6773. Which had eight vanes cracked over the allowable limits. TM55-1520-211-35, Figure 5-320 reads, "Cracks up to a cumulative length of 7/8 inch are acceptable on two vanes". NI nozzle was replaced and condemned item turned into supply.

16. Assisted E Co. 725th Trans. Co. (ADS) Engine Shop personnel, inspecting and evaluating a hot end, and overhaul of a #3 and #4 bearing package.

17. Set up maximum trim on UH-1D 66-1148, flew test flight for proper topping and vibration check. Aircraft released for flight.

18. Inspected engine on UH-1D 64-13627, T-53 L11B LE12758 for major FOD. Trailing edges of 4th and 5th stage blades were bent, blades were blended out, but appeared to be ragged and out of limits on the number that could be changed. Found a slight compressor rub between 3rd & 4th stages. Recommended the engine be changed. 697:00 hours since new, no overhauls.

19. Advised Ray Cantu, DAC, 34th Gen. Spt. Op., by telephone (30 Oct 67) of the shortage of asbestos seals that are required to perform hot end inspections, and of a requirement for NI nozzles in this area. Nomenclature found in TM55-1520-210-35P, FSN 5330-993-9578, P/N 1-300-052-01, Figure 219, Index 3, Packing, Material. 20th Tech Supply has a required balance of 220, zero on hand, 225 are due-in. TM55-1520-210-35P, FSN 2840-839-6773, P/N 1-110-030-36, Figure 216, Index 15, NI nozzle turbine assembly. 20th Tech Supply had one substitute item on hand, no established level, yet 27 are due-in.

20. Inspected UH-1H 66-16122, T-53 L13 LE15179 for combat damage. 1st stage Transonic blades damaged beyond repair. Awaiting word from investigating board.

21. In reply to your letter, Subject: Request for information/monthly reports, dated 25 Aug 67. The following is submitted.
Item i. Yes, I received a copy from Ray Cantu, 34th Group.
Item j. Yes, I am assisting maintenance personnel in the proper procedure of filling these forms out.
Item k. Appraising all personnel on the importance of using this new system. This unit has received all but one type of tag and label, and are striving to fully implement this system by 15 Nov 67. All shops are utilizing tags and labels. Approx. 70% completed to date.

6-6 Maintenance Performance Report 1478-R page 3

HEADQUARTERS U. S. ARMY VIETNAM
OFFICE OF THE CIVILIAN PERSONNEL DIRECTOR
SAIGON AREA CIVILIAN PERSONNEL OFFICE
APO SAN FRANCISCO 96243

LETTER ORDERS: 267-67   6 November 1967

SUBJECT: Travel Orders - PCS to CONUS

TO: Mr. Wayne A. Kuschel
          Equip Spec1 (Aircraft Propulsion Equip), GS-12
          FP# NU34788

1. On the call of the port commander, you will proceed from the Directorate of Maintenance, U. S. Army Aviation Materiel Command, with duty station at Saigon, Vietnam to Fort Sill, Oklahoma.

2. Travel by military or commercial aircraft authorized outside CONUS. Within CONUS travel via commercial air, bus, rail and/or POV authorized. If POV is used, reimbursement limitation in accordance with par C-6151-2, Vol II, JTR applies. Circuitous route travel for personal reasons will not increase travel time nor increase amount of per diem allowed. In lieu of subsistence, maximum per diem authorized.

3. You will perform 5 days TDY at Hq USAAVCOM, St. Louis, Missouri prior to reporting to new duty station.

4. 20 work days, chargeable to annual leave authorized in Riverside, Calif.

5. Split shipment of 11,000 lbs of HHG is authorized from overseas duty station and Riverside, California to Fort Sill, Oklahoma. One express shipment of NTE 350 lbs is authorized from overseas duty station to new duty station. If this 350 lbs is shipped as other than free checkable baggage, it will be considered as part of the maximum weight allowance. 166 lbs hand baggage authorized when traveling via military/commercial air. Temporary storage of HHG NTE 60 days is authorized. Non-temporary storage of HHG authorized.

6. Shipment of POV from overseas duty station is not authorized.

7. Required immunizations for re-entry into the United States will be obtained prior to departure from overseas duty station.

8. Travel of following dependents authorized from Riverside, California to Fort Sill, Oklahoma.

6-7 Staying in practice, receiving another travel order

Gussie M. Kuschel   Wife

Address: 4175 Adams Street, Riverside, California

9. Travel is necessary in the public service. Fund Citation: 2182020
060-8040 P2300-210(F) S23-204 81A3F CC 14 23L0.10223.A011MA UMA; P2300-220(2)
S23-204 81A32 CC 14 23L0.10223.A016MA FIA

WILLIAM A. METHVIN
Civilian Personnel Officer

DISTRIBUTION:
50 - Indiv
 2 - SACPO, APO 96243
 1 - DAC Payroll, APO 96243
 5 - Hq USAAVCCM, St. Louis, Mo.

6-7 Staying in practice, receiving another travel order page 2

Mr. Wayne Kuschel
20th Trans Co (ADS)
APO San Francisco 96353

Dear Mr. Kuschel:

You have been selected to attend the Maintenance Management
Course at Ft. Lee, Virginia starting on 7 Jan 68 and ending on 16 Feb 68
This course is designed to assist military and civilian managers to become more proficient in mid-level management positions within the Army
maintenance system.

We realize that this may cut short your planned annual leave but
we know that you will not want to miss this opportunity for management
training in your career field. Individuals scheduled to attend this
training course must have demonstrated high potential for managerial
development and we feel that you possess a sincere desire to improve
your ability relative to management.

Request you complete the inclosed DD Form 1556, Request for Enrollment at DOD Logistics Management Courses (6 copies) and OSM Form 54,
Service Agreement for Employees assigned to training. Please return
these forms as soon as possible so that they may be forwarded for approval
action.

We will notify you of any actions required and of the status of
your enrollment.

If you have any questions or need any assistance, please feel free
to contact this office.

Sincerely yours,

E. BARTLEY
Act Asst Chief
Technical Assistance Division
Directorate of Maintenance (MMP)
D F Pittman/mal/2072

2 Incl
as

Action Officer

6-8 Letter assigning me to St. Louis Missouri and school

HEADQUARTERS U. S. ARMY VIETNAM
OFFICE OF THE CIVILIAN PERSONNEL DIRECTOR
SAIGON AREA CIVILIAN PERSONNEL OFFICE
APO SAN FRANCISCO 96243

LETTER ORDERS: 324-67   30 November 1967

SUBJECT: Amendment of Orders

TO: Individuals Concerned

NAME	LO	DATE
CHARLES T. RUNKLE	258-67	3 Nov 67
CHARLES J. GRIMES	259-67	4 Nov 67
PRESTON S. RUSSELL	260-67	1 Nov 67
JOHNNIE O. WOOD	261-67	4 Nov 67
ROGER L. HARMER	265-67	8 Nov 67
FREDERICK C. DEMAREST	266-67	6 Nov 67
WAYNE A. KISCHEL	267-67	6 Nov 67
ARTHUR K. MAGNUSON	268-67	6 Nov 67

Above LO, pertaining to each individual, is amended to add the following paragraph:

    10. Required minimum period of service in this command curtailed at the request of CG, AVCOM, St. Louis, Missouri under the provisions of par C4.005-31, JTR, Vol II, per message 11-226 AMSAV-RCS dated 21 November 1967.

WILLIAM E. MURK
Acting Civilian Personnel Officer

DISTRIBUTION:
  30 - Indiv
   2 - SACPO, APO 96243
  25 - Hq USAAVCOM, St. Louis, Mo.

6-9 Amended letter orders

LETTER ORDERS: 339-67   12 December 1967

SUBJECT: Amendment - LO 267-67

TO: Individual Concerned

SO LO 267-67, dated 6 November 1967, pertaining to Mr. Wayne A. Kuschel is amended to read as follows:

1. Para 1 which read: "to Fort Sill, Oklahoma" is amended to read: "St. Louis, Missouri".

2. 2. Para 5 which read: "Split shipment of 11,000 lbs of HHG * * * to Fort Sill, Oklahoma," is amended to read: "Split shipment of 11,000 lbs of HHG * * * to St. Louis, Missouri."

3. Para 8 which read: "Travel of following dependents * * * * * to Fort Sill, Oklahoma," is amended to read: "Travel of following dependents * * * * * to St. Louis, Missouri."

WILLIAM E. MURK
Acting Civilian Personnel Officer

DISTRIBUTION:
  50 - Indiv
   2 - SACPO, APO 96243
   5 - Hq USAAVCOM, St. Louis, Mo.

6-10 My Individuals Concerned Travel Orders

MAINTENANCE PERFORMANCE REPORT

	1. REPORTING PERIOD
	FROM 1 November 67 TO 30 November 1967

	TYPE OF REPORT		
3. TO Headquarters U.S. Army Aviation Material Command Attn: AMSAV-FIT	X MONTHLY		X DA CIVILIAN
	SPECIAL		X MILITARY
	OTHER		

4. FROM *(Name, Grade-Rank-Title, Address, and Signature)*

Wayne A. Kuschel GS-12 Equipment Specialist
20th Trans. Co. (ADS)
APO San Francisco 96353

DATE 1 December 1967

Wayne A. Kuschel

PART I

5. UNIT(S) OR ACTIVITY SUPPORTED

520th Trans. Bn.
20th Trans. Co. (ADS)   725th Trans. Co. (ADS)

6. BASIC WEAPON (OR EQUIPMENT) SYSTEM ON WHICH ASSISTANCE WAS RENDERED

T-55 L7
T-53 L9, L11, L13

7. WERE PROBLEMS ENCOUNTERED THAT COULD NOT BE RESOLVED?
(If Yes Explain in Item 13)   ☐ YES   ☐ NO

8. INDICATE PROBLEMS ENCOUNTERED IN AREAS 6 THRU 9 BY LISTING NUMBER OF REPORTS SUBMITTED FOR EACH

a. TOOLS AND TEST EQUIPMENT	4	e. TAER		0
b. TECHNICAL PUBLICATIONS	1	f. MALFUNCTION		2
c. SUPPLY AND REPAIR PARTS	5	g. OTHER *(Specify)*		0
d. CHECKS AND ADJUSTMENTS	1			

9. **MANPOWER AND TRAINING DATA**

							COMP	PAID
a. DAYS WORKED THIS REPORTING PERIOD	30	b. ANNUAL LEAVE HRS	0	c. SICK LEAVE HRS	0	d. OVERTIME HRS		172:30
e. TOTAL HOURS SPENT W/UNITS IN ITEM 5	32:30	f. HOURS OF FORMAL TRAINING CONDUCTED	0			g. NUMBER OF PERSONS TRAINED *(Formal)*		0
h. HOURS TRAVEL TIME	30	i. HOURS OF OJT	40			j. NUMBER OF PERSONS TRAINED *(O/T)*		20
k. HOURS SPENT PERFORMING ACTUAL MAINTENANCE FUNCTIONS *(Explain in Item 13)*								283:30
l. OTHER *(See Instructions)* Instructed pilots & maint. personnel on gas turbine engine								

10. WERE PROBLEMS AND VISITS DISCUSSED WITH THE COMMAND G's/S's
AND OR HIS MAINTENANCE OR MATERIEL READINESS OFFICER?   ☐ YES   ☐ NO

11. NAME, TITLE AND ADDRESS OF PERSONNEL CONTACTED OTHER THAN ROUTINE

MAJ. E. Draper, C.O. 1/17th Cavalry Di An

MAJ. R.L. Brown, C.O. A Co. 801st Maint Co. Vin Loi

MAJ. J. W. Noble Maint. Officer, A Co. 801st Maint. Co. Vin Loi

PART II

12. THE SERVICES REPORTED ABOVE WERE PERFORMED IN A (SATISFACTORY) ~~(UNSATISFACTORY)~~ MANNER
(If Unsatisfactory, Attach Explanation)

DATE	NAME, TITLE AND GRADE OF DESIGNATED SUPERVISOR	SIGNATURE
Dec 1967	William M. Ridings Maj. TC Maintenance Officer	*William M Ri...*

ORGANIZATION AND ADDRESS

20th Trans. Co. (ADS)
APO San Francisco, 96353

AMC Form
5 Oct 66   1478-R

6-11 Maintenance Performance Report 1478-R

1. Inadequate helicoil inserts and tools are proving to be a problem area, components are removed from the engine and turned into supply channels. If units had helicoil kits to repair components time and money would be saved. Recommend that all GS and DS units research their facilities and requistion equipment to support the area. Reference TM AVN 23-15.

2. TDY to Dau Tieng to assist 188th A.H.C. on engine problems. This unit had ten T-53 L13 engines in shipping containers, ready to be turned into supply, all had FOD. Maintenance personnel are a re blaming the Sand-Dust separator for all the FOD. I inspected UH-1H 66-16126, T-53 L13 LE14260 for FOD. Two problems were encountered, it had emitted 1½(approx.)quarts of oil through nose section into the air filter lower assy, a nd very severe FOD. Upon inspecting inlet area, one washer was missing from the mounting ring assembly. Recommend that personnel perform a more thorough cleaning and policing of the plenum area.

3. Inspected UH-1D 64-13627, T-53 L11 LE11610 for a #2 carbon seal leak. Engine was repaired.

4. Assisted a ccident investigation board, Major Johnson, 269th Cmbt. Avn. Bn. in evaluating cause of power failure on UH-1D 64-13820, T-53 L9A LE06115. A thorough inspection was performed. Oil samples were analyzed and revealed a perservative oil was used, it had very little lubricating quality resulting in seizure of PT package.

5. Inspected UH-1D 65-122, T-53 L11 LE11398. Recommended engine change because #1 carbon seal was leaking oil out of the bleed band.

6. Several replacement nozzles(gas producer N1) are being received through supply channels without the time being recorded on 2410.

7. Inspected engine on UH-1D 64-13603, T-53 L11 LE10212. Hot end inspection revealed N1 nozzle cracked beyond limits. Replaced nozzle, engine serviceable.

8. Inspected engine on UH-1H 66-16122, T-53 L13 LE15179. Removed for FOD. Had 40:00 since new.

9. T-53 L13 LE15301 engine received from supply, that had physical evidence of being dropped, no tag on can indicating this. Shipping container was also damaged. Engine returned to supply a nd forwarded to test stand for required run-up on test stand.

10. Assisted on high EGT problem on UH-1C 66-513, T-53 L11 LE10072. Cleaned inlet housing which lowered EGT to limits. Engine had 80:00 until hot end inspection due. Recommend vaporizers be cleaned in accordance with TM's. I've been assisting units on pulling flow dividers and cleaning off the carbon build-up. This has alleviated most of EGT problems. (However make sure all dividers are installed properly, otherwise exit legs will burn off).

FOR HWP USE			
DATE RECEIVED	FOLLOW UP REQUIRED ☐ YES ☐ NO	SUSPENSE DATE	
ACTION ASSIGNED TO		DATE REPLY MAILED	
REMARKS			

6-11
Maintenance Performance Report 1478-R page 2

11. Assisted 3/4 Cavalry with a "no start" of engine, UH-1C 65-9459, T-53 L9 LE06280 replaced fuel sta rt nozzles, engine made serviceable. Recommend information be sent out to all units to turn into supply for overhaul, or testing of all fuel start nozzles removed from aircraft engines.

12. Major Ha rold W. Byars, Maintenance Officer, 392nd Trans. Det. APO 96353 should receive honorable mentioning. Major Byars has worked hard to achieve engine T80's. the later part of November 1967, UH-1D 65-12885, T-53 L11 LE12102 was removed for T80 of 1211:00 hours.

13. Damage is being done to canon plugs, because maintenance personnel are using canon plu pliers, and overtorquing them. Recommend that personnel use proper method, finger tight and then safety.

14. Visited Hq. Troop, 3/17th Cavalry, Di An APO 96289, and instructed maintenance personnel on proper cleaning of Sand-Dust separator and the prevention of FOD. Personnel a re under the opinion that the Sand-Dust separator is to solve all FOD problems. All maintenance personnel were well indoctrinated with proper cleaning and policing policies.

15. Assisted 3/17th Cavalry on visiting Lai Kai on maintenance recovery of UH-1C 66-640, T-53 L11 LE12667. Had a suspected power loss at 500 feet. Maj. Draper hovered the helicopter, all systems were checked for operation. Engine was thoroughly checked out. I accompanied it on test hop, no indications of any malfunctions. Aircraft was returned to Di An for maintenance check of all electrical systems and NII govenor charge.

16. Assisted Accident Investigating Board, Capt. Shwend, 269th Cmbt. Avn. Bn. on UH-1C 66-15173, T-53 L11B LE12601. O/H at ARADMAC. Aircraft settled and made contact with the water.

17. Visited 93rd Med. Evac. Hospital at Long Binh, instructed four pilots and maintenance personnel on T-53 L13 ga s turbine problems.

18. 520th Trans. Bn. (AM&S) Maj. Clements, called for my assistance to correct a high temp. and high EGT on Commanding General's Big Red One's UH-1H 66-16930 T-53 L13 LE15064. Sand-Dust separator required cleaning, briefed personnel on proper method called for on the Daily inspection. Problem was resolved, when I located a tube from the customer air, which wa s vented into the oil cooler compartment. After plugging this line we flew a test hop, all gaugex readings were in normal limits.

Wayne A. Kuschel, DAC
20th Trans. Co. (ADS)
APO San Francisco 96353

6-12
Photo showing compressor blade damage

CHAPTER 7-
MY MAINTENANCE MANAGEMENT
COURSE AND POSITION'S GAVE ME
PROMOTIONS

Upon arriving at Travis Air Force Base, my red passport was stamped December 19, 1967. For official business use, and become a U.S. citizen once more, my wife was waiting, and I happily assumed my role as a new person arriving back in the United States. It was freezing, 32 degrees and all I had on was a thin white short-sleeved shirt, black nylon sweater, and black cotton slacks. All were very thin for this type of cold weather since it was 120 degrees in Vietnam the day I departed.

Just a few days and Christmas would be here. We followed all the requirements of returning stateside. Our duty station AVSCOM was notified, then we proceeded to our home in Riverside, California for a short leave to regain one's sanity. I had numerous friends coming to our home at 4175 Adams Street, Riverside, California to welcome me home. My big chore was to get our household goods shipped to St. Louis, Missouri. I went to March Air Force Base for their assistance in shipping requirements. My leave was approved and a definite reporting date in St. Louis, Missouri was established. On the designated date all household goods were picked up and we locked the doors and got on the road towards St. Louis, Missouri. Weather was treacherous, especially in Flagstaff, Arizona ice and snow was the culprit, 18 inches deep on the average. My English Bulldog, Sissy, got anxious to use the outdoors, so in a small rest area near Flagstaff, Arizona I opened the door and she jumped out into the snow. She looked like a submarine under water, she was having a ball. When we got her quieted down, we had to towel her down. She was dripping wet. We then pulled in for lodging around midnight because there wasn't much farther my old body could go.

The next day as we traveled towards St. Louis, Missouri the snow was in the higher elevation or altitude and getting warmer in some areas, except when we hit the Four Corners area in New Mexico. That was the worst area in the United States at winter time. Very smooth, glazing ice, so slippery you couldn't stand up on the ice.

Traveling was very slow to the east until we reached Oklahoma City, Oklahoma then it was fairly fast until we got into Missouri around Fort Leonard Wood, more ice. I remember a small yellow 1964 Chevy that passed our car while I was making a new trail or path in the right lane, this little Chevy was slipping and sliding but he was driving at least 55 mph when he passed me. I told the wife he was an accident waiting to happen. About three miles down the road there he was in the ditch bleeding, with the police on hand.

Upon arrival in St. Louis, Missouri we went to the Motor Inn Motel and received temporary lodging. We were looking for quarters close to my work, so I could walk to and from without a lot of travel. We settled on the 30 Plaza Square apartments and got a two bedroom apartment. Our English Bulldog, Sissy took to apartment living like a champ. There was plenty of time for leash time and squirrel chasing.

On 5 January 1967, I reported in to the Division Chief. Mr. Bartley briefed me on the desires of the command for me to attend the United States

Army's Maintenance Management Course at Fort Lee, Virginia in March 1968. Mr. Bartley again reiterated since I had a college degree they wanted to utilize my skills because I was the only one of the one hundred thirty seven Equipment Specialists in the 1670 career fields that had four years of college. I was assigned as the supervisor/manager of Propulsion Systems. That gave me the responsibility for serving as the command's representative on all UH-1 (Huey) propulsion and maintenance problems.

After being dismissed I reported into the Granite City Army Dispensary at the Mart Building for chest pain. The doctor could not find the cause. However to alleviate the pain they issued (use as necessary) a 12 count of Metamucil to take three (3) times daily on a continuous basis. The pain could not be located by various doctors on duty between 1967 and my disability retirement 10 July 1979 (sometime after moving to Wichita Falls in 1980 a specialist from Chicago and Sheppard AFB doctors found I had a Hiatus Hernia and performed exploratory surgery whereby most of my problem was solved).

On my second day of duty I was asked to write a letter for the AVSCOM Commanding General's signature. This was the first time that this type of request was asked of me. If I knew the General it would have made it a lot easier to know his style of writing. This letter was to speak on vehicle usage in the Republic of Vietnam to better utilize the assigned vehicles, and coordinate the use of vehicles with other AVSCOM personnel and agencies. My supervisors gave me a pat on the back because the correspondence was outstanding. AVSCOM personnel would advise all agencies of time, where and when the vehicle would be used, i.e., if it would be used on base, or going to the hotels in Vung Tau. In other words, the personnel would look out for anyone needing transportation.

On my third duty day I ran into our double trouble bad boys (Parker and McElvaney) sitting in the mailing room. They knew I was a supervisor and had the authority of attending to any problem that might come up.

So they heckled a little, my skin was a lot tougher, than in the Vietnam era. The FBI and United States Army Criminal Investigators told Peck's black hat bad boys if any harm came to me they would have to answer for whatever crime was committed to silence me. They were required to go on trial in February 1968. Prior to this date I was required to answer all sorts of questions involving their participation in the black market, gambling and thefts. Before I left Vietnam I was requested to review a CID charge book approximately more than two inches thick with all the Vung Tau investigation findings in it. As far as I could tell about all the facts that happened were accounted for. In January 1968, the book I saw in official hands of the St. Louis, Missouri federal court had material that was entirely different. The book was about one inch thick and all the meaningful facts had been removed. It was useless in the present form. I gave my deposition to my superiors under oath to the best of my knowledge. To cut this story short, Pecks bad boys got three days suspension, but in my view it showed that they were both guilty of the charges. They were given stateside assignments and that's the last contact I had with them. Thank the good Lord! I don't think anyone should have to associate with this low class trash in their official duties as GS-12's. They should have been beyond reproach as career personnel.

My new supervisory position and Mr. Powers was to resolve all turbine engine and air frame problems or discrepancies within AVSCOM, any aviation unit in the USA or overseas, as expedient, and efficient as possible.

Then ensure to coordinate all information received, so all units know the facts and required maintenance would be completed in the shortest time available. There were approximately 7000 UH-1 (Hueys) in the system with all the flying time allocated within DOD aspects and budget limitations.

In addition to my assigned duties there were regulations that had to be kept current, such as armed forces schools to meet positions requirements and promotion advancements. Especially to enter the executive type management areas.

Whenever I was a supervisor over any personnel that required special training to maintain their efficiency on their job the person was then scheduled accordingly with plenty of time to attend any course. That way promotion would be acceptable, if warranted for advancement, if the person was fully qualified.

Our Technical Assistance office was assigned a summer hire during July 1968, a young lady 19 years old, very good typist and sharp as a tack on administrative correspondence. Nobody wanted to accept her because she was African-American and slightly overweight. I told my supervisor I would accept the responsibility for training her. Reason being, all the way through the T-53-L-13 Lycoming courses I attended there was an urgent need for an Army aviation gas turbine engine mechanics book for special tools required to work in sequence on all the T-53-L-13 gas turbine engine. Regardless of your expertise and abilities as an aviation propulsion mechanic, there were several special tools that were very similar in appearance that if used incorrectly would tear up the specific repair item or the tool itself. To alleviate this problem, this manual would illustrate with pictures and numbers for each step of the procedure to assist in preventing errors. The summer hire took on the book assignment, working very closely with me on typing, proofing, and tool photos, and in turn accomplished an outstanding worldwide guide. It was an excellent T-53-L-13 gas turbine information manual, so I had 500 copies made up for worldwide distribution. The completed manual didn't hit my desk before thunder and sparks from my supervisor had surrounded my area because I had used funds to bring the manual into existence. I didn't have the right without top management approval. So, I goofed.

I had a sore butt for all the problems that occurred. But it was well worth it to help the aviation mechanics and personnel. When the worldwide

United States Army Aviation Maintenance Companies found out that a valuable manual existed and was available to all aviation units utilizing T-53—L-13 engines, orders swamped the Director of Maintenance, Technical Assistance team for copies so all was forgiven on my part. "Good job, well done," said my supervisor, and I was thinking perhaps the aviation companies would save numerous dollars in complying with the contents.

The summer hire was very excited to receive a promotion from another federal agency and accepted the position. I bid her farewell for a job well done. I approve of the summer hire program wholeheartedly to acquaint young people with the federal programs available to them after graduation. Then it's up to them to decide on their future.

My new assignment was manager/supervisor of propulsion systems. The job had a lot of coordinating and problem solving. In addition, you might have to cross lines in several in-house disciplines and other outside commands, even working with the civilian companies manufacturing the assigned aircraft or parts combined on the major item. It was not an easy accomplishment, you made friends but sometimes you had to step on toes to get the end results finalized on time.

I was given orders on 20 February 1968 to pack my bags, that my Ft. Lee Maintenance Management school assignment course 68-4 was on schedule and that classes would begin in five days for a total of 42 days. Hastily in the early morning of 9 March 1968, [See travel orders to Fort Lee, Virginia 7-1] we gathered up the suitcases and health items required for the trip to Fort Lee, Virginia. In addition, my wife Marie was on liquid oxygen for her emphysema so I had to load the car with a large liquid oxygen tank and strap it down in case of an accident. Since Sissy, my buddy, bulldog was to accompany us, her food and bowls were in a special box. It was an excellent idea to strap everything down good since the bad weather was supposed to be severe as we were going east on Highway 70. In Pennsylvania, the eighteen wheelers were throwing large blocks of ice all over the highway so it was duck or swerve around the chunks of ice to prevent an accident.

When we arrived in Maryland we took Highway 83 south until we ran into Highway 95. Then it was a nice quiet trip to Fort Lee, Virginia. No mishaps, it was nearly 964 miles driving in one day. The wife and I arrive on time at Fort Lee, Virginia, and with a sick wife we were assigned quarters on the base. She had to visit Reynolds Army Hospital often for medication and examinations. The Maintenance Management course was one of the finest I had ever attended. My grades were exceptionally high. With the knowledge gained it would be used in my everyday life in the Maintenance Office. I was awarded my diplomas on 19 April 1968. My wife Marie had all the luggage ready for returning to St. Louis, Missouri. Sissy had enough of no catch-em squirrels and was sitting nearby where I parked the car, all we had to do was pack the suitcases and boxes in the trunk and depart. [See Copy of my diploma 7-2]

I had studied the return route and decided to go to Roanoke, Virginia and over the Allegheny mountains. What a rugged trip that was to be, straight up and essentially the same straight down. We found out one thing along the way. The meals were the "Old Style" down home cooking type; very flavorful and you never left a thing on your plate. Breakfast was a large piece of ham the size of a large plate, hash browns were special cooked and browned to perfection, scrambled eggs scrumptious to eat. In all of my service life that was the best food-eating road. Of course, I bet we maxed out our belt length and I would never guess the calories involved.

So we traveled to our 30 Plaza residence in St. Louis, Missouri. Our days off at Fort Lee, Virginia were spent touring all the civil war areas that we had time for, or healthy enough for. They were all very educational and helped set our minds straight on history. There were several we wanted to see but the timing was bad so it was time to return to AVSCOM.

I can say one thing you could depend on the command personnel to keep you appraised of what they expected of you, and here is an excellent example by Major General John Norton [See Major General Norton's letter to me 7-3]

The next duty day I was at the Technical Assistance office answering phone calls to resolve some of the issues. It took hours to coordinate the in-house engineering and support results and call the company or unit back with the solution. I accomplished my job as effectively and efficiently as possible leaving a good name and a good producer as the end result. During October 1968, I was promoted without grade increase to Acting Chief, Far East Branch. Since we had worldwide assignments, the bulk of our personnel were in the southwest Pacific. This included the good old Republic of Vietnam area. My red passport was updated with visas, back on 29 June 1966 for all worldwide countries that we had Technical Assistance personnel and aircraft located within the countries. There was no excuse for a delay or walk-through of the red passport requiring overseas duty or visits. This was a common thing to be prepared to depart immediately to any worldwide location requested by aviation units.

Oh! I got my tail feathers singed numerous times because of lack of information in the office. It takes time to receive information from major aviation companies, then walk-by coordination within our organization, such as engineering questions and receive end results expeditiously. Those engineering people had to have all the facts, figures and facets or information of the problem, and then they would have to coordinate every item within their directorates. This takes time to complete. A very serious problem may take a complete day to eliminate but it's rewarding when you get a "well done" from the field.

I received on 1 November 1968 a lapel pin/tie-tack holder from Brigadier General Traylor from AVSCOM, Vice Commander, that showed I was assigned in a combat area service, in the Republic of Vietnam from

15 December 1966 to 16 December 1967, or a full year. [Brigadier General Traylor Presented my award 7-4]

On 7 April 1969, I was summoned to our Directorate's office to receive a Department of Army Commendation. [Presented to me by Brigadier General Traylor 7-5] My devotion to duty takes in my old duty station of Cu Chi, and my current job at the technical assistance division from 6 August 1967 to 5 August 1968. It showed me there was no pointing of fingers of end results about the effects of the United States Army Criminal Investigation Division in 1966-1968. It did not reflect on my personnel record with AVSCOM commanders and what they thought of my managerial abilities.

In addition, I have received numerous letters of appreciation and commendations for jobs well done. However in some cases I have correspondence but do not have pictures of personnel presenting the awards to me, so please forgive me.

On 5 February 1969 I received a certificate of achievement commending me for service in Vietnam presented to by Colonel Delbert L. Bristol, C.O. Logistics Support and in addition I was presented with the RVN medal for Service in Vietnam this correspondence was signed by Stanley R. Resor, Secretary of the Army, Washington, D.C. [correspondence and picture of awards 7-6 & 7-7]

I must have done a very good job because on 27 February 1969 I was again more or less promoted to acting assistant Chief, Technical Assistance Division, and also acting Chief, CONUS Branch (GS-13 position) filling two hats. I worked well with all colonels, 1, 2, 3, and 4 star generals, GS-15s and GS-16s, whoever I contacted. So I had lots of supporters in the United States Army Material command. Being a GS-12 and having these responsibilities gave me experience that could not be achieved or duplicated anywhere. Of course the decisions were getting tougher; trying to get the personnel to properly justify the contents of correspondence was another item that had to be dealt with. So a memo was prepared and submitted to all levels of the Directorate, which helped in good basic communication for everyone.

I had to brief Thailand personnel 27 February 1969 and several more dignitaries. This position was one busy place to be; in other words, a hot seat. I got a very appreciative letter for briefing Thailand through General Chesark, AMC Commanding Officer. It came into AVSCOM and Major General Hinrichs endorsed it to me through the Director of Maintenance, Technical Assistance office. [Letter of appreciation Thailand Briefing 7-8]

Several areas had positions for grade advancement; to get ahead I put my name in for GS-13s openings that I was experienced or qualified in.

During May 1969, AVSCOM released a vacancy announcement for a GS-301-13 System Manager within the Special Items Management Office (SIMO). I didn't realize that I had been selected from AVSCOM merit promotion job opportunity number 35-69-51, dated 16 June 1969, until the correspondence came through my office on 29 June 1969. This was an indication that I was changing occupation code GS-1670-12 and promoted to a GS-301-13. The civilian personnel officer supplied me with a notification of personnel action and a job description for a System Management specialist job number 10924[Copy of SIMO Promotion GS-301-13 7-9]

I was introduced to GS-14 Mr. Ed Laughlin, who was recently promoted to that grade within the Budget Finance Office. Since he was the outgoing systems manager from 1968-1969 for the YO-3A aircraft, the command approved a two week transfer of all YO-3A aircraft functions and assets to me as the new YO-3A system manager. I was furnished a charter as the AVSCOM YO-3A System Manager and a YO-3A program transfer of responsibilities as YO-3A Systems Manager. [Charter for YO-3A System Manager 7-10]

What I am writing regarding the YO-3A silent aircraft was written bit by bit during my book writing of my experience as such, on what I remember during the time that I was involved in being the System Manager and the Light Observation Helicopter PM YO-3A project officer from 1969 through 1975. That time frame is during the later time when I was associated or assigned with other AVSCOM Directorates such as Technical Data, Cataloging and Standardization (TDC&S), Light Observation Helicopter-Project Managers Office (Configuration Management Division Identification and Control Branch, Special Items Management Office (SIMO), Cargo Aircraft Assistant Manager (CH-47 aircraft), Utility Division Assistant Manager (UH-1 & United States Army Presidential Bell, VH-IN Twin Huey) (SIMO), Directorate for Weapons Systems Management, Utility Division (UH-1 & VH-IN Division).

The command, regardless of where I was assigned, tasked me to be the AVSCOM YO-3A Project Officer for any requested information regarding the YO-3A aircraft. My duties entailed all types of management and records, keeping tabs of all facets on the ongoing YO-3A aircraft program. Then advising the responsible personnel of their input or corrective action. My new job description for my current position pointed out the areas of my responsibilities, and to insure the integration for life cycle management of one or more selected highly complex Army aircraft systems.

On our first round robin tour of the west coast regarding Lockheed Missile and Space Command and their subsidiaries, Ed and I decided to stay at the Golden Palace and eat at their Chinese eatery. Ed said he knew all about Chinese food and I let him go ahead and order part of the meal. Ed decided to order his special meal and I did the same. The Chinese waiter explained to Ed what his order consisted of for both of us. I didn't pay too much attention because of my concern trying to read some YO-3A correspondence, but when I heard what Ed ordered I started to laugh because the fermented beans was about as bad as Poi was for me in Honolulu, tasted like wall paper glue (my own judgment). We had lots of hee-haws and fun eating our Chinese meal, then we departed for our motel rooms to be ready for tomorrow.

My duty assignment would be working as AVSCOM's YO-3A system manager with Lockheed, Moffitt NAS, California, manufacturer of the previous two QT-2 aircraft in 1968, which were utilized in Vietnam as the "silent aircraft" mode to be sure it was feasible to continue on a new version, since the QT-2s were so productive in Vietnam during 1968 and returned to the United States for proper disposal by my office. DOD had approved the continuance of building a new type of silent aircraft, so Lockheed began to develop plans and locations for the manufacture of the airframe. Lockheed had several subcontractors such as Electro-Optical Systems (EOS) in Pomona, California. They were responsible for the mission equipment.

The United States Army Electronics Command at Ft. Monmouth, New Jersey, was responsible for overseeing all electronics, night vision, laser and infrared systems. The United States Air Force Procurement Office (AFPRO) would be responsible for all types of support between the United States Army and Lockheed to oversee all work accomplished by Lockheed concerning engineering items, airframe specifications, quality control, etc. One other factor that I did not know or realize was the YO-3A had a very, very high priority for the United States Army, being the leader of a tri-service agreement involving United States Navy, United States Marines and the United States Air Force.

To give a scenario of the YO-3A (to be), it was a night observation reconnaissance type military airplane with a length of 29' 4", wing span of 57', gross weight of 3,700 lbs., (this weight was a major factor in all additions or reductions of items required in the YO-3A configuration), crew of two (pilot and systems operator), power was a Continental I0-360 210 HP, 6-cylinder opposed engine with an endurance of five hours, quiet cruise speed was proposed for nearly 70 knots. [Pictures of YO-3A and me (several pictures) 7-11]

The finalized contract contained 11 aircraft to be manufactured for the United States Army. The YO-3A program had intense pressure on Lockheed and other activities to stay on schedule to manufacture, test aircraft, mission equipment, train personnel and the aircraft had to have a low decibel acoustical noise factor for a silent aircraft to fulfill the operation missions required in Vietnam. There was much more testing that had to be accomplished than any one person could comprehend or understand. In other words, the YO-3A aircraft had to be a complete package and be in-country to the Republic of Vietnam on a proposed future date.

Background history on the YO-3A silent aircraft: Lockheed was interested in the quiet aircraft in mid-1965 and accomplished information from QT-2 and Prize Crew imposed in night reconnaissance in Vietnam. The list of unknowns was long and the answers were hard to come by, such as sensors, ranges, acoustics detection, distance, time, aircraft type, power required, weight range and a quiet platform.

Department of Defense John Foster requested help. Lockheed had lots of problems solved utilizing facts obtained by the QT-2 in Vietnam. Lockheed was the ideal company to comply with Mr. Foster's request and was available to begin manufacturing a plane that would utilize a Schweitzer glider airframe model 2-32. This was the first aircraft to meet most of the engineering requirements. It was to be flown and tested at a special California site for security reasons and only at night so no one would see it and divulge or convey any accurate characteristics on the YO-3A. [YO-3A aircraft pictured in Republic of Vietnam 7-12]

Most of the YO-3A acoustics testing was conducted during the night time at a United States Naval Air Station, Crows Landing near Patterson, California, and other sites if selected by Lockheed. The aircraft was almost undetectable at 1,000 feet altitude. It would sound like a covey of birds flying. There were numerous flights to determine the best performance and acoustics, between three and six fixed pitch propeller blade. All the engineering personnel and test data picked the six propeller blades for the YO-3A aircraft. The blades were all handcrafted out of birch wood. If my mind can relate, a Mr. Fahlin handcrafted the blades for incorporation on the YO-3A aircraft.

Another area that we were all concerned with was the type of paint to be applied to the aircraft. There were several methods used to evaluate it and many paint companies to consider who had their own product. The paint had to adapt as a (stealth) "can't see" coating which was classified because of radar detection, so no one could purchase it from the producers. The paint which was utilized on the YO-3A was a light gray-blue color which cost the United States Army a bundle to test and apply to each aircraft.

There are so many facets involving the YO-3A that I can't begin to bring out all the bits and pieces, as my memory lacks the ability to go back 35 years and remember lots of little details but I'm trying to do the best that I can with good results, and provide interesting reading.

There was very limited aviation engineering information or "solid" data, words to define what was meant by aircraft "acoustical" measurement. There was limited knowledgeable information contained in the new DOD proposal for procurement of the YO-3A aircraft. Lockheed had to go through all types of defining acoustical testing of aircraft, their equipment, trailer, and gas generators. In addition, Lockheed purchased a large trailer worth nearly one million dollars to accomplish the unknown acoustics. The trailer was moved to selected locations for the YO-3A to fly in different configurations and register acoustical data.

When I became the YO-3A System Manager to replace Ed Laughlin we had a hectic two weeks for indoctrination to coordinate his thoughts and ideas into my head. What a chore that was going to be for me to be qualified. I can honestly say this was a fast, expeditious moving project. I found out that I wasn't an instant brain on the project and yet the project I heard of was low on funds. So Ed assisted by going through all the steps and disclosed the facts when we visited the United States Army Material Command in Arlington, Virginia.

The Material Command YO-3A project manager, LTC Lucas was appraised about the latest figures. Next we visited Mr. Long, the Assistant Secretary for the Army at the Pentagon. He was briefed on the program and the possible funding problems on the horizon. All knowledgeable information and correspondence was disseminated to concerned offices for their compliance and assistance. Because of the foot dragging in Congress the funds ran out. No one could agree as to where the funds would come from. My contact for YO-3A project funds was Senator Strom Thurman of South Carolina. Senator Thurman had no answers as to when funding would be available.

When Ed and I reported the funding information to AVSCOM, it started everyone contacting all personnel to make them aware of the impending money problems. I was called into the AVSCOM Commanding General's Office (Major General Norton), where he asked me of my experience in procurement contracts. I advised him I had limited experience while in the Strategic Air Command but with this fast moving program I could use any help that I might receive. The General asked me how I felt to have LTC Edward Browne take over and I would be his assistant or YO-3A Project Officer. I told General Norton that it would be outstanding as LTC Browne was the Light Observation Helicopter (LOH) Project Manager and had an excellent staff of personnel to assist in the continuation of the required YO-3A aircraft. Presently I had no staff personnel to assist me, but the Command gave me help for meetings or problem-solving from all of the AVSCOM Directorates. All I had to do was request personnel, which was an unthinkable statement. You could never depend on the personnel to stay on the YO-3A aircraft.

The General said he would set everything in motion and my charter would be revoked and to go to work in the LOH-PM office and meet the personnel. It wasn't long before LTC Browne and I were in meetings to come up with strategic maneuvers to work with all the commands and especially with Lockheed. LTC Browne reiterated AVSCOM's concerns and immediately stated I would be the AVSCOM YO-3A contact and control point on all correspondence and actions required.

I also found a friend. Al Bayliss was more or less a clean-up man in the engineering office. I asked him if he would like to work as an aero-engineer on the YO-3A project. Al Bayliss replied, "Yes. I was going to ask you for a job!" So I went to LTC Browne and he approved putting Al Bayliss on our project. So by slow coordination, the YO-3A team members were being assigned their primary duties with additional duty as the YO-3A aircraft team.

After a short period we had seventy eight AVSCOM personnel from all directors on our YO-3A team to keep it on track. That's the priority that a PM office has on the support of assigned aircraft systems, constant observation from designated branches.

Again I was called into the Directorates Maintenance Office, Colonel Vaughn C. Emerson on 22 August 1969 to receive an official commendation for the period 11 August 1968 to 10 August 1969. Guess I had done an outstanding job in the Technical Assistant Office. [Picture of award ceremony 22 August 1969 7-13]

When LTC Browne learned about the funding as being zilch or zero funds left to accomplish the remaining manufacturing of the YO-3A, he started setting up management meetings with higher headquarters and the Assistant of the Army Office in the Pentagon. He got to speak with Representative George H. Mahon (D-Texas), who in early 1970 was

Chairman of the House Appropriations Committee. There were very deep conversations regarding how much would be needed to finish the YO-3A program and where the funds would be taken from. I do know that it was a bittersweet situation, and if LTC Browne didn't acquire the funds to finish the program that there would be hell to pay. I won't say the complete statement. So AVSCOM and Lockheed agreed on a continued (fixed) contract. This YO-3A program had a lot of ups and downs in keeping on our goal of getting it into Vietnam in early 1970. There was lots of test flying, testing mission systems, acoustics, paint and combining of equipment into the airframe to be accomplished as soon as possible. There were lots of unknown situations yet to come into being.

AVSCOM designated the United States Air Force Procurement (AFPRO), located near Moffitt NAS as the watchdog over Lockheed. It was an outstanding choice. It was my privilege to coordinate all efforts with CPT Chidester or Mr. McLaughlin, who both did an outstanding job. Mr. McLaughlin was on top of all the production work Lockheed was putting out. In other words, staying on top of everything that Lockheed was doing, and then relaying the results to AVSCOM LOH-PM office, and coordinating the results with all AFPRO personnel to insure everyone was on the same sheet of paper.

Colonel Browne and I became the best of friends. This included all the LOH-PM personnel, since I was a retired officer I respected his office and all the responsibility he was handling. I knew how to do the necessary functions without bothering him and only needed his help when I required his approval or signature. While Colonel Browne and I were on road trips, it was like a three-ring circus; one to Washington, D.C., two to San Francisco, and three to Pomona, California.

When Colonel Browne was in Washington D.C. (most likely for meetings on funds, maintenance problems, etc.), I was on the west coast keeping all logistics and program problems to a minimum. Then we would get together in the AVSCOM LOH-PM to keep personnel coordinated on all our accomplishments and keep schedules on track with all ends tied up. It's unbelievable how busy a key member would be on this YO-3A project. With 11 aircraft on contract there was never a dull moment to relax.

The tri-services (Army, Navy, USAF, Marines) were required to coordinate and sign off correspondence requirements for their own specific service, which was a hefty requirement. Contact points were hard to keep up with; changing personnel was the big problem. Finally we had acquired a sufficient number of YO-3A's to begin the proposed flying program. That meant fly the aircraft from Moffitt NAS to Hunter-Liggett Field near Fort Ord, California and operate out of that AAF base. We had to hold all types of meetings with other Army Command personnel from Fort Monmouth, New Jersey and Ft. Belvoir, Virginia on the mission equipment, laser and infrared designator plus communications.

When you think everything was going along good, watch out, because a baseball bat was going to hit you. One screwy thing after another was always thrown into the ring of confusion. Then in the middle of things we had to hold procurement meetings with Lockheed to see what the final configuration was going to be. A full item by item (line by line) determination of cost and use requirement was to begin immediately with Lockheed coming into AVSCOM at St. Louis, Missouri.

When Lockheed arrived, they had five contract officers and three attorneys, plus the rest of their team. We, on the other hand, had one procurement officer, one legal officer and two helpers, which should show that if you want the whole bundle, Lockheed came prepared to do battle with the Army's best experts. We had outstanding Army personnel on our team and could hold their own regarding procurement decisions proposed by Lockheed. The only time Colonel Browne or I interrupted the meeting was if they got off track or if they could not resolve a difference, problem or impasse.

My thought when I began in June 1969 when I was introduced to the Lockheed personnel was that they were geniuses, so they thought. They were Lockheed corporate gung ho personnel that had to produce results to stay on the project. When Ed Laughlin briefed me in the beginning on Lockheed Engineering personnel he said they had the best part of sixty engineers salaries paid from YO-3A project funds. All the information that I could obtain from talking and briefings I wrote up or took notes, so I could go through them when I returned to AVSCOM. There was no more to be gained at Lockheed so they flew us (United States Army personnel), down to Electro-Optical Systems (EOS) at Pomona, California. They were the company that was manufacturing the mission equipment. Again we began attending meetings and were taken through the special area where the mission equipment was put together, being tested, and other facets. We returned to San Francisco, California for one more day at Lockheed, then returned to AVSCOM in St. Louis, Missouri.

About a week later I took a team of three AVSCOM personnel to Lockheed. Our AVSCOM engineer Dwight Brown was one that liked to play tricks on people. He knew that Bob Abbott was playing golf late One Saturday afternoon, so Dwight purchased a trick golf ball. He followed Bob around until everyone's eyes were off the green and he picked up Bob's ball and put his trick ball in its place. It was Bob's turn to hit the ball into the cup from about two feet away. Bob got his putter and got near the ball, squared off, and the ball curved around the cup. Bob was playing for dinner, and a trick ball is a No! No! When he saw what happened he swung the putter full blast and hit the ball out into space. Bob came to me and said he wanted to repay Dwight for his golf ball trick, and asked me if I could get his key and he would put cellophane on top of his commode. That way when Bob took Dwight to the pizza parlor he would feed him an abundance of beer. Bob wouldn't let him wee-wee until we got him back to his motel room, then Dwight would wee-wee all over the place. Before this could go into operation Dwight had to fly back to AVSCOM in St. Louis, Missouri for a high priority engineering requirement. Bob said there would be another day to even the score.

When I returned to St. Louis, Missouri, Dwight was sitting near my desk fiddling with a light bulb that had a battery and bulb inside. He explained that you put a piece of aluminum foil in your mouth, then put the light bulb in your mouth, move the foil across the two points on the base and the light would burn. Dwight asked me to hide it in my desk for him. A few days later the time was ripe for Dwight to impress my secretary. He said, "Let me have the bulb." Well, I always had extra bulbs in my desk for our lighting of the area so I gave one of my real bulbs to him. He had the foil in his mouth. He called the secretary over and made a bet with her that he could light the bulb. I didn't dare look at Dwight; otherwise, I would have burst out laughing so I started to read a piece of correspondence. All the time Dwight was twisting the bulb like a contortionist, putting it sideways trying to light it. Anyway I let it go on. After the secretary had left I pulled my desk open and said I bet I gave you the wrong bulb. He said some nasty words and left my area. Because of our hours, 14 to 18 hours per day, we had to loaf a bit and have some fun, a wee bit of loafing and then back to work.

On one of my west coast visits we had to go into Patterson, California, then to Crows N.A.S. Landing for the YO-3A testing. I was given the opportunity to fly in the YO-3A July 1969 with Lockheed's test pilot, Mr. Q.B. Burton. I got a flight suit and went to the aircraft, climbed in the front seat and buckled up. I had the mission equipment going and as we took off I uncovered the headpiece and as we climbed up to 1,000 feet I admired the YO-3A flying characteristics. Mr. Burton let me fly it, then it was time to use the mission equipment. I looked through the scope and saw the hair on the tip of a cow's ear move and twitch. You could almost see the minute detail of each hair. It was an amazing time to see such a perfect picture from the new type of double-dove mission equipment installed on the YO-3A aircraft. My mind was on what the personnel would be able to see on night missions in Vietnam. Time would tell but I hoped it was as good as my observation on my flight.

I could think of all the work that involved the operation of the mission equipment. Everyone had cooperated in an outstanding manner. There were lots of people on the "red eye" airlines for personnel to be there (anywhere a person on the YO-3A was required) for our first meeting in the morning affair. I can truthfully say there had to be lots of meetings to keep the YO-3A airplane on schedule without any mishaps and then meet all the logistics points. The evening of the day I flew in the YO-3A, there were several critical tests. One was to see how well the scope did its job on picking out a minimum of light from a distance of one mile.

A Lockheed man was placed in the center of an orange grove after it got dark, where no light would get to him. At the designated time, the YO-3A pilot headed towards the orange grove about a mile away. The weapons observer picked up the illumination without any difficulty. It was a success! For the first time operation of the mission equipment at night, this system was well ahead of its time. We had a dinner celebration in Patterson, California. The restaurant provided the biggest and best T-bone steaks on the west coast. So the people said, time would tell. I can say it was one of the best steaks I'd had in a long time.

My thought was that LTC Browne would pick up the United States Army's meal tickets as no discussion about paying were mentioned prior to the dinner and we would give LTC Browne the amount of our meals.

That night on our way to our lodging in Menlo Park, Colonel Browne said Lockheed picked up the tab for our dinner and he wanted no gratuity or favors, so we should tell him what price our meal cost (if we could remember) and give it to him. Colonel Browne then sent a personal check to the Vice President of Lockheed for our dinner. It was a very good and rewarding feeling to not be in the debt to any company or organization, whereby a slip of a tongue an investigation could begin, and where it stops no one knows. Lockheed apologized, the intent was for a "Thank you, Army" for your support of the program and we appreciate it. At least Lockheed got the Army's point of view of no more offering of gratuities

The Army and Lockheed were very happy it had finished an important milestone so we moved on toward another big milestone. Setting up the YO-3A ground school and flying training, this contemplated all kinds of areas coming together so we could get the aircraft into Vietnam by March 1970. We knew there was one big mass of work yet required to complete and coordinate the shipping of the YO-3A and crews into Vietnam.

LTC Browne and I flew the "red eye" TWA express back to St. Louis, Missouri. On the flight back we accomplished writing several high priority messages to get out first thing the next morning. After arriving at the LOH-PM office, about 0300 we then shuffled through our mail and early after personnel began arriving dictating to the secretary those important high priority letters, and made final decisions in order that no stop gaps existed in our incoming and outgoing YO-3A requirements. We contacted our AVSCOM team members for their input and approval for the logistical and engineering support items to field and train personnel. Then and only then, did we depart for home late in the afternoon for some well-deserved rest. This will enable a person to get his vitamins, to begin work tomorrow, at the first sign of the sun, creeping up on the wall across the street. It seems like my routine was up at 0530, work by 0700, then work at the office until 1800 or 1900, take your brief case home and work until 2200 (at least), then hit the bed for that courage to get up the next morning. Working in any program manager's office is a lot of dedicated late and longer than normal hours, which no one gives any credit for you doing. Your job description reads "and anything more required to accomplish the mission." Also, "performs other duties as assigned" (without asking questions).

It's a "so what," that's your job, you asked for it when you got in the PM's office. There are a lot of people who are selected for the PM's office because of their superior ability to achieve end results. The percentage rates of personnel who are interviewed for project manager duty versus the number of persons selected are in the low, low rate for acceptance because a person's lack of qualifying experience. When we talk of all the long hours one person can work in any office or on any project, just remember we never were paid for overtime. Your annual salary is what you received, nothing more.

There were lots of occurrences where people knew the supervisors and tried to manipulate a position whereby a promotion could be gained. Most of the supervisory positions that I held I did not have time to hold hands and lead people through their everyday jobs. But they got on the train, so to speak, at full speed. There was no training time available. My obtaining the best trained personnel was by utilizing the position information on the two-page job description and questioning each of the candidates on his/her merit or knowledge of the work position they were applying for. I had to have my logistics people ready to immediately assume full responsibility for their position. Most of the requirements were to travel to units in the field to assist in resolving or bring back to AVSCOM full facts of the problem, whereby management would provide a sound coordinated resolution and expedite the corrective action to the field.

To show how far my diversified job carried me, the office had received a bill of lading for YO-3A kneeboards for pilot and mission equipment operators. The personnel had to have the item to complete the prescribed Lockheed flying school course. It was detrimental that I find the box of kneeboards. The box was somewhere in Pan Am's cargo hangar at the San Francisco Airport. I flew to San Francisco, rented a car, then drove to Pan Am's main office. I presented my credentials and introduced myself to the number one person in charge. He put two other personnel on the job to trace the box with the kneeboards. We checked most of the cargo area and one of Pan Am's men said they had checked the north corner yesterday. I flatly told them all corners would be checked again as the manifest or bill of loading indicated the box was signed for by Pan Am and that was it, we would check all areas, period. Guess where the box was located? In the north corner, so close to the wall and under the biggest box, which no one wanted to move. There was work to be done to retrieve the box for the program. After three hours we had the box and I signed for it and left for the AFPRO Office at Moffitt NAS.

The time was here when I was asked to supervise or manage the YO-3A training program from the west coast starting at Moffett and Hunter-Liggett Army field or Fritschze Army Air Field. My temporary orders were for ninety days and a continuance until the project was finished, which was 159 days to finalize the entire program.

All actions between Lockheed and AFPRO, AVSCOM and LOH-PM, and LTC Brown's office were to be well coordinated, with no loose strings left dangling. LTC Browne and I worked with all elements to keep the aircraft production line and the acceptance of items by AFPRO from Lockheed, to be expedited to the United States Army for the YO-3A program and then deployment on the date specified. This continually held AVSCOM for in-house meetings to ensure that the program stayed on schedule. The training program was getting close to completion and only a few weeks were left to pull all facets together to deploy the YO-3A to Vietnam on schedule. Colonel Browne advised me we had to proceed to Lockheed and review the complete program. The next day we flew from St. Louis, Missouri Lambert Airport in a TWA aircraft to San Francisco, California airport where we landed late in the evening. We acquired a rental car. Upon getting to our assigned motel we found out that my reservations were not made, lost or thrown into the trash can.

The motel clerk called around, and there were no rooms to be found. LTC Browne told me there were two beds in his room and that I was welcome to use the extra bed. We got along fine. I found out that he was one grand friend. He could be called on anytime to assist in any way possible. From that time on we were the best of friends and if he called me today I would give him the shirt off my back (Lieutenant Colonel Edward M. Browne retired as a Major General, from the AH—64 (Apache) Program, and is currently living in Melbourne, Florida).

On a later day my schedule showed that I had to be on the west coast immediately for an extended period of time to coordinate and schedule all functions remaining that Lockheed had to accomplish, and what the United States Army was responsible to provide in order to meet all schedules required for the deployment of the YO-3A to Vietnam in early 1970.

On arrival at the San Francisco airport I rounded up my baggage, then rode a government vehicle to downtown San Francisco and picked up a government rental, a 1970 four door AMC ambassador. We had a contract for thirty days, that way the transportation would be a lot cheaper for our driving to Fort Ord, and to Fritschze Army Air Field near Fort Ord, Salinas, California. I was given maps of the whole area. Coming out of downtown San Francisco through the maze of concrete roads I got into the lane for Watsonville, California. It was a beautiful road with the scenery of pine trees and Pacific Ocean water. After a couple of hours of driving I arrived at Fort Ord and checked in with the United States Army Aviation unit that was to support our YO-3A aircraft.

It is hard to describe in detail all the efforts that actually went into this program. We couldn't go home and forget about it because we had a target date to get these "quiet" aircraft into Vietnam by early 1970. So, the latest technology would be tested to ensure the next generation of the "quiet" aircraft would be able to upgrade into a feasible family of classified silent aircraft.

While I was at Fort Ord, there were a bunch of hippy or yippy groups that overran some of Fort Ord's areas. I received a call from Moffitt NAS that two YO-3As would do a night flyover to pinpoint the hippies for the ground personnel, and the military police would be notified to clear them off the post. It was a very productive night. The clean-up was 100% effective with all camp areas cleaned up and unwanted personnel off the post. This was the first time the YO-3A aircraft was utilized using the mission equipment to accomplish a very important task requested by the Army in Washington D.C. There were lots of patting personnel on the back for a job well done.

I sat through some of the training classes and I thought Lockheed did a superb job on their curriculum that they had put together in a short period of time. The Army students were very harmonious in each of their assignments. They took great pride in the maintenance course. These aircraft were unique to any other aircraft in the Army inventory.

In writing the stories in this book, "All or Nothing", I did not mention many times about the tri-service agreement involving the Army, United States Air Force, Navy and Marines. They were hand-picked for their pilot abilities, size and weight, and if they passed all the flying night requirements, and in addition all personnel were selected for their background, experience, maturity, willingness to go into a combat role in Vietnam. These energetic pilots and mission equipment operators were outstanding personnel, with lots of questions, being asked about this new type of silent aircraft, conditions in Vietnam, areas to being assigned and so forth. The YO-3A had a great team and bunch of talented crew members to be associated with. I knew most of the pilots and operators.

Every system was new in originality as there were only eleven YO-3A aircraft that were put into the special "silent" aircraft category. One area that had to be addressed was the aircraft weight limitation. A special engineering meeting was held each month to ensure no overweight problems would arise. For each one ounce increase in weight, it had to be justified, documented and signed off by the engineering committee.

I heard through a Vietnam grapevine that the Viet Cong already knew there were new types of spy planes coming in to the country. Of course we had some west coast newspapers that were trying to outguess what the end product manufactured by Lockheed was all about. They mentioned the mission equipment could see through rocks, trees, or whatever their imagination could come up with, and at one time, I had a newspaper booklet of all the guessing games that a variety of newspapers could invent or come up with. It was an 8"x10" book and an inch and a half thick with views, artist drawings, anything in the news. Since this was a classified project, no one except the Department of Defense could give out any security information. They were very reluctant to provide the other side any information to alert them of the aircraft capabilities.

While I was TDY on the west coast, I spent numerous days chasing down and eliminating problems within our jurisdiction. There were numerous phone calls to all of the agencies from east coast, west coast and Vietnam, from sun up to sun down, then after duty hours if that alone can be defined. In any project manager's office there are exceptions to any rule and your patriotic feeling makes it possible to work any number of hours to achieve the end goal with perfect results.

LTC Browne and I met on the west coast and drove to the YO-3A graduation party at Carmel, California. It was a superb gathering. Now it was time to fly the aircraft to a designated location, disassemble them for shipment in several United States Air Force cargo aircraft to Vietnam.

My job on the west coast was about through and I returned to St. Louis, Missouri with an approved detail to the Light Observation Helicopter (PM), since the YO-3A program was over. My position within the Special Items Management Office (SIMO) had been abolished, so my friend LTC

Browne had a GS-13 position in Configuration Management that I was assigned to, until a sound position or permanent position was available.

On 31 August 1971, I received a letter of appreciation from Colonel Marr of all the YO-3A aircraft tested and evaluation during their deployment to Republic of Vietnam in early 1970.

Colonel John E. Baker the LOH's Program Manager expressed his appreciation of my being the YO-3A Project Officer on the AVSCOM control point. [Letter of appreciation from RVN ACTIV office Colonel Marr and Colonel Baker LOH-PM 7-14]

Next I was placed on a temporary assignment as a team member for logistics requirements at Granite City Depot to clarify and define the objectives for a new family of light observation helicopters—scout type, involving four major aircraft companies for their competition. This was an honor to work on this type of project as Logistics Specialist. Limited personnel get the opportunity to be selected to perform on this type of high priority program.

1. TYPE OF TRAVEL ORDERS

[X] TDY, UCMR PROPER STA. [ ] PCS (Civilian only) [ ] CONFIRMATORY ORDERS

2. NAME OF REQUESTING OFFICE	3. TELEPHONE EXT.	4. DATE
Dir of Maintenance, Tech Asst Div	2072/71	20 Feb 68

5. FIRST NAME - MIDDLE INITIAL - LAST NAME	GRADE	SERVICE NUMBER	ARM OR SERVICE (Military) POSITION OR TITLE (Civilian)	SECURITY CLEARANCE
WAYNE A. KUSCHEL	GS-12	DAC	Equip Spec	SECRET

6. ORGANIZATION AND STATION	9. ITINERARY [ ] CIPAP
USAAVCOM (MI-4021) St. Louis, Mo	WP from St. Louis, Mo to Ft Lee, Va and return to St. Louis, Mo

7. TO PROCEED O/A	8. APPROXIMATE NUMBER OF DAYS
10 Mar 68	42 Days

10. PURPOSE OF TEMPORARY DUTY
To Attend USAIMC Maint Mgmt Course 68-4

11. TRANSPORTATION AUTHORIZED
[ ] COMMON CARRIER; [ ] AIR [ ] SURFACE [ ] WATER [ ] AS DETERMINED BY TRANSPORTATION OFF. (Military only)
[ ] GOVERNMENT OWNED: [ ] VEHICLE [ ] AIRCRAFT [ ] VESSEL
[X] PRIVATELY-OWNED VEHICLE AT RATE OF_____ CENTS PER MILE [ ] TPA-TMDAG
[X] REIMBURSEMENT LIMITED TO COST TO GOVT OF TRAVEL BY USUAL MODE OF TRANSPORTATION, INCLUDING PER DIEM. (Civilian only)

12. PER DIEM AUTHORIZED (Civilian Personnel only)
[ ] MAXIMUM AUTHORIZED BY CPR T-3 [X] OTHER RATES OF PER DIEM (Specify)*See remarks

13. TRANSPORTATION OF DEPENDENTS (Civilian Personnel only)
[ ] EMPLOYEE REQUESTS TRANSPORTATION OF DEPENDENTS WHOSE NAME(S) AGE(S) AND RELATIONSHIP(S) APPEAR UNDER REMARKS
[ ] TRANSPORTATION AUTHORIZED BY GOVERNMENT [ ] VEHICLE [ ] AIRCRAFT [ ] VESSEL
[ ] TRANSPORTATION AUTHORIZED BY COMMON CARRIER (Commercial Air, Rail, Bus, Vessel)
[ ] TRANSPORTATION AUTHORIZED BY PRIVATELY-OWNED CONVEYANCE

14. SHIPMENT OF HOUSEHOLD GOODS (Civilian personnel only)
[ ] EMPLOYEE HAS DEPENDENTS AND IS AUTHORIZED MOVEMENT [ ] EMPLOYEE DOES NOT HAVE DEPENDENTS AND IS AUTHOR-
OF HOUSEHOLD GOODS NOT IN EXCESS OF 7000 POUNDS NET IZED MOVEMENT OF HOUSEHOLD GOODS NOT IN EXCESS
WEIGHT OF 2500 POUNDS NET WEIGHT

15. REMARKS (Use this space for special requirements, delay, authority for issuance, names of dependents, designation as courier, superior accommoda-
tions, excess baggage, etc.)
Reporting Time: NLT 2100 hours, 10 Mar 68. Class begins 0800 hours, 11 Mar 68.
Class ends 19 Apr 68. POV equipped with seat belts. Govt quarters available.
*Total expenditure for this travel claim will not exceed $511.50. SOURCE CIT NO 206
Advance of funds NTE $480.00 is auth. (Subj to reduction by paying office IAW JTR
Vol II para 8404).
TRAVELER IS DIRECTED THAT HE WILL COMPLY STRICTLY WITH THE PROVISIONS OF DOD DIR
5500.7 REGARDING ACCEPTANCE OF GRATUITIES IN ANY FORM.
Traveler must proceed within 8 days of WP date or the orders become invalid.
CDORD _____ Civ Pers Div, Pers and Trng

16. ADMINISTRATIVE APPROVAL	FOR USE OF APPROVING OFFICE ONLY
	18. AGENCY
HARRY J. DOLD, Acting Deputy Director	U. S. ARMY AVN MATERIEL COMMAND
Directorate of Maintenance (DMP)	19. ORDER NUMBER/REFERENCE
(Name, grade or title)	AMEAV 68-1261
17. FISCAL APPROVAL (Chargeable to)	20. DATE: 23 Feb 68
2182020 6A 7041 P2200-218-220	21. APPROVED. TRAVEL TO BE PERFORMED IS NECESSARY IN THE PUBLIC SERVICE. WP.
844-055 (2270.1210)	
	FOR THE COMMANDER:
NAME, GRADE OR TITLE	NAME, GRADE OR TITLE
	Barbara A. Kannels
	for WALTER J. TOBIN, CIV TO

DA FORM 662, 1 OCT 61   PREVIOUS EDITIONS ARE OBSOLETE.   5

7-1 Travel orders to Fort Lee, Virginia

United States Army
Logistics Management Center

Fort Lee, Virginia

This

Diploma

is awarded to

Mr. Wayne A. Kuschel

for successful completion of the

Maintenance Management Course

Given at Fort Lee, Virginia, this 19th day of April 1968

Donald L Cooper Jr.

WL Tate

7-2 Copy of my diploma

OFFICE OF THE COMMANDING GENERAL
U.S. ARMY AVIATION MATERIEL COMMAND
12TH AND SPRUCE STREETS
ST. LOUIS, MISSOURI

MAILING ADDRESS
P.O. BOX 209, MAIN OFFICE
ST. LOUIS, MISSOURI 63166

AMSAV-G(F)   12 March 1968

Mr. Wayne A. Kuschel
Technical Assistance Division
Directorate of Maintenance

Dear Mr. Kuschel:

    The efforts and contributions you and other DAC Equipment
Specialists have made to ensure the success of our technical assistance program have been outstanding. I have received many letters of
commendation and appreciation attesting that supported units are
pleased with the services being provided by the AVCOM Equipment
Specialists.

    In your demanding assignment, I must rely on you to exercise
tact, sound professional judgment and a sense of urgency. We here at
AVCOM can assist you in another quality you must exercise; timely
dissemination of information.

    To aid you in providing assistance, I have directed the entire
command to make available any reasonable service which will accelerate
or improve your support to commanders. In return, I ask that your
reports be sufficiently detailed, clear and comprehensive to permit
reply without having to ask for further clarification. Remarks,
discussions and recommendations should be included so that a better
evaluation and timely response can be made by the appropriate AVCOM
elements. Your information is given two major considerations; first,
solve the immediate problem; second, long-term corrective action.
Factual accuracy is the key.

    I appreciate the fine job you have done and assure you of my
full support in accomplishing the mission at hand. Let's agree that
we still have room for improvement.

                                Sincerely,

                                JOHN NORTON
                                Major General, USA
                                Commanding

7-3 General Norton's letter

7-4
Brigadier General Traylor Presented my award

DEPARTMENT OF THE ARMY

WAYNE A. KUSCHEL

IS OFFICIALLY COMMENDED

FOR

AN OUTSTANDING PERFORMANCE AWARD FOR THE PERIOD 6 AUGUST 1967 THROUGH 5 AUGUST 1968. DURING THIS PERIOD, MR. KUSCHEL HAS DISTINGUISHED HIMSELF BY PROVIDING THE UTMOST IN TECHNICAL ADVICE AND TRAINING TO THE USERS OF ARMY AIRCRAFT, WHILE SERVING IN THE REPUBLIC OF VIETNAM AND CONUS ASSIGNMENTS. HE IS A CONSCIENTIOUS INDIVIDUAL AND VOLUNTARILY ASSISTS ANYONE PRESENTING A PROBLEM, TECHNICAL OR OTHERWISE. HIS LOYALTY, DEVOTION TO DUTY, HONESTY AND PERSONAL HABITS ARE ABOVE REPROACH. MR. KUSCHEL IS A DISTINCT ASSET TO THE U.S. ARMY AVIATION SYSTEMS COMMAND AND THE FEDERAL SERVICE.

29 MARCH 1969

JOHN P. TRAYLOR, BRIGADIER GENERAL, USA
DEPUTY COMMANDING GENERAL
U.S. ARMY AVIATION SYSTEMS COMMAND

DA FORM 2445, 1 JUN 61

7-5 Presented to me by Brigadier General Traylor

DEPARTMENT OF THE ARMY
US ARMY AVIATION SYSTEMS COMMAND
PO BOX 209, ST. LOUIS, MO 63166

AMSAV-L-ATS   7 April 1969

SUBJECT: Outstanding Performance Award

Mr. Wayne A. Kuschel
Field Assistance Directorate
Technical Assistance Division

1. We congratulate you upon receipt of this outstanding performance award. Your performance in such an energetic, enthusiastic and professional manner as reflected by this award is to be commended.

2. We urge you to maintain the high standards you have established and apply them in your future assignments. The Army needs men possessing your qualifications and abilities and by applying yourself as you have demonstrated, you are making a significant contribution to the successful accomplishment of our field assistance mission.

3. A copy of this letter will be placed in your Official Personnel Folder.

4. You will be advised later of the date and time of presentation.

FOR THE COMMANDER:

1 Incl   ROBERT L. MC CARTHY, Act Asst Chief
Outstanding Performance Award   Technical Assistance Division

7-5 Page 2

EMPLOYEE PERFORMANCE RATING

(Civilian Personnel Regulation 400, Chapter 430.C) Emp No. 39011

1. NAME (Caps) LAST - FIRST - MIDDLE	MR. - MISS - MRS.	2. POSITION TITLE, NUMBER AND GRADE
KUSCHEL, WAYNE A.	MR.	GS-1670-12 Equipment Specialist (Aircraft Propulsion Equipment) JN 9202

3. NAME AND LOCATION OF EMPLOYING OFFICE

U. S. Army Aviation Materiel Command, Directorate of Maintenance, Technical Assistance Division, Technical Support Branch, Field Section St. Louis, Missouri

4. RATING PERIOD	FROM	TO
[A] OFFICIAL PERFORMANCE RATING	08-06-67	08-05-68
[ ] PROBATIONARY OR TRIAL PERIOD RATING		

The above named employee and the immediate supervisor have discussed the performance of the former during the rating period shown. The discussion included consideration of any major strengths and deficiencies in the employee's performance, and actions which both supervisor and employee can take to improve such performance, including training, self-development, and on-the-job assistance.

Any deficiencies which are the basis for adverse action, including action to withhold a step increase or to give an unsatisfactory rating, are described in detail on the reverse of this form or on attached sheets.

THE ADJECTIVE RATING RECOMMENDED FOR THE PERIOD IS:

[XX] OUTSTANDING   [ ] SATISFACTORY   [ ] UNSATISFACTORY 1/

SUPERVISOR'S SIGNATURE	DATE
John P. Morris	31 Oct 68

EMPLOYEE'S SIGNATURE 2/

Wayne A. Kuschel

THE OFFICIAL RATING ASSIGNED FOR THE PERIOD IS 3/:

[X] OUTSTANDING   [ ] SATISFACTORY   [ ] UNSATISFACTORY

APPROVING OFFICIAL'S SIGNATURE 3/	DATE
JOHN P. TRAYLOR, BRIG GEN, USA, DEP COM GEN	29 Mar 69

FOOTNOTES:

1/ Unsatisfactory rating requires a prior 90-day warning as discussed in CPR 400, Chapter 430.C.

2/ Employee's signature on the form indicates only that the evaluation discussion has taken place, and that he or she is aware of the rating recommended. It does not constitute agreement with the rating. Employees have the right to have ratings reviewed under procedures described in CPR 400, Chapter 430.C.

3/ An Outstanding rating requires justification, review by local Incentive Awards Committee, and approval by the Commanding Officer. An Unsatisfactory rating must be reviewed by the Civilian Personnel Officer for regulatory compliance prior to approval. A Satisfactory rating requires approval by the supervisor of the recommending supervisor.

4/ When a copy of this form, signed by approving official, is given to the rated employee it constitutes official notification of the performance rating for the period shown.

DA FORM 1052 JAN 57   PREVIOUS EDITIONS OF THIS FORM ARE OBSOLETE.

EMPLOYEE'S COPY 1

7-5 page 3

TASKS	PERFORMANCE STANDARDS	ACTUAL PERFORMANCE
1. Provides technical advice and assistance.	a. Ascertains and resolves maintenance and supply problems in the field. Must provide effective results 90% of the time.	During this reporting period, Mr. Kuschel was the Technical Assistance Division's propulsion specialist within USAAVSCOM and RVN. He has directed and assisted in resolving maintenance and supply problems presented by USAAVSCOM technical assistance personnel located with Army field and support units. Through his own knowledge, experience and judgment, his determination and resolutions have been correct 97% of the time. Through observation and review of direct and written communications, he has recommended many maintenance and operational changes to procedures which when followed by field personnel, were instrumental in raising the operational readiness posture of the units using his supported equipment. Through his knowledge of field problems, he has recommended product changes and improvements which have aided in raising the effective support furnished by aviation technical assistance personnel. He flew numerous test flights as an observer in RVN to evaluate and determine corrective action required to expedite restoring aircraft to an operational ready status. He has been correct in his determination and corrections of flight problems involving propulsion equipment 100% of the time.
	b. Observes operations in the field and investigates malfunctions of aircraft systems equipment.	
	c. Assists commanders in averting breakdown or deadline of equipment.	
	d. Advises, assists and instructs in accomplishing maintenance, adjustment, repair, servicing, testing, processing, packaging, preservation, assembly, in-house maintenance and modification of aircraft and related accessoreis of his assigned type of aeronautical equipment.	
	e. Inspects and furnishes analysis of aircraft damage and recommends repair methods, repair levels, or aircraft salvage. Findings and recommendations must be correct and adopted 90% of the time.	
	f. Recommends product changes and modifications and prepares and submits to AVSCOM, in a timely manner, all unresolved problems for resolution. Must maintain 85% effectivity and efficiency.	

7-5 page 4

TASKS

2. Provides technical instruction.

PERFORMANCE STANDARDS

g. Makes occasional flights as technical observer to determine causes of aircraft malfunction, improper flight control rigging, improper weight and balance, etc. Must be correct 95% of the time.

a. Instructs Military and civilian maintenance personnel on the job by demonstration or overseeing troops or utilizes formal classroom type facilities and instruction material.

b. Develops own POIs, researches and assembles information for classroom training purposes.

c. Instructs field personnel to assure that proper methods techniques, tools, publications, manuals, preventative maintenance procedures, production control and quality control maintenance directives, etc., are employed.

d. Assembles and prepares on request of installation commanders or upon direction of higher authority, or as a result of observation in the field, a wide variety of information from TB AVNs, ARs,

ACTUAL PERFORMANCE

Mr. Kuschel demonstrated his technical and educational ability when he was assigned as a T-55 AAMTAP instructor. With a minimum training period, he was qualified as a T-53-L11/L13 instructor and assigned the responsibility of team coordinator. Through his own initiative, he prepared and conducted formal training classes on all systems of the gas turbine engine. His classes contributed directly to the maintenance effectiveness of the attendees. Not only did he instruct in proper maintenance procedures but he rendered invaluable assistance in areas of technical supplies. Mr. Kuschel always strived to improve his method of instructing abilities, by incorporating new maintenance and instructional techniques which resulted in maximum retention by each student. He demonstrated the use of engine special tools used in conjunction with technical manuals or publications, in addition, always rendered invaluable assistance in

2

7-5 Page 5

249

TASKS

PERFORMANCE STANDARDS

SRs, etc., utilizing practical experience ingenuity and know-how. Distributes or processes assembled information or data as directed by local authority.

ACTUAL PERFORMANCE

all areas concerned with technical, supply, safety and operational procedures. Mr. Kuschel is constantly researching all available in-house resources for new ideas and necessary information in which he can develop, prepare POI for the Army Aviation Mobile Technical Assistance Program (AAMTAP). His guidance in the implementation of this valuable training aid has improved the abilities of the T-53 propulsion instructors, whereby, the overall efficiency of the mechanic skill level was increased, enabling the using organization to derive, the final benefit in aircraft availability. Mr. Kuschel prepared a student hand out booklet for AAMTAP training which incorporated the tear-down and assembly of the hot end on T-53-L13 engines. It was recognized that the inexperienced individual in the units engine shop required more guidance because of this new type engine. There were approximately 35 special tools required and a set sequence to utilize these tools, otherwise damage to the engine would take place. One T-53 instructor had Vu-graphs made from his handbook and instructs all facets of the tear-down and assembly of the engine.

3

TASKS	PERFORMANCE STANDARDS	ACTUAL PERFORMANCE
3. Organizes and conducts conferences and meetings.	a. Is considered to be an above average speaker and presents material in a clear cut pattern so as to communicate ideas to his audience or other conferees. b. Dresses with proper decorum in order to present a good appearance to his audience and to bring credit to the Command. c. Prepares conference agendas, arranges for guest speakers and chairs the conference when required or when situation warrants services as toastmaster.	Mr. Kuschel is well abreast and conversant on maintenance topics, he plans well in advance and presents his material in a logical and well organized manner. The sincerity and enthusiasm that he displays contribute greatly to his effectiveness. His overall appearance and dress at all functions are of the highest standards and contribute to the effectiveness of his presentation. He has prepared and coordinated the necessary administrative requirements for personnel visiting his duty station. His knowledge of protocol procedures assists in the preparation for these visits and of conducting them.
4. Keeps abreast of new developments and informed on latest maintenance techniques, policies and procedures.	a. Is a technical expert and advisor on assigned aircraft or aviation equipment. Must provide effective results 90% of the time. b. Has working knowledge of all regulations pertaining to maintenance and supply of assigned aeronautical equipment. c. Is familiar with the latest developments, regulations and ideas, operational and mechanical problem areas, and criteria requiring extensive knowledge of peculiar maintenance requirements, design changes and construction of his assigned type of aeronautical equipment.	On all systems that Mr. Kuschel supports, his management and technical direction has proven effective and correct 95% of the time. His knowledge of regulations pertaining to maintenance and supply on assigned propulsion equipment is to be commended. He continually strives to increase proficiency in this area. Assigned maintenance specialists continually call on him for information pertaining propulsion related regulations. The fact that personnel continue to do this is evidence that his background and knowledge are extensive and a valuable asset and is to be commended for his continued efforts. His knowledge of Army and Command organizational channels assists in the prompt and efficient dispatch of all maintenance and related technical items.

4

7-5 Page 7

TASKS | PERFORMANCE STANDARDS | ACTUAL PERFORMANCE

TASKS

5. Conducts scheduled and non-scheduled visits.

PERFORMANCE STANDARDS

d. Must be knowledgeable of Command Army organizational channels.

e. Maintains close liaison with US Air Force, US Navy, manufacturers and other activities operating similar equipments.

f. Makes periodic trips to manufacturers or training agencies to maintain current knowledge and to keep abreast of design and production changes which may have an effect on field level maintenance and logistical support.

a. Visits aeronautical maintenance activities, as required, on a scheduled or non-scheduled basis.

b. Completes arrangements for visits, secures approval of authority for visits. Travel will be made by commercial or military aircraft as directed by superiors or authority.

ACTUAL PERFORMANCE

Although his base of operation was firmly established, his visits to aircraft maintenance activities, in his area, has added greatly to the effectiveness of their operation. He resolves many potential problems on these scheduled or unscheduled visits. On trips to various operations, in his area of support, he displayed initiative by arranging the necessary transportation requirements associated with the visits. He maintains a passport with certain visas and current international vaccination on record and stays abreast of changes in diplomatic personnel, in his area, in order to better satisfy any emergency travel requirements.

5

7-5 Page 8

6. Prepares reports.

a. Submits activity reports at predetermined intervals, (normally every 30 days) to USAAVSCOM Technical Assistance Program Manager.

b. Reports will indicate clearly and factually the nature of tasks accomplished, troubles encountered, corrective measures taken or adapted, recommendations made and to whom made, and any other pertinent information related to general adequacy of maintenance, facilities, parts, supply, tools and publications. Reports must reflect 90% clarity, detail and completeness.

c. Problems or information furnished in reports should not be general in nature. Information must contain sufficient detail to enable USAAVSCOM action and/or resolution.

d. Reports should be submitted in accordance with AR 700-4 in a clear and concise manner.

e. Reports will be submitted through established channels to USAAVSCOM.

Mr. Kuschel is constantly reviewing and researching reports from field technicians and engineering personnel, which he analyzes for problems in the supply, maintenance and technical area. He is able to ascertain what is required without difficulty and gather all facts pertaining to the problem or request before he takes required action. In preparing status reports on technical matters, trends, task accomplished or replies to correspondence, he is able to indicate clearly and functionally what the problem is and corrective measure to be taken or adopted. All his reports or correspondence reflect 100% clarity, factual and completeness. He always uses established channels and insures that all effective personnel and elements are informed of problem and action taken or required. He also makes timely follow-ups to insure problems are resolved.

6

7-5 Page 9

253

TASKS

7. Works for program and group results.

PERFORMANCE STANDARDS

a. Contributes to good morale to the extent that no official and no more than two unofficial reprimands, (either written or verbal), are received from any source during a 12 month rating period for failure to observe any of the elements which constitute the employee's individual responsibilities.

b. Cooperates with superiors by willingly accepting assignments and instructions relating to areas of assigned responsibilities.

c. Cooperates with co-workers by treating them in a courteous manner and freely exchanging information toward improved efficiency and success of overall program.

d. Is industrious, volunteers services when scheduled work is completed.

e. Demonstrates dependability by unquestionable use of sick and annual leave.

f. Carefully observes all post and official rules and regulations.

ACTUAL PERFORMANCE

Mr. Kuschel has excelled in all areas and did not receive any official or un-official reprimands during this rating period. He has never abused his sick leave and plans his annual leave to fit in with his workload. In all manner, his work and personal conduct are beyond reproach. He is always willing to accept responsibility and tasks which are assigned to him and many times has volunteered to assist other personnel. His loyalty to the Army and this Command is commendable, always shows courtesy, politness, respect for authority and other workers and is willing to accetp con-structive criticism.

7

7-5 Page 10

TASKS	PERFORMANCE STANDARDS	ACTUAL PERFORMANCE

PERFORMANCE STANDARDS

g. During emergencies, works whatever hours or under whatever conditions are necessary to assist supported units in obtaining maximum readiness posture.

h. Demonstrates loyalty to the organization (Command and program), shows common courtesy and politeness and proper respect for authority, causes no dissension among fellow employees and accepts constructive criticism readily.

i. Readily accepts cross-training to new aircraft or aviation equipment in accordance with program requirements. Accepts necessary assignment changes with little or no difficulty or dissension.

8

7-5 Page 11

255

SUPERVISORY CONTROLS

Work is performed in an assigned area overseas or within CONUS under the general direction and administrative supervision of a supervisor located in St. Louis, Missouri. Detached duty station results in incumbent's receiving broad policy guidance outlines on objectives to be accomplished at time of assignment. Has full responsibility for work activities while on assignments and has wide latitude in exercising independent judgment in the interpretation and implementation of applicable maintenance policies and procedures. Adequacy of performance is judged through analysis of written reports, oral reports, and personal visitation.

MAJOR DUTIES

As a representative of the command with duty station located overseas or within CONUS, incumbent serves as a topmost technical expert and advisor in the maintenance of a specific series of reciprocating or turbine propulsion equipment used in the make-up of Army aircraft. As such, he furnishes expert and specialized advice, assistance, and instructions to Department of the Army personnel in maintenance, adjustment, repair, servicing, testing, processing, packaging, preservation, assembly, in-storage maintenance, and modification of his assigned aircraft propulsion equipment.

1. Maintains continuing contact with the command and close liaison with the U. S. Air Force, the U. S. Navy, and aircraft manufacturers to assure constant cognizance of the latest maintenance engineering data, such as engineering change proposals, blueprint changes, microfilm, factory bulletins, and other data pertinent to his assigned type of aircraft propulsion equipment. Develops and submits proposed changes to DA maintenance publication, maintenance procedures, and practices. Investigates, analyzes, and corrects diverse and complicated operational and mechanical problems requiring intensive knowledge covering maintenance and construction of his

7-5 Page 12

assigned type of Army aircraft propulsion equipment. Investigates deficiencies for the purpose of establishing areas that should be reported for equipment improvement. Makes occasional flights as technical observer to determine causes of malfunctions, such as improper fuel adjustment or flow, improper ignition system operation, origin of unusual noises, unusual vibrations, improper valve train adjustment or functioning, abnormal rpm indications, etc.

2. Researches and assembles information for classroom training purposes and based on practical experience and ingenuity, conducts classes (including lectures and demonstrations) for maintenance and operational (military and civil service) personnel in the maintenance and operation of assigned type of aircraft propulsion equipment. Further, effects training required by instructing all Department of the Army personnel or by training of maintenance personnel and overseeing their subsequent training of other troops. Conducts on-the-job training by demonstration and/or overseeing troops conducting maintenance at actual site to insure proper methods and techniques are used. Slants training toward preventive maintenance to avert engine breakdown and deadline of equipment. Also, assembles and prepares on request of installation commanders, direction from higher authority, or observation in the field, a wide variety of information from technical and administrative publications (including TO's, TM's SB's, TAB's, AR's, SR's, etc.).

3. Represents the command at Army supply and maintenance conferences National Guard conferences, and other top level meetings and conferences to discuss maintenance and operating procedures and is empowered to make commitments which obligate the command to a course of action. Renders technical advice and assistance to accident investigation boards in determining cause or probable cause of accidents, corrective and/or preventive action to be taken, and recommends applicable product changes and modifications. As required, inspects and furnishes analysis of engine damage and recommends repair methods, repair levels, and/or engine salvage. Makes periodic trips to manufacturers or training agencies to maintain current knowledge of assigned propulsion equipment and to keep abreast of the latest maintenance and operating procedures.

4. Prepares and submits written reports at predetermined intervals to the command, indicating clearly and factually the nature of tasks accomplished, trouble encountered, corrective measures taken or adopted, recommendations made and to whom made, and any other pertinent information related to the general adequacy of maintenance facilities, parts supply, tools, and publications.

Performs other duties as assigned.

NOTE: Travel for TDY will be made by commercial or military aircraft as directed by superiors. Involves temporary assignments requiring world-wide travel.

(Title and grade are established in accordance with position classification standards and guides referenced in Item 3. These referenced materials are available for your review in the Civilian Personnel Office.)

7-5 Page 13

THE
UNITED
STATES
OF
AMERICA
AWARDS

WAYNE KUSCHEL

THE MEDAL
FOR CIVILIAN SERVICE
IN VIETNAM

Washington, D. C.   Stanley R. Resor
                                 Secretary of the Ar

7-6

7-6 page 2

DESCRIPTION AND SYMBOLISM OF
THE SERVICE IN VIETNAM AWARD

OBVERSE
******
DESCRIPTION

On a disc 1 3/8 inches in diameter a dragon with its head to the left
and tail in an s-shaped loop to the right encircling the handle of a
flaming torch placed diagonally across the center from lower right to
upper left circumscribed with the words "Vietnam" above the "Service"
below in raised letters.

SYMBOLISM

The dragon, a symbol of many beneficent forms in Vietnam, is used in
conjunction with a flaming torch of liberty indicating our country's
aim to help maintain the cause of freedom among liberty loving peoples
of the world.

7-7

REVERSE
****
DESCRIPTION

On a disc 1 3/8 inches in diameter the shield from the United States
coat of arms flanked by two branches of olive bearing altogether
thirteen leaves and thirteen olives and enclosed by a circular inscription
containing the words "Government of the United States."

SYMBOLISM

The shield at center expresses the authority of the United States. The
olive branches symbolize our country's aim of world peace.

RIBBONS

The blue in the ribbon design alludes to the United States Government
and yellow and red are from the flag of the Republic of Vietnam.

This medal for Civilian Service in Vietnam has been awarded to and
will be presented to the following individuals at the appropriate times:

Edward Blalock   Orval Bennett
Roger Little   Wilford Cashwell
A. Robert Shaak   Joseph Kerekes
Clyde Davis   Jack Hayes
Charles Willis   Orville Gandee
Charles Gerau   Kenneth Warren
Forrest Hall   Willard Warren
Preston Russell   Wayne Kuschel
Charles Grimes   Charles Reed
Arthur Green
Raymond Pettigrew
George Barnes
Finis Melton
Wayne Goins
Glenn Perry
Arthur Magnuson
William Watlington
John Duggan
Lyman Wilmore
John Duffy
Charles Snipes

NOTE: The requirement for the above medal is to have spent 365 days in
RVN. If you feel that you are eligible for this medal, you are not on
this list and have not received this medal, please notify us at AMSAV-L-
ATS, ATTN: Mr. Charles Cox.

7-7 page 2

261

AMSAV-L-A (21 Mar 69) 3d Ind
SUBJECT: Letter of Appreciation

Headquarters, US Army Aviation Systems Command, P. O. Box 209,
St. Louis, Missouri 63166, 1 July 1969

TO: Mr. Wayne Kuschel, Field Assistance Directorate, Technical
Assistance Division

1. It is indeed a privilege and pleasure to forward the inclosed
correspondence. My hearty congratulations are extended to you upon
recognition of your outstanding performance during the visit of
representatives from Thailand.

2. The manner in which briefings were conducted and the interest in
the Field Assistance Program displayed by you while in contact with
the Thai Officers are indicative of your vast knowledge of the overall
mission responsibility of this Command and sincerity in improving
materiel readiness worldwide.

3. A copy of this correspondence will be placed in your Official
Personnel Folder.

1 Incl
nc

VAUGHN C. EMERSON
LTC, GS
Director of Field Assistance

4

7-8 Letter of appreciation Thailand Briefing

AMSAV-CL(GCS) (21 Mar 69) 2d Ind
SUBJECT: Letter of Appreciation

Headquarters, US Army Aviation Systems Command, P. O. Box 209,
St. Louis, Missouri 63166

2 5 JUN 1969

THRU: Director of Field Assistance

TO: Mr. Wayne Kuschel, Field Assistance Directorate

1. It gives me great pleasure to add my congratulations for your successful reception and briefing of the officers from Thailand.

2. Your accomplishment reflects the high standards you possess and demonstrates an awareness of the importance for mutual trust between free-world service members. I encourage you to continue to display the professionalism that makes you an important member of the AVSCOM team.

3. A copy of this correspondence will be placed in your Official Personnel Folder.

1 Incl
nc

ROBERT J. DILLARD
Colonel, TC
Deputy Commander for
Logistics Support

3

7-8 page 2

AMSAV-G (21 Mar 69)   1st Ind
SUBJECT: Letter of Appreciation

Headquarters, US Army Aviation Systems Command, P. O. Box 209, St. Louis, Missouri 63166 2 JUN 1969

THRU: Deputy Commander for Logistics Support

        Director, Field Assistance

TO: Mr. Wayne Kuschel, Field Assistance Directorate

1. The attached letters from Major General McCown and General Chesarek are forwarded with my sincere appreciation for your contributions to the successful reception and briefing of the officers from Thailand.

2. You were largely responsible for the cordial and accommodating atmosphere which prevailed during the visit of these officers - assuring them that they were welcome in our Command. The type of attention and consideration you displayed is necessary to maintain the rapport and feeling of mutual trust between our country and the countries of the world. Congratulations for a job well done!

3. A copy of this correspondence will be placed in your Official Personnel Folder.

1 Incl
nc
                              JOHN NORTON
                              Major General, USA
                              Commanding

2

7-8 page 3

264

DEPARTMENT OF THE ARMY
HEADQUARTERS UNITED STATES ARMY MATERIEL COMMAND
WASHINGTON, D.C. 20315

IN REPLY REFER TO

AMCPT-MS

21 MAR 1969

SUBJECT: Letter of Appreciation

Major General John Norton
Commanding General
US Army Aviation Systems Command
Post Office Box 209
St. Louis, Missouri 63166

1. It is indeed a pleasure to forward the attached letter from the Commander, US Military Assistance Command, Thailand and Joint US Military Advisory Group, Thailand.

2. Major General McCown's letter speaks for itself and I congratulate you, Brigadier General John P. Traylor and all other members of your staff responsible for the service which merited this recognition. The outstanding manner in which the visitors were welcomed to your command, and the informative briefings provided them during their visit, reflects great credit upon each of you and this Command.

3. Copies of this correspondence have been forwarded to the Department of the Army for inclusion in your official personnel records. Request you assure that copies of the complete correspondence are made a matter of record in the official files of General Traylor and all other individuals directly concerned.

1 Incl
as

F. J. CHESAREK
General, United States Army
Commanding

7-8 page 4

265

MACTJ4

27 FEB 1969

General F.S. Besson, Jr
Commanding General
United States Army Materiel Command
Washington, DC 20315

Dear General Besson:

We have recently had two groups of officers from Thailand complete
an extensive tour of logistics facilities in the United States, Japan,
Korea and Taiwan. Vice Admiral Jit Sanghkadul, Director of Joint
Logistics, Supreme Command Headquarters the senior member, was
interested in observing all aspects of logistics and learning as much
as possible during the time available. He was accompanied by four
members of his staff and my personal representative, LTC James B.
Woodruff who serves as the MACTHAI Logistics Advisor/Liaison
Officer. A second group of five Thai officers also visited organiza-
tions to obtain specific information for use in the Helicopter Single
Manager Program.

It is very clear from my discussions with Admiral Jit and as indicated by the actions which are currently being undertaken that this
was a most informative and successful jointly funded project. The
benefits should far exceed the cost. I therefore feel it has been a
sound investment which will contribute to the systematic development and increasing self-sufficiency of Thailand as a Free World
Force. The primary reason for this success has been the special
attention and sincere interest shown by your key personnel. I wish
to acknowledge those individuals.

First of all I wish to recognize Major General John Norton of your
United States Army Aviation Systems Command, Brigadier General
Traylor, his deputy and staff. They provided a warm and cordial

7-8 page 5

MACTJ4   27 FEB 1969
General Besson

reception for both groups on their first official visit in the United
States. Each briefing was tailored to provide specific information
which was needed and applicable to Thailand.

Colonel S. M. Burney, Commander of Anniston Depot and his staff
were visited to obtain information on repair and overhaul of ordnance,
equipment. During their stay in Anniston, arrangements had been
made to visit the residence of Mr. Charles Berman to see his extensive collection of firearms and other weapons which proved to be
unusual and informative. Colonel Burney's cordial reception, comprehensive tour and briefings greatly improved Admiral Jit's understanding of the materiel and manpower resources needed to operate
such a facility.

I wish to commend each of the officers and their staff along with
Major General Woolwine and Major General Schlitz of your staff for
their support, sincere interest and cooperation. Admiral Jit was
very favorable impressed by these officers and your management
system. As a result I expect him to diligently work to improve their
logistics system and increase the capability of their personnel. This
in turn greatly facilitates our mission accomplishment and enhances
the Free World's security. Thank you for this fine and needed assistance.

                         Sincerely,

                         Hal D. McCown

                         HAL D. McCOWN
                         Major General, USA
                         Commander

2

7-8 page 6

| STANDARD FORM 50 Rev. Dec. 1961 U.S. CIVIL SERVICE COMMISSION FPM Ch. 295 | Approved Exception | **NOTIFICATION OF PERSONNEL ACTION** (EMPLOYEE - See General Information on Reverse) | jj (PM) L-SF-6-131-69 |

(FOR AGENCY USE)

1. NAME (CAPS) LAST – FIRST – MIDDLE	MR. – MISS – MRS.	2. (FOR AGENCY USE)	3. BIRTH DATE (Mo., Day, Year)	4. SOCIAL SECURITY NO.
KUSCHEL, WAYNE A.	MR.	39011	12-06-23	

5. VETERAN PREFERENCE 2	1. – NO 3. – 10 PT. DISAB. 5. – 10 PT. OTHER 2. – 5 PT. 4. – 10 PT. COMP.	6. TENURE GROUP 1	7. SERVICE COMP. DATE 02-01-56	
9. FEGLI 1	1. – COVERED (reg. only-declined opt.) 3. – WAIVED 2. – INELIGIBLE 4. – COVERED (reg. and opt.)	10. RETIREMENT 1 1. – CS 4. – NONE 5. – OTHER 2. – FICA 3. – FS		11. (FOR CSC USE)

12. NATURE OF ACTION 702		13. EFFECTIVE DATE (Mo., Day, Year)	14. CIVIL SERVICE OR OTHER LEGAL AUTHORITY
CODE Promotion		06-29-69	Reg. 335.102

15. FROM: POSITION TITLE AND NUMBER	16. PAY PLAN AND OCCUPATION CODE	17. (a) GRADE (b) STEP OR OR LEVEL RATE	18. SALARY
Equipment Specialist (Aircraft Propulsion Equipment) JN 9202	GS-1670	12 03	pa $12,986

19. NAME AND LOCATION OF EMPLOYING OFFICE
US Army Aviation Systems Command, Logistics Support Activity, Field Assistance Directorate, Technical Assistance Division, Conus Branch, St. Louis, Missouri

20. TO: POSITION TITLE AND NUMBER	21. PAY PLAN AND OCCUPATION CODE	22. (a) GRADE (b) STEP OR OR LEVEL RATE	23. SALARY
Systems Management Specialist JN 10,924	GS-0301	13 01	pa $14,409

24. NAME AND LOCATION OF EMPLOYING OFFICE
US Army Aviation Systems Command, Logistics Support Activity, Systems Introduction Directorate, Future Weapon Systems Division, St. Louis, Missouri

25. DUTY STATION (City–State)	26. LOCATION CODE
St. Louis, Missouri	24-7080-510

27. APPROPRIATION	28. POSITION OCCUPIED 1 – COMPETITIVE SERVICE 2 – EXCEPTED SERVICE	29. (FROM)	APPORTIONED POSITION (TO) STATE
23L0.10211.A011SE	1		1 – PROVED 2 – WAIVED

30. REMARKS
☐ A. SUBJECT TO COMPLETION OF 1   YEAR PROBATIONARY (OR TRIAL) PERIOD COMMENCING _____
☐ B. SERVICE COUNTING TOWARD CAREER (OR PERM) TENURE FROM _____
SEPARATIONS: SHOW REASONS BELOW, AS REQUIRED. CHECK IF APPLICABLE ☐ C. DURING PROBATION

Selected from AVSCOM Merit Promotion Program Job Opportunity Number 35-69 S-1, dated 16 June 1969.

31. DATE OF APPOINTMENT AFFIDAVIT (Accessions only)	34. SIGNATURE (Or other authentication) AND TITLE FOR THE APPOINTING OFFICER
32. OFFICE MAINTAINING PERSONNEL FOLDER (If different from employing office)	M. DITTMAN,
33. CODE 19 EMPLOYING DEPARTMENT OR AGENCY AR 00 DEPARTMENT OF THE ARMY	Chief, Civilian Personnel Division
	35. DATE 06-27-69 2298

6 PART
50-131-13

1. EMPLOYEE COPY

7-9 Copy of SIMO Promotion GS—301-13

3. CITATION TO APPLICABLE STANDARD AND ITS DATE OF ISSUANCE	4. TITLE Systems Management Specialist		
	5. PAY SCHEDULE GS	6. OCC. CODE 301	7. GRADE 13
8. EVALUATION APPROVAL Title, pay schedule, code and grade of this job have been fixed in accordance with Department of the Army official policy and grade level standards.	SIGNATURE *Anton Imhof Jr.* ANTON IMHOF, JR.		DATE 3 Feb 69

9. SUPERVISORY CONTROLS, DUTIES, AND WORKING CONDITIONS *(Indicate percent of time for each duty, where pertinent.) (Continue statement of duties, etc., on reverse side if necessary.)*

SUPERVISORY CONTROLS

Works under general administrative and program direction of the division chief who issues policy guidance and provides broad outlines of goals to be achieved, indicating areas for particular attention, and techniques to be applied. Refers to superior questions of a policy nature, those of a precedent-setting nature and those considered to be controversial. Works independently in planning, organizing and executing activities. Work is reviewed for compliance with policies and the degree of success in mission accomplishment attained.

MAJOR DUTIES

Serves as a systems manager within a future weapons systems management office with responsibility for insuring the integration of life-cycle management of one or more selected highly complex Army aircraft systems. As an off-line manager and control point for assigned system(s) is delegated the authority and responsibility for assuring that all necessary life-cycel plans and actions, (research, development, contract definition, production, logistical support plans, material planning studies, etc.) are undertaken in an effort to (a) insure timely availability of equipment to the Army's inventory and (b) to insure that issuances and support requirements will be available in a proper time frame to accomplish the Army's mission for field support of assigned system(s). As the Systems Manager, keeps subject matter specialists advised of program requirements and directs and monitors their actions to insure that all actions are accomplished in a timely manner to meet program objectives. Incumbent must possess a comprehensive knowledge of aircraft systems, the interfunctional Command relationships, together with extensive managerial ability, initiative, tact, and diplomacy in order to attain program objectives within allocated funds and time periods required.

1. Is charged with responsibility for coordinating, monitoring and insuring the integration of all actions necessary to provide overall management for system(s) for the purpose of maintaining a well-balanced program to accomplish stated objectives.

10. JOB CONTENT APPROVAL *(Complete on organization file copy only.)*		
ORGANIZATION LOCATION		
THIS STATEMENT ACCURATELY DESCRIBES THE WORK REQUIRED IN ONE POSITION OR IN EACH OF A GROUP OF POSITIONS IN THE ABOVE ORGANIZATION.	THE ABOVE DESCRIPTION, WITH SUPPLEMENTAL MATERIAL, IS ADEQUATE FOR PURPOSES OF EVALUATION.	
SIGNATURE OF APPROVING SUPERVISOR *B. Stein* 2/13/69	SIGNATURE OF ANALYST *Martha Gayfield*	
11.	REAUDIT APPROVAL	
DATE		
SUPERVISOR'S APPROVAL		
ANALYST'S SIGNATURE		

DA FORM 374 (1 JUN 61)   PREVIOUS EDITIONS OF THIS FORM ARE OBSOLETE.

7-9 page 2

Insures effective and full accomplishment in all functional areas which are directed or assigned responsibility of AVSCOM. System management efforts are directed to systems requiring attention based on the following typical criteria: Programs managed are highly complex; involve continuous management control problems, many of which are controversial; have high military priority to meet a serious deficiency; have a significant impact on the economic stablization responsibilities of the Command and involve major and continuous planning and coordination throughout all phases.

2. Reviews programming documents received from Project Managers and/or higher echelons to determine effect on assigned programs. Through analysis and evaluation of current programs, budgets, state-of-the-art, etc., formulates changes to plans, programs, resources and related matters to assure effective balances and full accomplishment of objectives. Is responsible for development and implementation of system management policies and procedures and for managerial direction of delegated activities. Is held responsible for the analysis, evaluation, and implementation of AMC's program as it affects assigned systems from a systems management standpoint. Recommends changes in programming to Project Manager and/or high headquarters. As the controlling point, reviews and determines feasibility of proposed changes to determine impact upon assigned system(s) as well as possible effect on other areas. Provides staff supervision over projects which involve coordination and/or assistance from functional organizational elements, field activities, other government agencies, contractors, and other commodity commands.

3. Reviews significant actions and phasing data to ascertain progress of mission accomplishment and to identify milestones. Insures the conduct of periodic system management and functional review and analysis with operating functional elements, field agencies, and other commodity commands to determine program status, insure orderly and efficient support of system(s) and to detect before-the-fact potential slippage and problem areas. Discusses with functional directors problems arising from their continuous review of progress in assigned areas. Conducts comprehensive evaluation of programs utilizing various management tools such as line-of-balance techniques and Program Evaluation and Review Techniques (PERT) and available data collected through reports, etc. Initiates programs of corrective action and insures that results are consistent without compromises.

4. Serves as the Logistic Support Activity and Command representative at high level conferences and meetings with representatives of USAMC, DA, other commands, services, agencies and private contractors on matters required to effectively manage assigned system(s). Makes presentations, participates in the analysis and discussion of management problems and makes recommendations or commitments which often result in major replanning or reprogramming at higher echelons. When directed, visits industrial plants, tactical units, other federal agencies and field activities, both within and outside CONUS, for the purpose of insuring proper and adequate program accomplishment.

Performs other duties as assigned.

(Title and grade are established in accordance with position classification standards and guides. These materials are available for your review in the Civilian Personnel Division.)

DEPARTMENT OF THE ARMY
US ARMY AVIATION SYSTEMS COMMAND
PO BOX 209, ST. LOUIS, MO 63166

AMSAV-GL(L-SF)   **8 JUL 1969**

SUBJECT: Charter as AVSCOM Systems Manager for the YO-3A Aircraft System

Mr. Wayne Kuschel
Systems Introduction Directorate
US Army Aviation Systems Command
St. Louis, Missouri 63166

1. You are hereby appointed AVSCOM Systems Manager for the YO-3A Aircraft System. This appointment includes disposition of the two QT-2 aircraft.

2. Your mission is to plan, coordinate and assure execution of a life cycle program for this aircraft and to assure that funds for which AVSCOM has responsibility are appropriately planned and programmed. You are responsible for the development and maintenance of a Master Plan, when appropriate, for the execution of that portion of the YO-3A program as applies to AVSCOM, to include the schedule for phasing out centralized systems management. You will prepare for publication and will maintain current an AVSCOM Special Order designating individuals within AVSCOM who will have specific functional responsibility in connection with the YO-3A system.

3. You are authorized to report directly to me; the Deputy Commander for Research, Engineering and Data; or the Deputy Commander for Acquisition, when in your judgment Command action by one of us or higher authority is necessary. You will report weekly by means of a status report.

4. You will maintain or assure necessary coordination with:

   a. All elements of AVSCOM.

   b. US Army Electronics Command.

   c. US Army Test and Evaluation Command.

   d. US AMC Human Engineering Laboratories.

   e. US Army Combat Developments Command.

7-10 Charter for YO-3A System Manager

AMSAV-GL(L-SF)   8 JUL 1969
SUBJECT: Charter as AVSCOM Systems Manager for the YO-3A Aircraft System

    f. National Aeronautics and Space Administration (NASA).

    g. The Defense Supply Agency, and any other DOD agencies concerned
with the development, production or support of Army aircraft.

5. You will be stationed at AVSCOM, assigned to the Systems Introduction
Directorate, Future Weapon Systems Division, from the Chief of which you
will receive general guidance and administrative support.

6. Your appointment will continue until the YO-3A aircraft is fielded
and complete logistics support management by AVSCOM is transferred to
the Materiel Management Directorate.

7. This Charter supersedes and cancels "Charter as Commodity Manager for
the QT-2/3/4PC Aircraft Systems", addressed to Mr. Edward P. Laughlin,
dated 16 May 1968.

                                    ROBERT J. DILLARD
                                    Colonel, TC
                                    Deputy Commander for
                                    Logistics Support

DISTRIBUTION:
Office chiefs and directors
PM's and heads of USAMC Fld Ofc and
activities located at HQ, USAAVSCOM
CO's of USAAVSCOM sub-activities
Resident agencies
CG, AMC
CG, ECOM
CG, TECOM
CG, CDC
CO, Human Engineering Laboratories
Director, NASA Langley Research Center

2

7-10 page 2

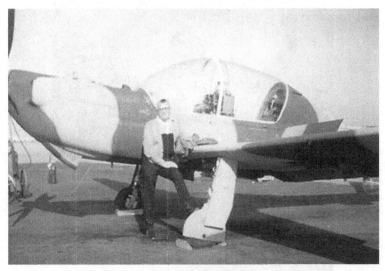

7-11 YO-3A

7-11 YO-3A

7-11 YO-3A

7-12
Various YO-3A aircraft pictures

DEPARTMENT OF THE ARMY

WAYNE A. KUSCHEL

IS OFFICIALLY COMMENDED

FOR

OUTSTANDING PERFORMANCE OF DUTY DURING THE PERIOD 11 AUGUST 1968 THROUGH 10 AUGUST 1969.
DURING THIS PERIOD, MR. KUSCHEL DISTINGUISHED HIMSELF BY PROVIDING TOPMOST TECHNICAL ADVICE
AND ASSISTANCE TO USERS OF ARMY AIRCRAFT. HIS DEVOTION TO DUTY AND OUTSTANDING EFFORTS IN
RESOLVING MAINTENANCE PROBLEMS HAVE BEEN REFLECTED IN THE HIGH RATE OF AIRCRAFT AVAILABILITY
WITHIN HIS AREA OF SUPPORT. HIS ACTIONS HAVE CONTRIBUTED GREATLY TO THE SUCCESS OF THE
ARMY MISSION.

22 AUGUST 1969

VAUGHN C. EMERSON, LIEUTENANT COLONEL, GS
DIRECTOR OF FIELD ASSISTANCE
US ARMY AVIATION SYSTEMS COMMAND

DA FORM 2446, 1 JUN 61

7-13 Picture of Award Ceremony 22 August 1969

277

7-13
Picture of Award Ceremony 22 August 1969

CONTROL NUMBER						DATE OF BIRTH			DATE OF APPRAISAL			INSTRUCTIONS FOR COMPLETION
						DAY	MONTH	YEAR	DAY	MONTH	YEAR	Do not complete Control Number (Col. 1 - 6).
1	2	3	4	5	6	7 8	9 10	11 12	13 14	15 16	17 18	Complete Date of Birth and Date of Appraisal
						0 6	1 2	2 3	3 0	1 2	7 0	(Cols. 7 - 18). Use numbers.

NAME (Last, First, Middle Initial)   **SOCIAL SEC NO.**   **DOD COMPONENT**   **CAREER FIELD CODE**

KUSCHEL, WAYNE A.   Army

POSITION TITLE, CSC SERIES AND GRADE

System Management Specialist GS-301-13

NAME AND LOCATION OF EMPLOYING ACTIVITY

USAAVSCOM, Logistics Support Activity,
Systems Introduction Directorate, St. Louis, Missouri

CAREER FIELD

SECTION I - CAREER APPRAISAL

THIS SECTION IS TO BE USED TO APPRAISE THE EMPLOYEE'S POTENTIAL CAPABILITY AS JUDGED AGAINST ESTABLISHED CHARACTERISTICS AND SKILL REQUIREMENTS FOR PROGRESSION IN THE CAREER FIELD.

CARD COLUMN	APPRAISAL ELEMENTS	CODE LEVEL	NUMERIC CODE LEVELS:
	ENTER CODE WHICH MOST NEARLY DESCRIBES THE EMPLOYEE'S POTENTIAL CAPABILITY. PARTICULAR CONSIDERATION WILL BE GIVEN TO THOSE COMPONENTS FOLLOWING EACH ELEMENT IN PARENTHESES.		4. Outstanding 1. Marginal 3. Above average 0. Unsatisfactory 2. Average IDENTIFY SKILLS AND CHARACTERISTICS ESTABLISHED AS REQUIREMENTS, AND UPON WHICH DETERMINATION OF CODE LEVEL IS BASED.
19	1. TECHNICAL COMPETENCE (Soundness of decisions, solutions and recommendations, quality of work produced.)	4	Work produced is of highest quality and recommendations and decisions are without exception sound and workable.
20	2. QUANTITY AND TIMELINESS (Meeting of schedules and deadlines accomplishing of workload in order of priority.)	4	Consistently exhibits keen awareness of relative priority of actions and governs his efforts accordingly.
21	3. WRITTEN COMMUNICATION (Expression of ideas in a clear, precise and convincing manner.)	4	Written communications are exceptionally clear and convincing.
22	4. ORAL COMMUNICATION (Expression of ideas in a clear concise and convincing manner. Consider both face-to-face and conference situations.)	4	In both formal and informal briefing and discussion situations expresses himself in a positive and confident manner.
23	5. COOPERATION (Exercising tact and diplomacy and maintaining effective relationships, working harmoniously with others, considering other view points and being willing to give assistance.)	4	His ability to work harmoniously with groups typified by a wide range of discipline, organization and position and to successfully elicit the whole-hearted cooperation of all concerned is particularly noteworthy.
24	6. STABILITY (Maintaining composure and effectiveness under pressure and adverse and changing conditions.)	4	Maintains poise and effectiveness under the most adverse conditions.
25	7. SUPERVISION AND ADMINISTRATION (Development of employees, respect, loyalty and cooperation gained, effectiveness of delegation of authority, distribution of work, coordination and control of diversified activities, assuring conformance to high standards, planning and organization.)	4	Has no current supervisory responsibility but his demeanor and performance as a project leader indicate potential for an outstanding supervisor.
80		5	

DD FORM 1559 1 MAY 66

7-13 Award Ceremony 22 August 1969

279

1. CAREER GOALS - STATE CAREER GOALS IN TERMS OF ACHIEVEMENT DESIRED WITH RESPECT TO THE FOLLOWING POSSIBILITIES. IT IS NOT NECESSARY TO SUPPLY COMMENT FOR ALL CATEGORIES LISTED BELOW. EMPLOYEES OBJECTIVES SHOULD BE DISCUSSED ONLY IN THOSE AREAS THAT REALLY APPLY; THAT IS, SUPPLY ENOUGH INFORMATION TO FULLY ESTABLISH CAREER GOALS. OTHERWISE, ANY ONE OR MORE (but not all) OF SUB-ITEMS "a" THROUGH "f" MAY BE LEFT BLANK. IF FURTHER EXPLANATION OF THESE GOALS IS NEEDED, OR IF TIME, PLACE AND/OR SEQUENCE OF ATTAINMENT ARE MATERIAL TO THEIR PROPER EXECUTION, USE LAST ITEM "OTHER GOALS".

a. FUTURE JOB ASSIGNMENTS (Include functional specialties, grades and/or titles which represent career goals)	b. FUTURE DUTIES (Include specific duties or groups of duties not necessarily embraced by known functional job titles)
Assignment to positions of increased complexity and responsibility in the field of program management.	
c. FURTHER KNOWLEDGE AND SKILLS (Identify desired capabilities and/or knowledge or disciplines to be acquired)	d. ROTATIONAL JOB ASSIGNMENTS (Include other capacity in which it is desired to apply experience and knowledge)
Updating in the latest configuration management procedures and techniques.	
e. ORGANIZATION, MISSION (Include kinds of organization in which assignment is desirable)	f. OTHER GOALS (List other factors not accounted for in above items)

7-13 Award Ceremony 22 August 1969 page 2

SECTION II - CAREER PLAN (Continued)	
2. TRAINING AND DEVELOPMENT - WITH RESPECT TO FURTHER TRAINING AND DEVELOPMENT, CONSIDER NEEDS AND PLANS TOGETHER. THIS INFORMATION IS TO BE FURNISHED THROUGH JOINT EFFORT OF SUPERVISOR AND EMPLOYEE.	
a. TRAINING NEEDS (What does the employee need with respect to any or all of the following:)	b. TRAINING PLANS (What actions can be taken with respect to any or all of the following to accommodate these needs?)
(1) SUBJECT MATTER KNOWLEDGE

Increased knowledge in the latest management techniques and thinking with particular emphasis upon project management. | (1) FORMAL EDUCATION (e.g., what college courses, etc.) |
(2) SPECIAL SKILLS	(2) DOD SPONSORED COURSES (includes local training)
(3) EXPERIENCE	(3) JOB ASSIGNMENTS DETAIL, PROMOTION REASSIGNMENT
(4) ORIENTATION	(4) ON-THE-JOB ACTIVITY (i.e., present position)
(5) PERSONAL DEVELOPMENT	(5) OTHER SELF-DEVELOPMENT
(6) OTHER DEVELOPMENT	(6) OTHER TRAINING

7-13 Award Ceremony 22 August 1969 page 3

281

Wayne Kuschel is a highly dedicated and motivated individual who has consistently exhibited outstanding technical competence in the performance of all his duties. His personal initiative, resourcefulness and perserverence in the face of almost overwhelming obstacles have been significant factors in the successful accomplishment of the YO-3A program.

DATE	TYPED NAME, TITLE AND ORGANIZATION	SIGNATURE OF SUPERVISOR
3 May 71	JAMES F. MATTHEWS, Deputy Proj Mgr LOH Proj Mgr's Ofc	

2. EMPLOYEE COMMENTS
THE ABOVE CAREER APPRAISAL AND PLAN HAVE BEEN DISCUSSED WITH ME AND MY COMMENTS (if any) ARE AS FOLLOWS:

I concur

DATE	SIGNATURE OF EMPLOYEE
4 May 71	Wayne A. Kuschel

3. REVIEWING SUPERVISOR'S COMMENTS
TO WHAT EXTENT DO YOU AGREE WITH ABOVE CAREER APPRAISAL AND PLAN?

DATE	TYPED NAME, TITLE AND ORGANIZATION	SIGNATURE OF REVIEWER
5-4-71	EDWARD M. BROWNE, LTC TC LOH Project Manager	

4. CAREER ADVISOR'S COMMENTS

DATE	TYPED NAME, TITLE AND ORGANIZATION	SIGNATURE OF CAREER ADVISOR

Page 4

7-13 Award Ceremony 22 August 1969 page 4

INCENTIVE AWARD NOMINATION AND APPROVAL

For use of this form, see CPPM 1, Sec 12; the proponent agency is Office of the Deputy Chief of Staff for Personnel.

PART I - TO BE COMPLETED BY OPERATING OFFICE

1 EMPLOYEE'S LAST NAME, FIRST NAME, MIDDLE INITIAL	2 ORGANIZATION
KUSCHEL, WAYNE A.	USAAVSCOM, Field Assistance Directorate

3 PRESENT POSITION TITLE, GRADE AND SALARY	4 POSITION HELD DURING PERIOD COVERED IN NOMINATION (If different)
~~Equipment Specialist (Aircraft Propulsion~~	Equipment Specialist (Aircraft Propulsion Equipment) JN 9202 GS-1670-12

5 TYPE OF AWARD RECOMMENDED AND JUSTIFICATION

Furnish on reverse side or on an attached sheet of 8" x 10½" paper a factual statement of what the employee has done to warrant consideration for an award, indicating benefits resulting from the employee's performance and significance of special act or service. Include specific data required by applicable regulations for the type of award recommended. Attach a draft of a proposed citation to be included on commendation certificate written in the third person, and not exceeding 90 words.

a. HONORARY		b.	MONETARY	
CERTIFICATE OF ACHIEVEMENT	DECORATION FOR EXCEPTIONAL CIVILIAN SERVICE	QUALITY INCREASE TO: $ P.A.	DATES FROM: TO:	
CERTIFICATE OF APPRECIATION FOR PATRIOTIC CIVILIAN SERVICE	DEPARTMENT OF DEFENSE DISTIN-GUISHED CIVILIAN SERVICE AWARD	SUSTAINED SUPE-RIOR PERFORM-ANCE	DATES FROM: TO:	
MERITORIOUS CIVILIAN SERVICE AWARD	PRESIDENTIAL AWARD			
OTHER (Specify) X Outstanding Performance Award		SPECIAL ACT OR SERVICE	DATE	

6 NOMINATING OFFICIALS

TYPED NAME AND TITLE	EXTENSION NO.	SIGNATURE	DATE
CHARLES A. REED, JR Acting Chief, CONUS Branch	6591	*Charles A Reed Jr*	12 Aug 69
B. STEIN Chief, Future Wpn Sys Div	5784	*Nicholas J Clous*	15 Aug 69

PART II - TO BE COMPLETED BY CIVILIAN PERSONNEL OFFICE

7 TYPE AND DATE OF INCENTIVE AWARDS GRANTED DURING PAST YEAR (Except Length of Service and Suggestion Awards)

PART III - TO BE COMPLETED BY LOCAL INCENTIVE AWARDS COMMITTEE

8 ☑ RECOMMEND APPROVAL OF AWARDS AS FOLLOWS:				9 ☐ DISAPPROVED	
CERTIFICATE OF ACHIEVEMENT	CERTIFICATE OF APPRECIATION FOR PATRIOTIC CIVILIAN SERVICE	QUALITY INCREASE	SUSTAINED SUPER-IOR PERFORMANCE	MERITORIOUS CIVIL-IAN SERVICE AWARD	
DECORATION FOR EXCEPTIONAL CIVILIAN SERVICE	SPECIAL ACT OR SERVICE	DEPARTMENT OF DEFENSE DISTIN-GUISHED CIVILIAN SERVICE AWARD	PRESIDENTIAL AWARD	OTHER (Specify) *Outstanding Only*	

COMPLETE FOR MONETARY AWARDS RECOMMENDED

AMOUNT RECOMMENDED $	TANGIBLE MONETARY BENEFITS $	☐ INTANGIBLE BENEFITS	ESTIMATED FIRST YEAR SAVINGS $

10 DATE 18 Aug 69	TYPED NAME OF LOCAL COMMITTEE CHAIRMAN *C. Brewer*	SIGNATURE

PART IV - TO BE COMPLETED BY APPROPRIATE APPROVING AUTHORITY(IES)

ACTION LEVEL	APPROVED (If monetary, indicate amount)	DIS-APPROVED	ADDITIONAL CASH AWARD	SIGNATURE, TITLE AND DATE
11 INSTALLATION COM-MANDER OR DESIGNATED REPRESENTATIVE	X			*Vaughn Clemson 12 Aug 69*
12 MAJOR COMMAND REVIEW COMMITTEE				
13 COMMANDER OF MAJOR COMMAND OR DESIGNATED REPRESENTATIVE				
14 DEPARTMENT OF THE ARMY INCENTIVE AWARDS BOARD				1 3 AUG 1969

DA FORM 1256, 1 JAN 65

REPLACES EDITION OF 1 JUN 61, EXISTING SUPPLIES OF WHICH WILL BE ISSUED AND USED UNTIL 1 JAN 66 UNLESS SOONER EXHAUSTED.

7-13 Award Ceremony 22 August 1969 page 5

EMPLOYEE PERFORMANCE RATING

(Civilian Personnel Regulation 400, Chapter 430.C)

1. NAME (Caps) LAST - FIRST - MIDDLE	MR. - MISS - MRS.	2. POSITION TITLE, NUMBER AND GRADE
KUSCHEL, WAYNE A.	MR.	Equipment Specialist (Aircraft Propulsion Equipment) JN 9202 GS-1670-

NAME AND LOCATION OF EMPLOYING OFFICE
US Army Aviation Systems Command,
Field Assistance Directorate,
St. Louis, Missouri

4. RATING PERIOD	FROM	TO
☒ OFFICIAL PERFORMANCE RATING ☐ PROBATIONARY OR TRIAL PERIOD RATING	08-11-68	08-10-69

The above named employee and the immediate supervisor have discussed the performance of the former during the rating period shown. The discussion included consideration of any major strengths and deficiencies in the employee's performance, and actions which both supervisor and employee can take to improve such performance, including training, self-development, and on-the-job assistance.

Any deficiencies which are the basis for adverse action, including action to withhold a step increase or to give an unsatisfactory rating, are described in detail on the reverse of this form or on attached sheets.

THE ADJECTIVE RATING RECOMMENDED FOR THE PERIOD IS:

☒ OUTSTANDING   ☐ SATISFACTORY   ☐ UNSATISFACTORY 1/

SUPERVISOR'S SIGNATURE	DATE
Charles A Reed Jr.	08-10-69

EMPLOYEE'S SIGNATURE 2/
Wayne A. Kuschel

THE OFFICIAL RATING ASSIGNED FOR THE PERIOD IS 3/:

☒ OUTSTANDING   ☐ SATISFACTORY   ☐ UNSATISFACTORY

APPROVING OFFICIAL'S SIGNATURE 4/	DATE
Vaughn Emerson	12 Aug 69

FOOTNOTES:

1/ Unsatisfactory rating requires a prior 90-day warning as discussed in CPR 400, Chapter 430.C.

2/ Employee's signature on the form indicates only that the evaluation discussion has taken place, and that he or she is aware of the rating recommended. It does not constitute agreement with the rating. Employees have the right to have ratings reviewed under procedures described in CPR 400, Chapter 430.C.

3/ An Outstanding rating requires justification, review by local Incentive Awards Committee, and approval by the Commanding Officer. An Unsatisfactory rating must be reviewed by the Civilian Personnel Officer for regulatory compliance prior to approval. A Satisfactory rating requires approval by the supervisor of the recommending supervisor.

4/ When a copy of this form, signed by approving official, is given to the rated employee it constitutes official notification of the performance rating for the period shown.

DA FORM 1052   PREVIOUS EDITIONS OF THIS FORM ARE OBSOLETE.
1 JAN 67

OPERATING OFFICIAL'S COPY 2

7-13 Award Ceremony 22 August 1969 page 6

TASKS	PERFORMANCE STANDARDS	ACTUAL PERFORMANCE
1. Provides technical advice and assistance.	a. Ascertains and resolves maintenance and supply problems in the field. Must provide effective results 90% of the time. b. Observes operations in the field and investigates malfunctions of aircraft systems equipment. c. Assists commanders in averting breakdown or deadline of equipment. d. Advises, assists and instructs in accomplishing maintenance, adjustment, repair, servicing, testing, processing, packaging, preservation, assembly, in-house maintenance and modification of aircraft and related accessories of his assigned type of aeronautical equipment. e. Inspects and furnishes analysis of aircraft damage and recommends repair methods, repair levels, or aircraft salvage. Finding and recommendations must be correct and adopted 90% of the time. f. Recommends product changes and modifications and prepares and submits to AVSCOM, in a timely manner, all unresolved problems for resolution. Must maintain 85% effectivity and efficiency.	During this reporting period, Mr. Kuschel was assigned as Acting Chief Far East Branch, Acting Chief, CONUS Branch, Acting Asst Chief, Technical Assistance Division at USAAVSCOM, St. Louis, Mo. In addition to these assigned positions, he was utilized as the expert on gas turbine engines. He has directed and assisted in resolving administrative, maintenance and supply problems presented by USAAVSCOM technical assistance and field personnel located worldwide. Through his own knowledge, experience and judgment, his determination and resolution have been correct 97% of the time. Through observation and review of direct and written communications, he has recommended many maintenance and operational changes to procedures which when followed by field personnel, were instrumental in raising the operational readiness of field problems, he has recommended product changes and improvements which have aided in raising the effective support furnished by aviation technical assistance personnel. He has assisted on numerous test flights by trouble shooting the aircraft propulsion system, then evaluating and determining corrective action in order to expedite restoring aircraft to an operational ready status. He has been correct in his determination and corrections of flight problems involving propulsion equipment 100% of the time.

7-13 Award Ceremony 22 August 1969 page 7

TASKS	PERFORMANCE STANDARDS	ACTUAL PERFORMANCE
	g. Makes occasional flights as technical observer to determine causes of aircraft malfunction, improper flight control rigging, improper weight and balance, etc. Must be correct 95% of the time.	
2. Provides technical instruction.	a. Instructs military and civilian maintenance personnel on the job by demonstration or overseeing troops or utilizes formal classroom type facilities and instruction material.	2. Mr. Kuschel demonstrated his diversified technical and educational ability when assigned to the Technical Assistance Division. On many occasions he was called upon to instruct personnel performing aircraft maintenance at AVSCOM Flt Detachment, Lambert Field, St. Louis, Mo. He received recognition from military personnel for the exceptional job performance. Through his own initiative, he prepared and conducted formal training classes on all systems of the gas turbine engine. His classes contributed directly to the maintenance effectiveness of the attendees. Not only did he instruct in proper maintenance procedures, but he rendered invaluable assistance in areas of technical supplies. Mr. Kuschel always strived to improve his method of instructing abilities, by incorporating new maintenance and instructional techniques which results in maximum retention by each student. He demonstrated the use of engine special tools used in conjunction with technical manuals or publications, in addition, always rendered invaluable assistance in all areas concerned with technical, supply, safety and operational procedures. Mr. Kuschel is constantly researching all
	b. Develops own POIs, researches and assembles information for classroom training purposes.	
	c. Instructs field personnel to assure that proper methods techniques, tools, publications, manuals, preventative maintenance procedures, production control and quality control maintenance directives, etc., are employed.	
	d. Assembles and prepares on request of installation commanders or upon direction of higher authority, or as a result of observation in the field, a wide variety of information from TB AVNs, ARs, SRs, etc., utilizing practical experience ingenuity and knowhow. Distributes or processes assembled information or data as directed by local authority.	

2

7-13 Award Ceremony 22 August 1969 page 8

available in-house resources for new
ideas and necessary information in which
he can develop, prepare FCI for the Army
Aviation Mobile Technical Assistance
Program (AAMTAP). His guidance in the
implementation of this valuable training
aid has improved the abilities of the
T-53 propulsion instructors, whereby, the
overall effeciency of the mechanic skill
level was increased, enabling the using
organization to derive the final benefit
in aircraft availibility. Mr. Enschel
prepared a student hand out booklet for
AAMTAP training which incorporated the
tear-down and assembly of the hot end on
T-53-L13 engines. It was recognized that
the inexperienced individual in the units
engine shop required more guidance because of this new type engine. There were
approximately 35 special tools required
and a set sequence to utilize these tools,
otherwise damage to the engine would take
place. One T-53 instructor had vu-graphs
made from his handbook and instructs all
facets of the tear-down and assembly of
the engine. Personnel world-wide request
copies of this handbook to be used for
instructional material and indoctrinating
new personnel.

3

7-13
Award Ceremony 22 August 1969 page 9

TASKS

3. Organizes and conducts conferences and meetings.

4. Keeps abreast of new developments and maintains technical knowledge, policies and procedures.

PERFORMANCE STANDARDS

a. Is considered to be an above average speaker and presents material in a clear cut pattern so as to communicate ideas to his audience or other conferees.

b. Dresses with proper decorum in order to present a good appearance to his audience and to bring credit to the Command.

c. Prepares conference agendas, arranges for guest speakers and chairs the conference when required or when situation warrants services as toastmaster.

a. Is a technical expert and advisor on assigned aircraft or aviation equipment. Must provide effective results 90% of the time.

b. Has working knowledge of all regulations pertaining to maintenance and supply of assigned aeronautical equipment.

c. Is familiar with the latest developments, regulations and ideas, operational and mechanical problem areas, and criteria requiring extensive knowledge of peculiar maintenance requirements, design changes and construction of his assigned type of aeronautical equipment.

ACTUAL PERFORMANCE

Mr. Kuschel is well versed and conversant on maintenance topics, he plans well in advance and presents his material in a logical and well organized manner. The sincerity and enthusiasm that he displays contribute greatly to his effectiveness. His overall appearance and dress at all functions are of the highest standards and contribute to the effectiveness of his presentation. He has prepared and coordinated the necessary administrative requirements for personnel visiting his duty station. His knowledge of protocol procedures assists in the preparation for these visits and of conducting them.

On all systems that Mr. Kuschel supports, his management and technical direction has proven effective and correct 95% of the time. His knowledge of regulations pertaining to maintenance and supply on assigned propulsion equipment is to be commended. He continually strives to increase proficiency in this area. Assigned maintenance specialists continually call on him for information pertaining propulsion related regulations. The fact that personnel continue to do this is evidence that his background and knowledge are extensive and a valuable asset and is to be commended for his continued efforts. His knowledge of Army and Command organizational channels assists in the prompt and efficient dispatch of all maintenance and related technical items.

4

7-13 Award Ceremony 22 August 1969 page 10

TASKS	PERFORMANCE STANDARDS	ACTUAL PERFORMANCE
	d. Must be knowledgeable of Command Army organizational channels.	
	e. Maintains close liaison with US Air Force, US Navy, manufacturers and other activities operating similar equipments.	
	f. Makes periodic trips to manufacturers or training agencies to maintain current knowledge and to keep abreast of design and production changes which may have an effect on field level maintenance and logistical support.	
5. Conducts scheduled and non-scheduled visits.	a. Visits aeronautical maintenance activities, as required, on a scheduled or non-scheduled basis.	Although his base of operation was firmly established, his visits to aircraft maintenance activities, in his area, has added greatly to the effectiveness of their operation. He resolves many potential problems on these scheduled or unscheduled visits. On trips to various operations, in his area of support, he displayed initiative by arranging the necessary transportation requirements associated with the visits. He maintains a passport with certain visas and current international vaccination on record and stays abreast of changes in diplomatic personnel, in his area, in order to better satisfy any emergency travel requirements.
	b. Completes arrangements for visits, secures approval of authority for visits. Travel will be made by commercial or military aircraft as directed by superiors or authority.	

5

7-13 Award Ceremony 22 August 1969 page 11

289

a. Submits activity reports at predetermined intervals, (normally every 30 days) to USAAVSCOM Technical Assistance Program Manager.

b. Reports will indicate clearly and factually the nature of tasks accomplished, troubles encountered, corrective measures taken or adapted, recommendations made and to whom made, and any other pertinent information related to general adequacy of maintenance, facilities, parts, supply, tools and publications. Reports must reflect 90% clarity, detail and completeness.

c. Problems or information furnished in reports should not be general in nature. Information must contain sufficient detail to enable USAAVSCOM action and/or resolution.

d. Reports should be submitted in accordance with AR 700-4 in a clear and concise manner.

e. Reports will be submitted through established channels to USAAVSCOM.

ACTUAL PERFORMANCE

Mr. Kuschel is constantly reviewing and researching reports from field technicians and engineering personnel, which he analyzes for problems in the supply, maintenance and technical area. He is able to ascertain what is required without difficulty and gather all facts pertaining to the problem or request before he takes required action. In preparing status reports on technical matters, trends, task accomplished or replies to correspondence, he is able to indicate clearly and functionally what the problem is and corrective measure to be taken or adopted. All his reports or correspondence reflect 100% clarity, factual and completeness. He always uses established channels and insures that all effective personnel and elements are informed of problem and action taken or required. He also makes timely follow-ups to insure problems are resolved.

7-13 Award Ceremony 22 August 1969 page 12

TASKS

. ...ks for program and
. ...sults.

PERFORMANCE STANDARDS

a. Contributes to good morale
to the extent that no official
and no more than two unofficial
reprimands, (either written or
verbal), are received from any
source during a 12 month rating
period for failure to observe
any of the elements which constitute the employee's individual
responsibilities.

b. Cooperates with superiors by
willingly accepting assignments
and instructions relating to
areas of assigned responsibilities.

c. Cooperates with co-workers by
treating them in a courteous manner
and freely exchanging information
toward improved efficiency and
success of overall program.

d. Is industrious, volunteers
services when scheduled work is
completed.

e. Demonstrates dependability by
unquestionable use of sick and
annual leave.

f. Carefully observes all post
and official rules and regulations.

ACTUAL PERFORMANCE

Mr. Kuschel has excelled in all areas
and did not receive any official or un-
official reprimands during this rating
period. He has never abused his sick
leave and plans his annual leave to
fit in with his workload. In all manner,
his work and personal conduct are beyond
reproach. He is always willing to accept
responsibility and tasks which are assigned
to him and many times has volunteered to
assist other personnel. His loyalty to
the Army and this Command is commendable,
always shows courtesy, politeness,
respect for authority and other workers
and is willing to accept constructive
criticism. Mr. Kuschel assumed the additional responsibility for the Director
of Field Assistance for all AVSCOM
Operations center functions. In the eight
months that Mr. Kuschel was in this position
he received high praise from his superiors
for his outstanding accomplishments.

7

7-13 Award Ceremony 22 August 1969 page 13

291

TASKS | PERFORMANCE STANDARDS | ACTUAL PERFORMANCE

g. During emergencies, works whatever hours or under whatever conditions are necessary to assist supported units in obtaining maximum readiness posture.

h. Demonstrates loyalty to the organization (Command and program), shows common courtesy and politeness and proper respect for authority, causes no dissension among fellow employees and accepts constructive criticism readily.

i. Readily accepts cross-training to new aircraft or aviation equipment in accordance with program requirements. Accepts necessary assignment changes with little or no difficulty or dissension.

8

Mr. Kuschel, during his assignment in Systems Introduction Directorate, Future Weapon Systems Division, has performed his duties outstandingly.

7-13 Award Ceremony 22 August 1969 page 14

292

3. CITATION TO APPLICABLE STANDARD AND ITS DATE OF ISSUANCE	4. TITLE Equipment Specialist		
CSC, GS-1670, Jun 64	(Aircraft Propulsion Equipment)		
	5. PAY SCHEDULE	6. OCC. CODE	7. GRADE
	GS	1670	12

8. EVALUATION APPROVAL Title, pay schedule, code and grade of this job have been fixed in accordance with Department of the Army official policy and grade level standards.	SIGNATURE *Anton Imhof, Jr.*	DATE
	ANTON IMHOF, JR.	20 Aug 65

9. SUPERVISORY CONTROLS, DUTIES, AND WORKING CONDITIONS (Indicate percent of time for each duty, where pertinent.) (Continue statement of duties, etc., on reverse side if necessary.)

SUPERVISORY CONTROLS

Work is performed in an assigned area overseas or within CONUS under the general direction and administrative supervision of a supervisor located in St. Louis, Missouri. Detached duty station results in incumbent's receiving broad policy guidance outlines on objectives to be accomplished at time of assignment. Has full responsibility for work activities while on assignments and has wide latitude in exercising independent judgment in the interpretation and implementation of applicable maintenance policies and procedures. Adequacy of performance is judged through analysis of written reports, oral reports, and personal visitation.

MAJOR DUTIES

As a representative of the command with duty station located overseas or within CONUS, incumbent serves as a topmost technical expert and advisor in the maintenance of a specific series of reciprocating or turbine propulsion equipment used in the make-up of Army aircraft. As such, he furnishes expert and specialized advice, assistance, and instructions to Department of the Army personnel in maintenance, adjustment, repair, servicing, testing, processing, packaging, preservation, assembly, in-storage maintenance, and modification of his assigned aircraft propulsion equipment.

1. Maintains continuing contact with the command and close liaison with the U. S. Air Force, the U. S. Navy, and aircraft manufacturers to assure constant cognizance of the latest maintenance engineering data, such as engineering change proposals, blueprint changes, microfilm, factory bulletins, and other data pertinent to his assigned type of aircraft propulsion equipment. Develops and submits proposed changes to DA maintenance publication, maintenance procedures, and practices. Investigates, analyzes, and corrects diverse and complicated operational and mechanical problems requiring intensive knowledge covering maintenance and construction of his

10.	JOB CONTENT APPROVAL (Complete on organization file copy only.)	
ORGANIZATION LOCATION		
Directorate of Maintenance, Technical Assistance Division, Technical Support Branch		
	THIS STATEMENT ACCURATELY DESCRIBES THE WORK REQUIRED IN ONE POSITION OR IN EACH OF A GROUP OF POSITIONS IN THE ABOVE ORGANIZATION.	THE ABOVE DESCRIPTION, WITH SUPPLEMENTAL MATERIAL, IS ADEQUATE FOR PURPOSES OF EVALUATION.
	SIGNATURE OF APPROVING SUPERVISOR	SIGNATURE OF ANALYST

11.	REAUDIT APPROVAL					
DATE						
SUPERVISOR'S APPROVAL						
ANALYST'S SIGNATURE						

DA FORM 374 1 JUN 61   PREVIOUS EDITIONS OF THIS FORM ARE OBSOLETE.

7-13 Picture of Award Ceremony 22 August 1969
Job Description page 15

assigned type of Army aircraft propulsion equipment. Investigates deficiencies for the purpose of establishing areas that should be reported for equipment improvement. Makes occasional flights as technical observer to determine causes of malfunctions, such as improper fuel adjustment or flow, improper ignition system operation, origin of unusual noises, unusual vibrations, improper valve train adjustment or functioning, abnormal rpm indications, etc.

2. Researches and assembles information for classroom training purposes and based on practical experience and ingenuity, conducts classes (including lectures and demonstrations) for maintenance and operational (military and civil service) personnel in the maintenance and operation of assigned type of aircraft propulsion equipment. Further, effects training required by instructing all Department of the Army personnel or by training of maintenance personnel and overseeing their subsequent training of other troops. Conducts on-the-job training by demonstration and/or overseeing troops conducting maintenance at actual site to insure proper methods and techniques are used. Slants training toward preventive maintenance to avert engine breakdown and deadline of equipment. Also, assembles and prepares on request of installation commanders, direction from higher authority, or observation in the field, a wide variety of information from technical and administrative publications (including TO's, TM's SB's, TAB's, AR's, SR's, etc.).

3. Represents the command at Army supply and maintenance conferences National Guard conferences, and other top level meetings and conferences to discuss maintenance and operating procedures and is empowered to make commitments which obligate the command to a course of action. Renders technical advice and assistance to accident investigation boards in determining cause or probable cause of accidents, corrective and/or preventive action to be taken, and recommends applicable product changes and modifications. As required, inspects and furnishes analysis of engine damage and recommends repair methods, repair levels, and/or engine salvage. Makes periodic trips to manufacturers or training agencies to maintain current knowledge of assigned propulsion equipment and to keep abreast of the latest maintenance and operating procedures.

4. Prepares and submits written reports at predetermined intervals to the command, indicating clearly and factually the nature of tasks accomplished, trouble encountered, corrective measures taken or adopted, recommendations made and to whom made, and any other pertinent information related to the general adequacy of maintenance facilities, parts supply, tools, and publications.

Performs other duties as assigned.

NOTE: Travel for TDY will be made by commercial or military aircraft as directed by superiors. Involves temporary assignments requiring world-wide travel.

(Title and grade are established in accordance with position classification standards and guides referenced in Item 3. These referenced materials are available for your review in the Civilian Personnel Office.)

7-13 Picture of Award Ceremony 22 August 1969
Job Description page 16

AMCPM-LH (31 Aug 71) 2d Ind
SUBJECT: Letter of Appreciation

Office of the Project Manager, Light Observation Helicopter Systems,
PO Box 209, St. Louis, Missouri 63166 13 October 1971

TO: Mr. Wayne A. Kuschel, YO-3A Project Officer, LOHS Project
     Manager's Office

1. I am very appreciative of the commendatory comments which
Colonel Marr, Chief, Evaluation Div, ACTIV, and Major General Kornet,
CG, USAAVSCOM, have forwarded to me for the contributions made by
you in support of our YO-3A "Quiet Airplane" operational evaluation.
I proudly extend their personal thanks for your laudable performance.

2. It is indeed a pleasure for me to have your efforts as Project
Officer on the YO-3 recognized in this manner. You have demonstrated
your administrative competence and devotion to duty on this project
and your personal contributions have added greatly to the success
of the Light Observation Helicopter Systems Project Manager's Office.
I know I can expect your continued praiseworthy performance as noted
in basic correspondence.

3. The letter from Colonel Marr with indorsements will be included
in your official personnel records.

JOHN E. BAKER
COL, FA
LOHS Project Manager

4

7-14 Letter of appreciation from RVN ACTIV Office
Colonel Marr and Colonel Baker

AVIB-ED   31 August 1971

SUBJECT: Letter of Appreciation

Commanding General
US Army Aviation Systems Command
PO Box 209 Main Station
St. Louis, Missouri 63166

1. The Army Concept Team in Vietnam (ACTIV) conducted an operational evaluation of the YO-3A quiet airplane from 13 July 1970 through 31 April 1971. In both scope and magnitude this evaluation was one of the most extensive ever conducted by ACTIV. The purpose of this letter is to officially recognize the efforts and contributions of those who supported this program during the employment of this aircraft in the Republic of Vietnam.

2. On numerous occasions, unique and unexpected difficulties arose which required immediate and accurate analysis and rectification. The resolution of these problems dictated intensive management and a concerted personal effort on the part of the action officers assigned to the Office of the LOH Project Manager, Headquarters, USA Aviation Systems Command (USAAVSCOM). With few exceptions, problems were resolved in a responsive and accurate manner even though it was sometimes necessary in the interest of expediency to arrive at an appropriate solution without benefit of a thorough field analysis. The interest and professionalism exhibited by the USAAVSCOM YO-3A staff in the discharge of their individual and collective responsibilities immeasurably enhanced the degree to which the evaluation objectives were ultimately satisfied.

3. Although every member of the YO-3A aircraft team should be recognized, the following personnel are specifically commended for their wholehearted contributions to this program: Colonel Baker and Mr. Mathews, the project manager and deputy respectively, Mr. Wayne Kuschel and Mr. Harry Murphy. Mr. Kuschel responsively reacted to the requirements and demands placed upon him and served as the focal point for all YO-3A program related reports and actions. Mr. Murphy, the program logistician, served to coordinate support actions. Mr. Mathews capably acted in the absence of

7-14
Letter of appreciation from RVN ACTIV Office
Colonel Marr and Colonel Baker

AVIB-ED (Con't)   31 August 1971
SUBJECT: Letter of Appreciation

Colonel Baker to resolve urgent actions affecting the overall program.
Each of these personnel were responsive, sincere and devoted to the
task of supporting the YO-3A program in the best possible manner. Because of their wholehearted efforts the evaluation achieved the desired
results despite the inordinate number of adversities which arose.

4. Please convey to those responsible my congratulations and sincere
appreciation for their outstanding efforts in behalf of the ACTIV evaluation.

                               William K. Marr
                               WILLIAM K. MARR
                               Colonel, INF
                               Chief, Eval Div, ACTIV

7-14 Letter of appreciation from RVN ACTIV Office
Colonel Marr and Colonel Baker

CHAPTER 8-
WHAT A SURPRISE,
A PROMOTION TO GS-14

About two weeks into our competition to define the new light observation helicopter, I was approached by Barry Baines from AVSCOM civilian personnel office. Barry said jokingly, "I'm sorry to have to give you these papers, but you may become very happy. Congratulations, you've been promoted to a GS-14, Division Chief within the Technical Data Management Office, under Mr. Wayne Smith, the Director." I didn't know what to say. I was dumb-founded because of my prior meetings or interviews with Mr. Smith. [Promotion to GS—14 8-1 and Job Description]

To go back three or four months, I was given a time and date for Mr. Smith's office to interview me for this GS-14 vacancy position. But knowing how some of the Directors work, it's a formality to go through civilian personnel with paperwork and have interviews with the command's qualified personnel. I plainly asked Mr. Smith if he had a person sitting on this GS-14 position. He kind of avoided answering that question but he grinned. The subject changed to my B-36 aircraft flying experience and other Air Force aircraft and positions I held. He was impressed, so I thought, but that would not change his choice of who was to be selected to his directorate. I later heard the man's name who was submitted for the promotion. From what I heard from a good source, the Commanding General (MG Hinrichs) decided to promote some outsider, namely me. So this complete swap-around caught me off guard. Here I had 5 1/2 years of civil service time and promoted to GS-14. It was a good record for me, at least I thought.

I remember receiving my GS-1670-11 on 6 June 1966, GS-1670-12 on 12 August 1967, GS-301-13 on 29 June 1969 and now my GS-1670-14 on 5 March 1972, which was a record for me being promoted in civil service, or so I thought. It shows what a person can achieve or accomplish by good hard work, regardless of the time required.

Needless to say, knowing Mr. Smith from prior meetings I was reluctant to even approach his office and let him officially know I was his new Division Chief in his directorate. WOW! What a bad feeling in the pit of my stomach, that day of reporting. Mr. Smith was very curt and to the point. My feeling was he felt the command let him down, thinking only of himself. So he gave me the two-bit (25 cent) tour, then asked if I needed anything to begin. I said, "No!" However, I was still on official YO-3A detail to the Light Observation Helicopter Program Manager, that all the supervisors, CPO and Project Manager should resolve my detail problem. I was following instructions being on that LOH-PM team project and in a qualified position within that LOH-PM office.

My next pleasant surprise was meeting a very gracious, young petite lady. She was to be my division's secretary. Her name was Carol Hessenauer. From our meeting I could feel a good working relationship beginning. What I really appreciated was her honesty in speaking with me and the method she used to do her duties. She was one dependable person that I could rely on. This was because of our close relationship with the AVSCOM staff personnel. It proved true. She took care of protecting my back, safeguarding me from personnel who I knew were going to throw monkey wrenches into the works. We were trying to perform and achieve a workable division office. I can truthfully say Carol was well recommended by the Commanding General, AVSCOM, Chief of Staff, up and down the ranks, so what a relief to have a well-qualified secretary on my team.

The last phone call (January 2010) I had with Carol I asked if she had a spare picture of herself back when we were in TDC&S together she said if she could find one, she would send it to me for my book "All or Nothing".

She sure didn't lose any time in sending one, of course I picked the one where she was receiving an Outstanding Performance rating award and a step increase award in 1973 from my friend and Commander Directorate of Maintenance Colonel Wm Gene Phillips. [Carol Hessenauer good Illinois friend 8-2]

But I am not going to stop at that one picture, I want to show our splendid boss the Commanding General of AVRADCOM Major General Frank H. Hinrichs he was always behind and supporting his employees in all respects and honored them for worthy tasks that the employee earned. [Was an honor to be on the "Hinrichs" AVRADCOM team 8-3]

In my estimation Carol was worth her weight in gold. That was the value I would place on her for her experience, disposition, qualifications, for protecting our office, and her ability to do her everyday duties, which resolved all the battles that our five GS-13's were throwing more monkey wrenches into my decisions.

I may have been her boss, so to say, but she was a true friend and was vigil whenever she had any dealings with my Assistant Division Chief, Mr. Ramey, by never disclosing anything that I had going on or in the mill. This was an asset in what we had to put up with in the Assistant Division Chief and four GS-13s. Never in my career have I ever entered into a situation that had live tigers, five GS-13s and no cages for our survival.

I can say that Carol and the five assigned branch secretaries were on excellent terms. That's what it takes to maintain the working relationship from top echelon to the bottom level and keep all division correspondence on a secure need to know basis. In other words, don't broadcast any information that would give the answer away to the other side. Keep them in the dark, so management can do its job. Because our division had approximately two hundred personnel in grades of GS-4 through GS-13, there had to be 100% cooperation between all elements and personnel in my division. I assured myself this would be met or achieved as soon as possible.

When I began my supervision as the Division Chief, I had a feeling this was going to be a difficult task. Immediately the five GS-13s formed a clique to conspire within themselves. They were known as the Metro-Goldwin-Mayer (MGM) studio (Mozelwski, Goodwin, Monken), plus two, Ramey and Schacht. Every one of my personnel hated their branch supervisor's guts because of the baloney or nonsense they conveyed to these "working people". In eighteen months, before I took over the control of the division they had fifteen reported complaints or grievances of different violations. So when I learned some of the problems, I started going into the employees work stations and visiting with them, talking to them on what they were doing and what they were accomplishing toward a goal. We would sit down and go through the forms that they maintained and methods of improving their work skills. This was the determining factor in who I was going to send to school to improve their morale and groom for promotion.

All that the GS-13s ever expected was ten hours of work in an eight hour day from the employees, never discussing their careers, schooling or retiring. That was the supervisor's past problems that surfaced and why they had so many grievances in this division. Another reason that I enjoyed working with Carol was we could talk over problems and decide the best course of action to correct our division's faults. With her and the branch secretaries on best of terms it kept me from being degraded by the five GS-13s or undermining my authority. My assistant Division Chief, Mr. Ramey, was the one I had to fight fire with fire. He was Mr. Smith's favorite person to be promoted when I was selected instead for that assigned position and approved by the Commanding General. No one considered my background or experience. I had a Bachelor's Degree in Administration, I had computer programming under my belt, I had the United States Army Maintenance Management course, and several executive management courses. All the time these GS-13s stayed in their AVSCOM offices, never attending schools or events which was required for advancement to higher grades. Sure was dumb of them. I believe that Mr. Smith put them under his thumb to keep them in line (do what he wanted with them).

So to make things even between the GS-13s and myself, I proceeded to my civilian personnel contact, Mrs. M. Roberts, and requested an explanation of what I could do to accomplish my assignment as Division Chief. CPO allowed me to review all of my Branch Chiefs personnel records in a room adequate to spread out the records and satisfy my needs of making a sound decision of what to do and swap the GS-13s for cross-training for more experience and replacement factors within the division. My final determination was to nullify their current management abilities. They only had knowledge of their individual previous assigned branch tasks except for their daily sign-off duties. By cross-training all five GS-13s within the division, this would put them at a disadvantage of not knowing their newly assigned jobs. That way they would have to come down to my expedient learning level and we would be on the same sheet of experience or knowledge, so to speak. [Cross training of GS-13's 8-4]

This allowed me sufficient time to begin managing the Division and see where the problems were, and solve them on the spot. This gave the

Division time to gain more productive work from the excellent employees under my supervision. In addition, it allowed me to keep up my full managing of the GS-13 personnel and let them know what I was doing and the reason behind my decisions. There would be no transfers or promotions for about six months. It was now official and the five GS-13s were put on their new duty assignments immediately so I could study the basic problems that caused poor morale within my division personnel and alleviate it. It wasn't long and the workers began to react to my goal. It began to increase the correspondence and data output by my people. That was one goal we achieved for our command. These requirements, were good results for the working personnel that accomplished, the high standards for the division.

Since this approach was unique and never used in prior years within ASVCOM, it was going to be tried this one time to solve my Divisions personnel problems. I was putting my problem gang on the same level as myself, since I was new and needed a short period of time to be efficient to manage this data-producing office and become more productive. I didn't know how Mr. Smith would receive my decision of cross-training my personnel but I had the Commanding General on my side. Then a rumor was floating around that my Logistics Division was to be transferred to the Directorate of Maintenance. Under my breath I was happy to have my division under the United States Army Maintenance Directorate function. I was introduced to Colonel Phillips and we hit it off in an outstanding way. I respected and admired him for his cooperation in my running the division functions.

After I received my GS-14 promotion into the Directorate of TDC&S as Chief of Logistics Division, I had one more item to accomplish. It was an exit interview that was to advise the LOH-PM Manager, Colonel Baker, of problems that had to be addressed concerning himself, his personnel, and myself. There were too many back-stabbings from various personnel within his management area. One person would say something to another about a third party, and none of them knew the complete story.

But when they began stating that they were going to take my promotion away and give it to a worthy partner of theirs, I said baloney. For one thing, I had a four year college degree and was more eligible for the Supervisory Chief, GS-1670-14, which was different than a GS-301-14 in any logistics requirement, and that their partner or buddy was not fully qualified, period. Another factor overlooked when they opened their mouths and put their shoes in, was that I was fully qualified on both Department of Army and Army Material Command referral lists for any GS-14 position. Further, their buddy was not on the referral list in any shape, type or form. He was stagnating in his position as a GS-13 logistics specialist. He was even sitting on a higher grade position GS-14 in another project office and never received it because he didn't have a manager's knowledge to complete any project, especially outside the logistics area. He was a special buddy to a certain management person who would try to get the person, the underdog, promoted. I put in a lot of time as the YO-3A project officer (during 1969-1975) and any time a letter of appreciation was written and received in this headquarters, their underdog buddy was always placed in the letter as to how much logistics support he gave to the project. What a bunch of baloney and I could have said the actual words BS, and that is what I think of this man and his support.

I wrote four pages of exit interview statements concerning their LOH program managers, which were overall office problems that should have been alleviated or resolved in their managerial areas. I would bet my current paycheck that nothing was ever done and to this day would or still exist. So I had a clear mind when I exited the Light Observation Helicopter project manager's area to take over my new position. [Exit interview with Colonel Baker 8-5]

I was putting my trust in my employees and assisting in their personal problems. It eliminated a lot of controversies within the work area. Then each Friday at 1645 my secretary Carol would advise me it was time to have the personnel gather around the elevators and lecture them on the current programs. Then I would let the personnel get on the elevators early because the other four days at work they were always the last personnel to get on the elevators going down because the elevators stopped on the way up to the 9th floor and the employees filled the elevator going up, so I felt my personnel deserved at least one day of break.

By telling the personnel of the program's schooling and such, they were more productive and accomplished about 30% more work. The command let everyone know about this increase in the work load. After a couple of weeks of the elevator episode, I reported into Colonel Gene Phillips, Directorate of Maintenance, what I had done. He said, "Wayne, this is your division. Get your fanny out of here and run it the way you want to." In other words, do what I want to do. Guess he got a good word or so from my other job performances. Then to ensure my employees got relief from their assigned branch chiefs, I immediately began an open door policy whereby if they had a grievance or gripe I would have a chance to resolve it before it was a major problem or stretched out of proportions. My five GS-13 branch managers were very disgruntled about this decision. I held to my decision and won a victory of extreme importance with no new grievances throughout my time in the Technical Data Office.

As time progressed our division managerial skills excelled higher than expectations and the personnel were comfortable and happy in their work. AVSCOM's Commanding Officer was always praising the improvement shown in accomplishing the heavy division's workload. Since my swapping of branch chief positions, my problem gang had to gain experience on their new job assignments and increase their skills before the six months were up. This gave them little time to get together and start talking over old and new ideas on how to run my division. In other words, it kept them off guard to my advantage.

So it goes, when you're new on the job a short learning period had to be given to you. It's not possible to be at 100 mph the first instant you sit in the division position. If you're a manager, that skill is always there but the small details have to be dealt with. My Assistant Division Chief, Mr. Leonard E. Ramey, was a person who wanted to be a manager but hated working with any schedule, correspondence, or anything to do with work.

Regardless, in time I made these five GS-13s work as a Division team, unconcerned with the other small details which might belong to another branch chief. In fact, they would stay within their domain to accomplish their daily work load.

Let me reiterate about Carol Hessenauer. She was the most rewarding secretary I ever had. Her work was 110%, perfect on any subject she was assigned to do. The AVSCOM command staff had high regard for her because of her painstaking thoroughness of all correspondence prepared for the command, outside the command, higher headquarters or any civilian organizations. Command and staff personnel considered our division as the backbone of AVSCOM.

On 8 May 1973 I was given RIF paperwork by Mr. Bainter from civilian personnel, and he advised me 1 July 1973 that I was again in a Reduction In Force (RIF) condition and that Mr. William Gillespie had bumped me for veterans preference. I had orders to go back to the Technical Assistance Division as a GS-1670-12, where my "Republic of Vietnam Pecks black hat bad guys" were located. I advised personnel that I would resign if this was the best that could be afforded to me. [Photo—To Whom It May Concern 8-6]

Colonel Phillips was trying to help me with achieving a new position since the Reduction in Force (RIF) for my job was taking place. He wrote a letter "To whom it may concern" to show his opinion of my high points and how well I accomplished managing my division.

I was called into the Director of Maintenance on 29 May 1973, where Colonel William Gene Phillips presented me with an Official Commendation for my work with his and the Directorate's Office. [Picture receiving Department of Army Commendation 8-7][Department of Army Commendation with Colonel Phillips 8-8]

STANDARD FORM 50 Rev. Dec. 1967
U.S. CIVIL SERVICE COMMISSION
FPM. Ch. 295

Approved
Exception

NOTIFICATION OF PERSONNEL ACTION
(EMPLOYEE – See General Information on Reverse)

(FOR AGENCY USE)
dt ME 4485

1. NAME (CAPS) LAST – FIRST – MIDDLE	MR. – MISS – MRS.	2. (FOR AGENCY USE)	3. BIRTH DATE (Mo., Day, Year)	4. SOCIAL SECURITY NO.
KUSCHEL, WAYNE A.	MR.	39011	12-06-23	

5. VETERAN PREFERENCE			6. TENURE GROUP	7. SERVICE COMP. DATE
2	1. – NO 3. – 10 PT. DISAB. 5. – 10 PT. OTHER		1	02-01-56
	2. – 5 PT. 4. – 10 PT. COMP			

9. FEGLI		10. RETIREMENT	11. (FOR CSC USE)
1	1. – COVERED (reg. only-declined opt.) 3. – WAIVED	1	1. – CS 3. – FS 4. – NONE
	2. – INELIGIBLE 4. – COVERED (reg. and opt.)		2. – FICA 5. – OTHER

12. NATURE OF ACTION	13. EFFECTIVE DATE (Mo., Day, Year)	14. CIVIL SERVICE OR OTHER LEGAL AUTHORITY
702 CODE Promotion	03-05-72	Reg 335.102

15. FROM: POSITION TITLE AND NUMBER	16. PAY PLAN AND OCCUPATION CODE	17. (a) GRADE (b) LEVEL	STEP OR RATE	18. SALARY
PM(A) 11,644-S		13	03	pa $19987

19. NAME AND LOCATION OF EMPLOYING OFFICE
US Army Aviation Systems Command, Office of the Project Manager,
Light Observation Helicopter Systems, Configuration Management Division,
Identification and Control Branch, St. Louis, Missouri

20. TO: POSITION TITLE AND NUMBER	21. PAY PLAN AND OCCUPATION CODE	22. (a) GRADE (b) LEVEL	STEP OR RATE	23. SALARY
Supervisory Equipment Specialist (Aircraft) 12,736-S	GS-1670	14	01	pa $21960

24. NAME AND LOCATION OF EMPLOYING OFFICE
US Army Aviation Systems Command, Directorate for Technical Data, Cataloging
and Standardization, Technical Data Management Division,
St. Louis, Missouri

25. DUTY STATION (City-State)	26. LOCATION CODE
St. Louis, Missouri	29-7080-510

27. APPROPRIATION	28. POSITION OCCUPIED 1 – COMPETITIVE SERVICE 2 – EXCEPTED SERVICE	29.	APPORTIONED POSITION	
1MA	1	(FROM)	1 – PROVED 2 – WAIVED	(TO) STATE

30. REMARKS:
☐ A. SUBJECT TO COMPLETION OF 1 YEAR PROBATIONARY (OR TRIAL) PERIOD COMMENCING_____
☐ B. SERVICE COUNTING TOWARD CAREER (OR PERM) TENURE FROM_____
SEPARATIONS: SHOW REASONS BELOW, AS REQUIRED. CHECK IF APPLICABLE ☐ C. DURING PROBATION

Authority: DA Referral List 1 109L, dated 1 November 1971.

Para 88, Line 01
Comp Level: 057
Orgn Code: AXX

31. DATE OF APPOINTMENT AFFIDAVIT (Accessions only)	34. SIGNATURE (Or other authentication) AND TITLE FOR THE APPOINTING OFFICER
32. OFFICE MAINTAINING PERSONNEL FOLDER (If different from employing office)	*Gerald L. Black*
33. CODE 19 AR 00 EMPLOYING DEPARTMENT OR AGENCY DEPARTMENT OF THE ARMY	GERALD L. BLACK, Acting Chief, Civilian Personnel Division
	35. DATE 03-01-72 2298

6 PART
90-134-14

8-1 Promotion to GS-14

DEPARTMENT OF THE ARMY	1. INSTALLATION OR HEADQUARTERS OFFICE	2. JOB NUMBER
JOB DESCRIPTION (DA CPPM 1 and CPR P30)	US ARMY AVIATION SYSTEMS COMMAND	12736-S

3. CITATION TO APPLICABLE STANDARD AND ITS DATE OF ISSUANCE	4. TITLE Supervisory Equipment Specialist (Aircraft)		
	5. PAY SCHEDULE GS	6. OCC. CODE 1670	7. GRADE 14
8. EVALUATION APPROVAL Title, pay schedule, code and grade of this job have been fixed in accordance with Department of the Army official policy and grade level standards.	SIGNATURE ANTON IMHOF, JR.		DATE 3 Sep 71

9. SUPERVISORY CONTROLS, DUTIES, AND WORKING CONDITIONS (Indicate percent of time for each duty, where pertinent.) (Continue statement of duties, etc., on reverse side if necessary.)

SUPERVISORY CONTROLS

Works under general direction of the director who outlines responsibilities, broad objectives, and goals to be attained. Exercises broad authority with considerable latitude for the use of independent judgment in planning and directing the work of the division. Work is reviewed for accomplishment of overall objectives and conformance with basic policy.

MAJOR DUTIES

Serves as Chief of an Element (Division), which is subdivided into subordinate organized entities (Branches/Sections), and as staff advisor to the Director/Deputy Director. Possesses a comprehensive knowledge of the Provisioning Master Data Record (PMDR) and Federal Stock Number Master Data Record (FSNMDR) within the AMC Logistics Program-Hardcore, Automated (ALPHA) system, and exercises managerial, technical and administrative direction over subordinate elements through assigned supervisory personnel. Responsibilities include the technical/administrative direction of specific elements involved in Provisioning, Publications, Automated Data, and Integrated Management Programs which are used worldwide on all type of Rotary/Fixed Wing aircraft, Air Delivery/Life Support equipment, tools, ground support equipment, accessories, propulsion systems, trainers and other equipment required to support Army aviation. Data developed and maintained is used to support assigned equipment/systems through all stages from preproduction through disposal. Provides representation at Contractor Plants and on special projects or committees as required for determining the technical and policy requirements for maintenance, overhaul, rebuild and logistical support for assigned equipment/systems. Applies a practical technical knowledge of aircraft construction, maintenance, operation and repair; applies a good workable knowledge of the regulations, policies, operating and budget programs, practices and procedures. Interprets technical and administrative directives and develops proposed policy to cover new or changed requirements. Coordinates policy/procedures with counter-parts

10. JOB CONTENT APPROVAL (Complete on organization file copy only.)

ORGANIZATION LOCATION

THIS STATEMENT ACCURATELY DESCRIBES THE WORK REQUIRED IN ONE POSITION OR IN EACH OF A GROUP OF POSITIONS IN THE ABOVE ORGANIZATION	THE ABOVE DESCRIPTION, WITH SUPPLEMENTAL MATERIAL, IS ADEQUATE FOR PURPOSES OF EVALUATION.
SIGNATURE OF APPROVING SUPERVISOR	SIGNATURE OF ANALYST

11. REAUDIT APPROVAL

DATE							
SUPERVISOR'S APPROVAL							
ANALYST'S SIGNATURE							

DA FORM 374 1 JUN 61   PREVIOUS EDITIONS OF THIS FORM ARE OBSOLETE.

8-1 Promotion to GS-14 page 1

in other agencies of the Government and with contractors. Work is accomplished by
a staff of approximately 125-200 employees predominately in the Equipment Specialist
field in grades GS-09 through GS-13, together with supporting administrative and
clerical personnel.

1. Conducts a continuous appraisal of program progress, accomplishments, and
effectiveness, through a review of progress reports, program documents, studies,
reports, and by evaluation and consultation with subordinate supervisors. Plans and
makes functional assignments of work to subordinates and makes continuing evaluation
of division operations to assure that work is being accomplished in the most efficient
and expeditious manner and that all activities are effectively integrated into a
uniform and consistant work entity. Briefs subordinate employees and others as
required to insure consistant interpretation and correlation of policies, regulations,
and priority factors in the planning and execution of work. Determines training
needs and devises methods of accomplishing such training. Develops standards of
performance, prepares performance appraisals for supervisory personnel, and approves
or disapproves leave requests. Initiates personnel and position actions, attempts to
resolve grievances which cannot be resolved by subordinate supervisors, holds corrective
interviews, and takes administrative disciplinary measures as required in executing
the full scope of supervisory personnel management obligations.

2. Develops and applies policies and procedures for operation of the division to
conform with higher echelon directives and regulations and to promote efficiency,
economy, and conservation of materials and manpower. Reviews existing policies,
program plans, and schedules to insure that deficiencies and problem spots are identi-
fied and that appropriate action is taken to resolve them. Reconciles opposing or
conflicting concepts, plans or viewpoints in achieving integrated maintenance operations
within the organization and essential cooperation with other AVSCOM personnel
performing closely allied functions such as engineering, cataloging, procurement,
requirement, automatic data, etc. Outlines and evaluates projected requirements and
the impact on existing operations. Discusses and clarifies division responsibility
and allocates the responsibilities to be assumed by various branches, sections and
groups.

3. As the command's key technical provisioning data representative, maintains
executive level relationships and contacts with principal officials of the commodity
commands and industry to advance the concepts and application of maintenance doctrine in
the Department of Defense and Department of the Army Logistics Program, the Integrated
Item Reduction Programs, and the Single Manager Assignment Programs. As Staff Advisor
to the Director/s is frequently called upon to participate in or serve as leader of
conferences, as well as planning and policy-making committees which have command or
Department-wide significance and impact and where commitments rendered are accepted
as authoritative and binding. Participates in conferences with representatives of
Allied countries, e.g., Canada, Turkey, England, etc. providing technical expertise
and guidance in the provisioning and/or support of aircraft configurations/modifications
unique to the DOD system. Discusses with superior/s those recommendations or commitments
which have a major effect on the division mission. Utilizes a comprehensive knowledge
of division and directorate operations, operational requirements, applicable regulations
and directives, workloads, deadlines, priority programs, and operational trends in

8-1 Promotion to GS-14 page 2

conferring periodically or on call with the Director for the purpose of keeping him informed of the status of the program, advising him on problem areas, and/or making recommendations which will enable him to accomplish phases of the total directorate program.

Performs other duties as assigned.

(Title and grade are established in accordance with position classification standards and guides. These materials are available for your review in the Civilian Personnel Division.)

8-1 Promotion to GS-14 page 3

8-2 Carol Hessenauer good Illinois friend

8-3 Was an honor to be on the "Hinrichs" AVRADCOM team

AMSAV-FB   Employee Career Appraisals (DD Forms 1559)

Dir of PT&PD   Dir for Maintenance   17 Jan 73
Civ Pers Div   Tech Data Mgt Div   Mr. Kuschel/ch/3025
ATTN: AMSAV-RCR

1. Discussion between Mrs. M. Roberts, Civilian Personnel, and the undersigned,
16 Jan 73, regarding extending submittal of DD Forms 1559.

2. Request your approval of extending 1559 submittal to 15 March 1973, on the
following personnel:

   a. John A. Monken, GS-1670-13, Supervisory Equip Spec, SSN: ▬▬▬▬

   b. Edgar D. Goodwin, GS-1670-13, Supervisory Equip Spec, SS ▬▬▬▬

   c. Robert G. Schacht, GS-1670-13, Supervisory Equip Spec, S ▬▬▬

   d. Albert J. Mozelewski, GS-1670-13, Supervisory Equip Spec, ▬▬▬▬

   e. Leonard E. Ramey, GS-1670-13, Supervisory Equip Spec, SS ▬▬▬

3. Justification is that this Division is striving for exceptional qualification on
the present assigned Branch Chiefs. Subject Branch Chiefs are presently on a cross-
training program, and sufficient time should be afforded the individuals to handle
the management and supervision areas, this will enable the Division Chief to properly
rate the individuals.

4. In the event the Appraisal forms can be submitted prior to 15 Mar 73 they will be
hand-carried to CPO.

                              WAYNE A. KUSCHEL
                              Chief, Tech Data Management Division

                    8-4 Cross training of GS-13's

AMCPM-LH   24 March 72

SUBJECT: Items for Discussion with COL J.E. Baker, LOH Project Manager

COL J.E. Baker, Project Manager
LOHS

1. This letter along with a personal exit interview will apprise the
LOH-Project Manager of additional facts to debate the conversation that
took place 14 Mar 72, 1645 hours, in the Project Manager's Office, with
Mr. James F. Matthews being present. The conversation consisted of
intimation by COL Baker that he threw my name around literally during
a telephone conversation with Mr. Dittman, CPO, and that you (COL Baker)
felt the undersigned was not worthy of promotion ahead of Mr. Harry D. Murphy.
To be more explicit COL Baker, the Civil Service rules and regulations
are vastly different than military rules and regulations. It behooves you
to understand Civil Service regulations, and the fact that personnel are
eligible to file grievances against your Office over matters concerning
their professional careers or utilize other channels, including writing
to their Senators or Congressman.

2. The undersigned attempted to explain that there were two entirely
different career fields involved; a. GS-301-14 Logistic Management in
LOH-PM and; b. GS-1670-14 Supervisory Equipment Specialist in TDC&S
Director's Office. COL Baker retorted that he was going to see what could
be done to prevent the undersigned's promotion, since he felt Mr. Murphy
was qualified in the Equipment Specialists Career Field and deserved this
promotion. COL Baker, had you pursued this course and miracles happened
Mr. Murphy would have been assigned to TDC&S and not with the LOH-PM's
Office. However, I have had a Form 50 since 9 Mar 72, promoting me to a
GS-1670-14, in the Directorate of TDC&S. My qualification was a determining factor for selection to the position within TDC&S, the college
degree I earned in 1957 was the one main factor in my behalf. I'd like
to ask one question! While I was spending my hard earned Captain's pay
for a college degree, by attending night school, what was everyone else
doing with their time and money? Maybe everyone else is not inclined
towards self-development in their off duty time. (I believe in it).

3. One factor that was not discussed or brought out was the GS-1670-14
position was on a DA Referral List, dated 1 Nov 71 (undersigned interviewed
during Jan 72), and the GS-301-14 was on a AMC Referral List. The undersigned was listed on both DA and AMC Referral Lists.

8-5 Exit interview with Colonel Baker

4. Further, the undersigned was not given the benefit of a formal interview for the GS-301-14 position on the AMC Referral List. It appears an ulterior motive prompted Mr. Matthews and you (COL Baker) to ask me if I would accept the Logistics Management Division Chief's position in the event Mr. Murphy's promotion was rejected by AVSCOM, presumable for lack of qualifications. At that time I indicated I wanted the position and since two of us were competing for the same position this placed the LOH-PM management at a disadvantage, because Mr. Murphy advised the undersigned that if anyone was selected and promoted over him for the Division Chief's position, although they were better qualified, he would file a grievance based on the experience of the year or so he performed in that function. Based on my acceptance and also knowledge of AVSCOM's prerequisites which requires a college degree for promotion to GS-14, I would have also filed a grievance against the LOH-PM Office if not selected and promoted to this position.

5. As of this date, 17 Mar 72, I have not been advised or counselled by LOH-PM of their intent or reasoning for not providing a release date, so that I can assume the position that I was promoted to, that being Chief of Tech Data Management Division, TDC&S.

6. Since my detail to the LOH-PM Office (Aug 69) certain individuals are praised on their background experience, as you (COL Baker) brought out on Mr. Murphy, that he had over 25 years of faithful Civil Service background, which is commendable; however, allow me to toot my own horn. If anyone would take the time to review my record they would note that I haven't exactly been stagnant. I enlisted as a Private, 12 June 1940 and retired in grade of Major, 30 June 1960. I was promoted to every grade (except Staff Sgt) up through the ranks and had seven (7) years seniority as a Captain prior to promotion to Major for retirement, and all of this was attained by age 36½. The U.S. Army Aviation Materiel Command selected me with grade of GS-1670-11 in June 1966, I was immediately sent to Ft. Sill, Oklahoma for two weeks of T-55 Turbine Engine Training. Then sent TDY for 30 days to Ft. Rucker for on-the-line training, then assigned to Ft. Benning, Ga. as T-55 Engine Instructor. In Oct 66, AVSCOM requested that I go to Ft. Eustis, Va. for T-53-L13 Engine Training. Completed in Nov 66 and assigned as AAMTAP Team Coordinator and departed for RVN Dec 66 for a one year tour. Received promotion to GS-1670-12 in Aug 67 while in RVN. Reassigned as Turbine Engine Manager within Field Assistance, U.S. Army Aviation Materiel Command, St. Louis, Mo., Jan 68. Interviewed and selected for promotion to GS-301-13 as YO-3A Project Manager in June 69. In Aug 69 was detailed to the LOH-PM Office, as the YO-3A Project Officer, this lasted until 17 Apr 70, when I was placed on "excess" list because Systems Introduction was phasing out. This lead to my assignment to LOH-PM Configuration Management Division as a Branch Chief (never served in this position), Supervisory Equipment Specialist, GS-1670-13.

8-5 Exit interview with Colonel Baker page 2

7. COL Baker mentioned how hard Mr. Murphy had worked for promotion to
grade GS-14. COL Baker and Mr. Matthews were advised that I was sympathetic
regarding Mr. Murphy's potential promotion. However, I'm disputing the
idea that only Mr. Murphy works hard. There are many employees that
accomplish correspondence tasks at home for their office. Another view
would be to ask why personnel remain after 1630 hours, it could be that
automobile traffic is heavy and by waiting an hour or so, they can arrive
home at the same time and not battle traffic. At this point I would
recommend a cursory look into each Supervisors ability to accomplish task
assignments. Is the supervisor delegating tasks or does he accomplish
the difficult jobs himself for fear they will not get done, thereby limit-
ing supervision on other matters? The present scholastic philosophy is
this indicates poor management. Also everyone is forgetting the hectic
times spent on the YO-3A project, for example; on two separate days, there
were eighty calls and transactions, these were informally logged in from
all over the U.S. and RVN. I have been called by COC at all hours of the
night, and inturn have gone to the Mart Building to resolve problems caused
by these calls which required writing numerous messages, MFR's and DFs so
that operational posture was maintained. On one occasion I spent 5 weeks
at LMSC facilities working out management problems so that the YO-3A was
accepted on dates specified and inturn the deployment dates (established
nine (9) months prior) never slipped and were on time. To this mediocre
task (as everyone thought) one individual logged each team member as working
256 hours overtime, including Saturdays and Sundays. Of course my lower
grade personnel never had the opportunity of being paid overtime, and they
never requested anything in return for this exercise.

8. Another statement by you and Mr. Matthews was that Mr. Murphy was doing
an outstanding job for 2 to 3 years. Again, I'm disputing the facts that
Mr. Murphy is the only outstanding individual working 2 to 3 years on a
project or for that matter a given job assignment. There has been several
personnel doing an outstanding job without any fanfare; however, they are
in a class by themselves or minority known as steady pacers. They work in
a systematic atmosphere and when the paper work is turned in the task is
complete and no snowflake is delinquent. For additional information, I was
assigned the YO-3As Project Officer from Aug 69 thru July 71 in the PM's
Office. I also did an outstanding job and was personally advised by
LTC E.M. Browne for my effort, and that I would be given an outstanding
award. I can say this, I haven't received one little shred of paper to
indicate this (Mr. Matthews is aware of this statement). Conversely,
several personnel who made my task more difficult than it already was have
received awards, medals, commendations and pay for their futile efforts on
the YO-3A. One would have to assume that as long as you screw up a project
you'll receive acknowledgment and be rewarded.

3

8-5 Exit interview with Colonel Baker page 3

9. Another item that irritates other PM employees and myself is the
tardiness of performance appraisals. This is the only tool that an
employee has that gives him retention points. While all eyes are cast
upon one individual there are approximately 7 to 8 other deserving
personnel that have to wait for the one special individuals case to be
accomplished before the wheels of progress can begin grinding out the
tardy correspondence. Since my detail and then assignment to the LOH-PM
my experience has been that my performance appraisal was 5 months late
and the most recent one I signed Jan 72 has not been received in CPO to
date, 15 Mar 72. As the Project Manager it behooves you to get the lax
handling and tardiness of these reports corrected, so that deserving
personnel can receive their proper recognition.

10. There are several areas within the LOH-PM Office if not corrected
will deteriorate the overall efficiency, they are:

   a. How does a faithful Civil Service employee completing their work
in 40 hours compete for recognition, ie, outstanding awards, commendations,
SSPA, etc., versus an individual that puts in 70 hours per week and receives
the highest incentive awards and personal recognition from management.

   b. Conversation with employees indicates their belief that the Project
Manager does not approve outstanding awards, etc. This has a morale factor
involving all employees that are competing for special recognition.

   c. Promotions within the Project Managers is at a low ebb. There have
been many instances where there are vacant promotional areas and no one is
selected. Yet an individual that receives a call for an interview from an
outside source is immediately promised a higher grade or "he becomes
indispensable to LOH-PM".

11. My main objective in writing this letter was to provide the Project
Manager with constructive criticism to assist in improving the overall
program.

                              WAYNE A. KUSCHEL

                                    4

            8-5 Exit interview with Colonel Baker page 4

DEPARTMENT OF THE ARMY
HEADQUARTERS, US ARMY AVIATION SYSTEMS COMMAND
PO BOX 209, ST. LOUIS, MO 63166

AMSAV-F

1 1 MAY 1973

TO WHOM IT MAY CONCERN:

1. Mr. Wayne A. Kuschel has been an active member of my organization as Chief of the Technical Data Management Division for the past 10 months. Prior to that time I have had first hand knowledge of his abilities, his character, and his work since 1966. He can be justly described as an outstanding supervisor, employee, and a fine man, who uses his unique qualities and broad capabilities to inspire and lead others to perform any task assigned to him.

2. As a highly experienced and highly qualified individual, he was selected for promotion to GS-14, in 1972, chosen from a field of outstanding candidates. It is believed, by his superiors and co-workers, that his management ability and qualifications are unequaled in this Command. Having been selected he was appointed to the position as Chief of the Technical Data Management Division, Directorate for Maintenance. Prior to his appointment the morale of this Division had fallen to a very low state. Organizational cooperation and personnel enthusiasm had deteriorated to an unacceptable level and were in danger of adversely affecting this Command.

3. Mr. Kuschel, with insight and decisiveness, quickly took action to clear channels of communication, re-establish a cooperative atmosphere and through his own enthusiasm, managerial competence and eye to fairness and concern for the well being of his employees virtually lifted the morale of his personnel by its bootstraps and thus greatly improved working attitudes. His recognition and control of heretofore devisive factions within his Division were instrumental in improving the efficiency and capabilities of this Command.

4. I believe Mr. Kuschel's integrity, intelligence, and capabilities to be of the highest quality and I find him to be one of this Command's great assets. I offer this statement as my highest regard and confidence in this man.

Colonel, GS
Director of Maintenance

8-6 To Whom It May Concern

318

DEPARTMENT OF THE ARMY

WAYNE A. KUSCHEL

IS OFFICIALLY COMMENDED

FOR

EXCEPTIONAL PERFORMANCE IN EXECUTING THE MISSION OF THE TECHNICAL DATA MANAGEMENT DIVISION. MR. KUSCHEL'S COMPREHENSIVE KNOWLEDGE IN PROVISIONING, ARMY PUBLICATIONS, AND INTEGRATED MANAGEMENT PROGRAMS SIGNIFICANTLY IMPROVED THE CAPABILITY OF THE DIVISION. WITH EXTENSIVE KNOWLEDGE OF THE AMC LOGISTIC PROGRAM HARDCORE AUTOMATED SYSTEM, HIS EFFORT CONTRIBUTED TO THE ESTABLISHMENT OF A SOUND DATA BASE FOR THE FEDERAL STOCK NUMBER MASTER DATA RECORD. HIS SPLENDID ATTITUDE AND DEVOTION TO DUTY MADE HIM AN ASSET TO THE DIRECTORATE.

29 MAY 1973

GENE PHILLIPS, COLONEL, GS
DIRECTOR OF MAINTENANCE
US ARMY AVIATION SYSTEMS COMMAND

8-7 Department of Army Commendation

319

8-8
Department of Army Commendation

CHAPTER 9-
LOTS OF SUPERVISION REQUIRED
FOR AIRCRAFT SURVIVABILITY
EQUIPMENT

I visited Major General Hinrichs and told him my views and laid my career on the line. He stated that I had an exceptionally good track record and he would see if he could assist me. Then the civilian personnel office sent me a new position as a GS-301-13, Step 8, CH-47 (Chinook), and CH-54 Cargo Systems Assistant Manager of Heavy Helicopters. I don't know what transpired after I departed the Commanding General's Office, or the events leading up to the new GS-301-13 Systems Assistant Manager of Heavy Helicopters position. [Picture of CH-47 (Chinook) 9-1] This gave me the overall responsibility for the intensive management of one or more selected first line cargo aircraft. This was a switch in managerial abilities on current and modified helicopters requiring intensive lifecycle management because of the limited numbers of assigned six qualified personnel. The field personnel would report discrepancies to our office. Our program manager was LTC Sternat, a well-versed aviator type staff officer. He had a knack for resolving problems, so we fed dangerous situations or safety of flight items to him. The rest of my equipment managers resolved anything and everything that came in to the office marked for our immediate attention. Within AVSCOM, all Directorates had their personnel aligned with the command's types of aircraft, so it was an easy operation to receive assistance wherever it was needed. Being a senior staff advisor to my supervisors was a very envious position. All doors were open for my convenience on specific helicopter problems or managerial areas.

My next duty assignment I was picked for was the reorganization of AVSCOM. [AVSCOM Reorganization 9-2] Officer in Charge was LTC Parker, two Majors, Robb and Bryan, another GS-13, Don Ward and I (GS-13). Our efforts were such that we had to work all the various directorates into two major organizations, the United States Army Aviation Systems Support Command (AVSCOM Support) with a Major General commanding and the United States Army Aviation Research and Development Command (AVRADCOM) with another qualified Major General commanding. After numerous in-house briefings, sixteen hours per day for six days and endless weeks, it was getting tedious and hectic. I thought it would never become a reality. There were meetings with the Commanding General (MG Hinrichs, his Vice Commander (BG Mackmull), and Chief of Staff (Colonel Bristol). Every facet or detail was analyzed, hashed and re-hashed for pros or cons to eliminate the danger of higher headquarters denying or cancelling the project as not feasible for a workable aviation and support reorganizations. After several weeks of write, re-write, removing or adding specific regulations from AMC on what the end results would be, our command briefing personnel went to HQ AMC Arlington, Virginia to brief them on the first slice of the pie, so to speak, and receive their comments to incorporate into the next session of events.

Upon the command's briefing personnel returning to AVSCOM, we began incorporating AMC recommendations as close as they could be utilized by all of AMC commands. When all the AMC recommendations were incorporated, another briefing at HQ AMC was made ready for the specific time and date. This time our reorganization authority would take place across all the HQ AMC commands present. One specialized area which was set in motion was for a new Weapons System Management Directorate to be put in place. They would assume all the old and new specific types of equipment to ensure nothing in the management area was left out or fell through the crack. Our team received congratulations from the command and staff area, and again all of us were going to be up for grabs. [AVSCOM Reorganization Updated 9-3], [Recommended TDA Changes for WSMO 9-4]

After we finished the reorganization of AVSCOM to include a Weapons System Directorate and the commands under the HQ AMC, I received on 29 March 1974 a letter of commendation from the AVSCOM Command Section. (LTC Murray E. Parker) [Copy of Letter of Commendation 9-5]

Since the new Directorate of Weapons System Management became operational, it realized all the old commands functions into a new manageable unit with more command authority and a Colonel as the new commander. I was assigned to the Director of Weapons Systems Management as the assistant manager GS-13 of the UH-1(Huey) helicopter system. We were responsible for the executive life cycle management for the operational support of all assigned first line UH-1 (Huey) aircraft weapons systems. There were over 7,000 plus UH-1 (Huey) currently in the Army inventory, a regular old work horse. In addition to the UH-1's (Hueys), we had the VH-1N Presidential Aircraft Army One System. [Picture of UH-1 (Huey) and Presidential UH-1N Army One 9-6] This required our supervisor, Lieutenant Colonel Ulysses S. Large, Jr., to be on frequent classified temporary duty somewhere in Texas for the United States Army's support of the Presidential Aircraft Army One. We had the normal problems on the UH-1 (Hueys) since they were rolling up a tremendous amount of total flying hours worldwide. It meant parts were deteriorating or wearing out. With new decisions and engineering support required to prevent any disruptions in the flying capability of the helicopter, you cannot use a band aid to resolve this type of problem.

One thing really bothered me each year I had to fill out a "Confidential Statement of Employment and Financial Interests" Department of Defense Personnel DD Form 1555 1 March 1966.

If this form was so important for us GS-13 and above grades to fill out, why doesn't the United States Government utilize it to disclose the financial interests from the President on down, his Staff, Congressional personnel, designated Czars, Department personnel and all personnel above the grade of GS-13 or whatever pay level is determined beneficial.

Words in the Constitution of the United States of America in Article I, Section 9 "no money shall be drawn from the treasury, but in consequence of appropriations made by law and a regular statement and account of the receipts and expenditures of all public money shall be published from time to time".

Sounds like someone in the Treasury Department or of its likes should be giving us an accounting of a check and balance type of statement, let all of us U.S. Citizens know where the money is coming from where and how the money will be spent. That would be a good question and answer.

In addition, why are there so many problems of personnel not paying income taxes, why not garnish their earnings to pay the bad debt? That's all I heard of in the Armed Forces at meetings, etc.

My belief is being honest in offices or officials holding good paying positions, why not have them provide proof of earnings and some type of statement and make sure the exact amounts are displayed in newspapers around the United States of America. [Confidential Statement DD Form 1555 9-7]

After I became Assistant Manager on 9 June 1974 of the UH-1(Huey) Helicopter Division, the Drug Enforcement Agency (DEA) came to AVSCOM for assistance in destroying the current marijuana crop in the country of Jamaica.

The DEA requested three (3) UH-1 (Hueys) helicopters be provided and six months inventory of spare parts for the helicopters. I was in favor of assigning three (3) new UH-1 (Hueys) helicopters from the Bell Helicopter Company (BHC), in Hurst, Texas. These helicopters would be provided on the ongoing BHC contract. This was agreeable with Mr. John W. Starks, DEA Aviation Section. On 15 January 1975, the United States Embassy in Kingston, Jamaica sent Major General Hinrichs at AVSCOM a final situation report stating how pleased they were with our aviation support and that the mission could not have been successful without it. Then on 22 January 1975, a Drug Enforcement Agency (DEA) letter of appreciation was sent to AVSCOM Executive Officer for LTC Large, acknowledging the performance they felt merited special recognition and our competence, which did much to enhance the image of AVSCOM. [Letter of Appreciation 15 January 1975 9-8]

Since LTC Large and I were working closely with John Stark, Chief DEA Aviation Section, he made numerous telephone calls to our office with frequent visits to ensure adequate support was provided. We devoted as much time as necessary to cover all of DEA requirements. We had special handling or dialogue between the two organizations. They got what they needed to accomplish their mission. A few days later John sent me a box with a special note and how much he enjoyed our relationship and behold, there was a bottle of Jamaica rum inside with the DEA insignia attached. I asked John if I owed him any money because gratuities were out. He stated he bought the bottle before returning to the United States to show his appreciation for my support. So I had a small shot to try out the contents. It was excellent tasting; it took the best of two years to sip it dry.

Since the Utility Division, within the AVSCOM Weapons System Management Office had the largest segment of aircraft, the UH-1 (Huey) helicopter they were required to prepare for a full scale, program review for the United States Army's, Vice Chief of Staff, General Walter T. Kerwin, Jr. on the 14th of May 1975.

The Success of the review was passed down through channels to Lieutenant Colonel Ulysses S. Large, Jr., my supervisor, who in turn indorsed a Letter of appreciation to me.

The reader of my book "All or Nothing" can read my received appreciative remarks, in this letter. Especially the stated remarks "indicates your dedication and professional competence" and etc. It makes a person want to continue on the course of managing until his usefulness is no longer required and the persons career is finished, then he retires. [Letter of appreciation General Walter T. Kerwin Army Chief of Staff 9-9]

We had a problem in the tail rotor system. After months of coordinating and meetings to obtain funds for modifying the tail rotor, the go-ahead came through, so the advertisement to modify went to procurement to be put out on contract. Before the final go-ahead date, our UH-1 (Huey) office received notice that Mr. William Gillespie, a GS-14, Chief Logistics Maintenance office, used an electronic means to siphon off $120,000.00 for himself to purchase a computer for his Technical Data Branch. This irked LTC Large whole-heartedly and he reported it to the command section. It didn't sit well with anyone and Bill Gillespie got only a slap on the wrist. Where the recouped funds came from to get the high priority Safety of Flight item on contract I personally do not know, but the problem was resolved.

After a little over two years on this team I went for an interview in the Aircraft Survivability Equipment (ASE-PM) Program Manager's office to fill a division chief's GS-14 position. Again there were shenanigans being pulled, trying to promote from within that office. The local supervisors tried to keep their favorite person shielded from outsiders who had a valid claim for that position. My RIF was caused by a dang fool civil servant not capable of doing his duty or job, disliked by people he came in contact with, and was kept floating on "Command Personnel Detail" in limbo because he couldn't do his job as a supervisor. Yet the service kept him on the rolls and no one tried to fire him because he was an African-American and excess to the command's needs and requirements, or he would never have been on a long term loan basis. To prove that point, I was on LOH-PM detail from 18 April 1971 until 5 March 1972 when Mr. Smith, Director of TDC& S had to eliminate my position on the YO-3A aircraft and temporarily assign me to the LOH-PM office to get my service as his Chief of Technical Management Division. If the Directorates want you moved they work with the command and the civilian service officer until they get it done. Good kind words can change parts of the world if necessary.

I was listed on the AMC civilian personnel and DA referral list for GS-346-14 because of my Reduction in Force (RIF) status and my effective executive management training and capabilities in special positions. I was judged well qualified for any GS-14 position.

Regarding my losing my GS-14, these are my thoughts on my successor. Mr. William Gillespie, being African-American, and with an engineering degree, was given my supervisor GS-14 position in the Directorate of Maintenance Technical Data Logistics Division because he was made "minimum" qualified by the civilian personnel board for RIF situations. By him being qualified for one line only and no more than four inches long on my job description, #JN 12736-S, the job description itself was the best part of two pages long. This was because specific managers were afraid to take on the race issue and criticism that would arise from his qualification factors. This was for 1974. They didn't debate that subject for any reason, which I thought was totally wrong. I had an outstanding qualification factor for the GS-14 position, being in the Chief of Technical Data Division position for two years. Another thing in my thoughts, there were a GS-14 and a GS-15, both who were African-American that were on my side to remain as the Logistics Chief. These panel personnel knew Mr. Gillespie could not manage nor supervise personnel and yet the other civilian members on the board gave into letting Mr. Gillespie qualify for the established GS-346-14 position. It was getting the problem off their shoulders and not be in a lawsuit, to heck with my outstanding managerial ability.

After a couple months, the AVSCOM civilian personnel office gave me the chance to accept a position as Chief (GS-14) [Promotion to GS 14 9-9a] Logistics Management Division of the Aircraft Survivability Equipment Program Managers Office (ASE-PM). [ASE-PM staff personnel 9-10] Gee! Whiz!, they also had assigned a total of six personnel to control fifty-one aircraft survivability equipment systems (ASE) and to accomplish worldwide fielding requirements. I had the logistics control and approval of millions of dollars for all assigned systems, which included school and maintenance requirements for all ASE systems or projects. [General John R. Guthrie, comments on ASE program 9-11]

To elaborate, each of the fifty-one systems would be handled similarly to an individual aircraft, ship or whatever item, requiring constantly monitoring of 301 different points on the life cycle management system. The life cycle management is known as the "womb to the tomb" concept and it means exactly that. If you allow any one of the 301 check point requirements to fall out of phase or through the cracks, the complete life cycle would suffer. It would take extra time, money and effort to get it back on proper schedule or restore the life cycle to get it on track. There would have to be a combined in-house and command approval of corrective action to restart the program and lots of funds to correct the problem.

My Logistics Division was what a person would say "plucked clean and real mean" to properly be able to manage it. If one of my dedicated personnel had physical problems and someone wasn't there to pick up the program and run with it, the slippage had to be reported with the possible consequences and what corrective actions had to be taken. Most generally one of the assistant project manager's dependent on his workload might come to the rescue. I made an acquaintance or friend at the time in AVSCOM's Command Section Chief of Staff area. His name was Captain Gerald Green. He was one sharp and very intelligent person and aviator. Shortly thereafter he made Major (recently I contacted him and he had retired as a full Colonel, living in Illinois as a happy family man. He was highly educated and talented enough for any job assignment given to him. He was well gifted to take over any aviation position in HQ AMC). Colonel Green assisted me many times to expedite necessary action items.

Working in the ASE-PM as a Division Chief, we did achieve some high and low points. Everybody can't be perfect 100% of the time, but there were other personnel that expected a perfect record regardless of what it might take. During my time in the ASE-PM there never was a dull moment. I had one GS-12 named J.W. Dean. He came from Borger, Texas. He was one person that was perfect in all his dealings with his fellow persons or subordinates, and always fair and accurate in working with other commands. His work was 100% perfect any time of the day. You really had to hold him down to a slow speed when you gave him a job or assignment. He would achieve 100%; the best end results of any AVSCOM personnel. (I spoke with Colonel Gerald Green in October 1991. He was the UH-60 Black Hawk project manager. He told me that J.W. Dean was in his logistics area. That means he was either a GS-13 or 14, a well-deserved promotion).

The ASE-PM held meetings with other commands at their facility. Colonel Jack L. Keaton always took me along as a logistics team member so I could speak of any logistical requirements. I had to carry enough background material on whatever of the 51 systems that came into the discussion to give a firm answer or to contact our office and resolve it or get the action started. There were so many facets of our operation that it was totally impossible to keep ahead of in-house decisions, the contractor and his sub-contractors. It was tremendous and a taxing position. It's like being in the driver's seat without a steering wheel. If there would have been adequate qualified personnel staffing, it would have been a lot easier to control the division workload; whereby the various systems would have been assigned to a large group of personnel who would be dedicated to keep all systems on track or schedule. If one person went on leave or on sick leave, it left a void that no one could really fill. The only way I stayed ahead as far as I did was to keep questioning each system manager for his accomplishments and what actions he had taken or was working, the dates of completion, when the system tentatively would go to the field. All work had to be justified, on how the end item would be installed on the aircraft, and by whom, the United States Army or civilian contractors? There was lot of coordination that had to be accomplished to ensure proper installation of all assigned systems. The personnel were all superior workers (except Allen Chick) on accomplishing their workload.

I had to take exception to GS-9 Allen Chick. He was in a rear-end car accident and consequently had to be on sick leave or annual leave when needed. But I could not rely on his work schedule or take trips for his assigned systems of which he had 7 ASE systems to manage. After so long a period of time I had to submit justification correspondence for a physical on Mr. Chick. Either he had to be on duty full time to control his assigned programs or I would require a new replacement so that all high priority programs would not lapse into "no attention" and cause a catastrophic ending. There were too many actions required by many companies and Army Aviation units to field the equipment that Mr. Chick was assigned to accomplish. Regardless, I had to resolve this problem and Mr. Chick's sick leave so his programs would be covered 100% of the time.

As far as I was concerned my logistical personnel did an outstanding job regardless of what happened. No one could do more in the time frame allotted to get the equipment to the field. The main goal was of Aircraft Survivability Equipment to safeguard the crew members, then the aircraft. However, a lot of research and development had to be accomplished and improvements incorporated, then more test had to be performed to insure only the safest product would be put in the Army's inventory, let alone installed on other tri-services aircraft.

It was like a dream trying to manage the logistics area within the ASE-PM office. (I truly didn't believe I would last as long as I did, which was a total of Five (5) years including my retirement date of 10 July 1979). There were lots of problems between the various offices. It seemed like there were musical chairs being played because of the differences in people's personalities, and opinions, especially when a division chief went TDY, leave or school. The replacement or acting division chief would try and pull all types of actions that appeared as thorns in everybody's side, so the only way the acting chief could achieve a change was by implementing their desired feelings and putting his revisions into force. The acting chiefs never won any popularity contests, only got flack because of proposed changes which cancelled ideal procedure that had been in operation for a long period of time. The acting chief was able to implement changes to suit his self-esteem, things that would benefit his own position or duties, not thinking about consequences down the path, or the next day, next week or next year.

The project manager, Colonel Jack Keaton was one fine gentleman, very intelligent. He was well advised in all facets of United States Army

Aircraft Survivability Equipment policies and requirements and could relate to any subject within the confines of the United States Army and other working commands and all tri-service agencies involved in using this type of equipment or their improved, similar version of the United States Army's.

I can truthfully say that my prior experience in a Project Manager office qualified me to handle the logistical management element in the Aircraft Survivability Equipment. There was no time to transition into the Chief of Logistics position. It was an instantaneous reaction, like getting on a fast speeding automobile (that was not stopping) and going at least 100 miles per hour on all logistics topics or subjects contained within the Project Manager's office. I was acquainting myself on background information regarding numerous systems while on TDY trips to chair meetings since I was delegated the job of accomplishing assigned duties. This is one sticky piece of jargon saying I had to kick some butt in order to get people to move and do their duties. I was in an enviable position. If the personnel didn't do their duty towards the end result required in ASE accomplishment, I very tenderly requested their reassignment as our support personnel. This was the only method of getting the job done.

In this case you can't wear your heart on your (shirt) sleeve, but remember the end results are what I had to consider to get the high priority system into the field expeditiously as possible. Regardless of who gets stepped on or hurt, when the person could not accomplish the end results he was put aside or in a lesser responsible position depending on their career field and grade and what he could accomplish; in other words, have him reassigned as time was a very precious commodity.

On one occasion we were setting up an ASE-PM field office at Fort Monmouth to assist in alleviating any of these programs and expediting actions necessary to prevent any program system stoppage or slippages. I was interviewing GS-13s for logistics positions. There were several personnel at AVSCOM that wanted a chance to be interviewed and selected, as it was a big pay increase for everyday spending and for the high three years needed for retirement. I never knew who all the local candidates were but one stands out in my mind, a young lady, red-headed GS-12 from a command logistics area arrived at my office. After going through my two-bit requirement she flatly told me she would romp in the sack for a chance to acquire a promotion, besides it would be fun. With my tongue in check I quietly let the request slip by the wayside. After several trips to Fort Monmouth, I selected Ted Conti because of his vast knowledge in the electronics field and the methods he used to expedite and resolve problems in his command areas. Ted Conti was technically highly qualified to call support meetings within Electronic Command and coordinate with our ASE-PM and other United States Army team members to ensure all logistical areas were covered.

No one can truthfully say how many hours go into supporting systems, but it can be seven days per week with sixteen to eighteen hours per day spent on keeping systems on track. It is a known fact when you achieve a grade of GS-12 your supervisors expect your free time, with no overtime to keep or support the project or system. I can't dispute this requirement. To do so would bankrupt the government in overtime pay. I felt comfortable in supporting the system under my jurisdictions without added expenditures or funds for payment to employees. But there should be hard cold facts to substantiate these requirements, it being very controversial. I doubt if any regulation would be implemented to support the pay factor. It's different than being in a civilian company that has overtime rules.

The ASE-PM office was in support of all types of Army aircraft, fixed wing and helicopters to meet continuing battlefield threats. This entailed controlling developmental, production and fielding requirements encompassing the counter measures technology areas of Infrared, Radar, Optics and vulnerability reductions. One large factor involved was the total

ASE weight per system or equipment installed on each aircraft. This had a tremendous impact on the final aircraft configuration. With all of these programs, my division was overburdened with logistical programs and problems. We all had to stay within well-defined boundaries and on the same sheet of music. This meant the Army family and civilian companies had to agree on all facets and requirements of each system. Regardless of the importance of logistical support, it had a heavy impact on the future field support of each system. There were numerous studies and meetings to ascertain correct numbers of required parts, bits and pieces, total hours or time to do the maintenance.

I was called to Colonel Keaton's office on 20 February 1976 and received my 20 year service award and pin. Every time civilian personnel reviewed my records I would be authorized another award for seniority or longevity of service. These awards provided me with the strength and insight to do a much better job for Uncle Sam and I could say I had been there. The Logistics Chief position that I was assigned did not let me rest for the numerous past actions that kept coming into my office each day. My secretary was very proficient in sorting out the status of the correspondence. She had a knack at classifying the importance of each piece of correspondence, and provided a suspense on the ones that needed an endorsement or coordination by other offices.

Oh! There were times when I would lose some tail feathers because of a delinquent piece of correspondence and somehow dropped through the improper channels route. This was due to time constraints in getting all the offices to finalize the various personnel required to sign the paper work off. There were many times where it was necessary to go to the other commands or civilian contractor plants to insure the program was on track. Once a program event is not met on the required life cycle schedule it takes lots of extra meetings, phone calls, and personnel to review each task and determine corrective action to have it back on schedule.

The ASE-PM life cycle management had many tasks to be performed and each task had to be acted on when the time was due in order to keep it in step with all scheduled tasks and available aircraft worldwide, including installation time of items. However, all the ASE systems tasks being at different intervals on the life cycle management took the whole ASE logistics team to share in completing each step. It's not an easy situation to be in or faced with. Only a minimum of available man hours can be devoted to any particular area or problem without some other area slippage or problems developing.

On one occasion during June 1976 five of my assigned personnel were tentatively scheduled for TDY to several areas overseas for installation of ASE equipment, leaving only three persons including the division secretary to maintain all schedules and work load. There was no solution to my division's workload other than take care of the high priority items as they become known. I had to justify all change proposals, hopefully to adequately manage the various complex program areas.

With my limited time available for the overall management of the logistical office, on the 8th day of March 1976, I was notified that the ASE Deputy PM Mr. James C. Katechis and Mr. Herbert B. Murch were unable to attend an Executive Dynamics Seminar and that I would fill that space. The seminar was scheduled over a three-week period from 0830 to 1600 hours, covering five days. These seminars were utilized to provide executive managers with current methods to assist in all elements involving our personnel. After I received the official notice of attending this course, I proceeded to the Deputy Director's office and had Mr. Murch (engineering) present to justify my case and problems it would cause at that time. Regardless of my shortage of personnel and the length of the course, I could not convince them of my problems. They said the Logistical Division would run itself and they would assist in keeping it on time and schedule.

When I returned after the course ended, the paperwork and schedules were all screwed up. All that was mentioned was get into your work load and straighten things out. This shows how much assistance I received when I filled in for them for any type of education.

April 1976 was the time when I should have put in for thirty days of leave. Let the problems fall on the GS-15s to show a point that you do require sufficient personnel for worldwide equipment installation to keep equipment on schedule. However, this ensured us with proper abilities to accomplish our duties or dynamic leadership qualifications for problem solving and decision making that all systems stay on schedule. I can say whole-heartedly that a refresher course of instructions helped out managers to do their jobs more proficiently by bringing new types of ideas for division manager's abilities to assist each of us. There are so many aspects to managing a division or office that I don't know how to begin. I always analyze the complete office procedure and then go through each requirement, time frame, and files to acquire some knowledge on what had to be completed on scheduled dates, and keep your tail feathers dusted off for future problems arising.

Truthfully, good communication and good common sense plays a large role in sound management. Oh, a thorough knowledge of the job is an A-plus in accomplishing the end results. Regardless, when these problems arise, there are answers in a technical manual. Either you know it, have knowledge of it, or you have to apply well known good common sense in dealing with each subject.

When I was assigned to the ASE-PM, I was located on the eighteenth floor of the MART building located at 12th and Spruce in downtown St. Louis, Missouri. The project manager was located on the 17th floor and I used to keep the emergency stairwell hot by running up and down trying to put out the fires. Like I said before, there were so many problems that developed and immediate resolutions had to be given to prevent program slippage that there was no time for anything else to be done.

Mr. Robert Bubbla, a GS-13, was sitting on the vacant GS-14 Division Chiefs position which was in the process of being filled, or until a qualified GS-14 person was selected to assume the Chief's position. So I had several interviews before I was appointed. I had a very short period to get acquainted with the entire logistics area, which was determined to be a very complex logistics program. There was an undeterminable amount of fast action items that would require constant surveillance over all the life cycle management areas. While I was reviewing my assigned personnel for their specialized experience and background information to make certain that the best experienced man was on the most complex program, there were many actions that were on going, but by delegating out the "HOT" requirements it alleviated lots of anxieties that a new person coming on board received. You feel like heck, pulled through a keyhole at the end of the day when you had a chance to go over each system and what they really looked like on the life cycle chart. I always stayed late in the evening with Colonel Keaton or Mr. Katechis, PM. We would go over delicate security system problems and what my team had to do to keep the system going. The Colonel's four assistant program managers had lots of input. They also were available to provide assistance to any division that requested their help in eliminating the bottlenecks and I had numerous bottlenecks, so to speak.

I was appointed to a logistics team that LTC Dick Hazelwood headed up to take Special Aircraft Survivability Equipment to Germany and install on all assigned UH-1 (Huey) helicopters. We departed St. Louis in January 1978 for two or three weeks to complete the project. Dyna-Electronics was to install equipment across West Germany on specific aviation aircraft. Upon arriving at JFK International Airport on Long Island we loaded all baggage, supplies and tools on board a Pan Am 747 scheduled to land at

Frankfurt, Germany. The trip took twenty seven hours, with all of us being woke up every couple hours to eat. That was the most restless trip I have ever been on. At Frankfurt we were put on a bus to Kaiserslautern, where a combined United States Army, contractor maintenance, and in-country operations meeting was to be held. This would ascertain all problem areas that could possibly develop and the corrective action required to reduce ready aircraft scheduling problems, stoppages for supplies, or airframe installation problems. All areas of operation had to be considered because of hostile threats from communist East Germany. The aircraft had to be put into first line operation readiness immediately. This was the number one requirement for our installation team, to get the equipment installed on the aircraft/helicopter and have it flying as soon as possible. In case of problems or additional maintenance required, Dyna-Electronics had well qualified personnel to do our ASE system installation needs. Within two days, Dyna-Electronics teams were spread out across Germany in each of the Army's installation area or where the work would be performed. After two and a half days at Kaiserslautern we were taken to Frankfurt 7th Army Headquarters and assigned an office for control of our team. We were told about the does and don'ts while on German soil. Each team member was authorized a small Ford Corsica rental car to do their official duty. One of the first requirements I had was to assist Dyna-Electronics in having their tools released from the German impound section at Rhein-Main Airport. We had to use the Dyna Electronics Volkswagen bus because of the volume of cartons to transport, the equipment to special locations or center of the hub for fast installation of items onto each designated UH-1 (Huey). To get the particular equipment through customs I had to justify the United States Army's requirements for the special installation of classified ASE systems. The German security personnel were not curious, but were very sincere in assisting us in getting the crates out of the impound area to the trucks to haul them to maintenance area. That equipment saved the project time and money by getting it expedited out of the impound area. There were numerous pieces of correspondence that had to be coordinated and approved by the German Security personnel. The autobahn was something to see and ride on. Everyone traveled at 120 to 140 klicks or kilometers per hour. Of course the Porsches and Mercedes-Benz were always racing and trying to beat the other drivers. It was dangerous if you drove in the left lane and a car came up behind you and blinked their lights. It meant get over fast because I'm coming through. I saw numerous accidents from not getting out of a fast car lane. They just plow into the rear end and cared less of the consequence of the accident results. Life meant nothing to those careless people.

Since my military career began in 1940 I never had the opportunity to visit any European area until I was directed to be part of the ASE team scheduled to go into Germany for maintenance/installation of various ASE systems. We were advised to carry sufficient clothing for the winter time. I wholeheartedly accepted because I might never get another chance at seeing Germany. The whole team had to acquire AAA driver's licenses specifically for Germany and update our official "red" passports. The passports were hand-carried to Washington, D.C. for expeditious handling because of the close departure date. Trying to get Germany's United States Army units coordinated, because of their high priority, then schedule secret ASE installation and ensure Dyna-Electronics Corporation to be cleared through Heidelberg's 7th Army Corp to each aviation company was a tremendous task. Security was a very tight issue since there were numerous foreigners trying to acquire ASE equipment information from St. Louis of the dates we were scheduled to depart and complete the itinerary. There was lots of extra work put in at the office to coordinate all efforts to pull this project off without any problems or hitches.

My friend Jack Moore, one of my employees within the logistics division, was also scheduled to go because of his managing of critical

ASE systems that were scheduled to be installed in Germany. He also had a brilliant mind. He had a knack of looking and studying problems within his logistical assignment, developing updated plans and material to combat any problems arising at a later date. He was in a catch-22 situation where he could not be promoted to a higher grade until all facets of the civil service regulations were justified and then after three or four years of tried and true policies with a proven track record he still was not promoted. The grade structures could not be restructured for any one person regardless of his qualifications because higher headquarters would say "disapproved" for grade increases. You had to stay within the boundaries of the manning regulations, regardless of the man's capabilities. I did submit his name continually for a worthy promotion to GS-12, which he received in due time. Jack was elated that he was finally a grade higher. I feel it was late for him receiving a promotion, as he did an outstanding job from the time he was selected for the position. It's a rough situation to be an AVRADCOM spokesman. At designated meetings, some AVSCOM teams had up to eighty members to control. So the chosen chairperson had to be diversified with a complete knowledge of all AVSCOM functions and had to know when someone or an office had slacked off in their job accomplishment. I found numerous personnel who were really devoted and dedicated to their jobs. They would access the big picture requirement and apply corrective action when necessary to keep all actions in step with the complex programs. It seemed like the hard and dedicated workers never got credit where and when credit was due. They remained in their selected position and other personnel received the honor of a promotion. In my lengthy federal service, I never believed in this method but always tried to give just credit to the workers. I would never attempt to estimate how many "Letters of Appreciation" nor "Quality Step Increases" that I gave out, but the morale was such that the increased production spoke for itself.

Of course, sometimes the supervisor had a hard time to digest and swallow their belief in the individuals because some of the workers were not liked for their dependability or giving assistance when things began to fall through the cracks, so to speak. In my position I could not let anyone decline doing something to accomplish the end results of our systems, so I could protect our team personnel, regardless of the Directorate they were assigned to. I was not the most popular Chief in the AVRADCOM, ASE PM Office. I got the job done with stepping on toes or whatever the method that would achieve the end results. I had to go up against GS-15 and GS-16s to get the logistics back on track.

Our division Christmas party was something special. To show my appreciation for the tremendous work load my few employees accomplished, I was determined to have some type of a division party for my gratitude and let them enjoy the close working relationship. We worked all year to finish on schedule all projected items in the logistical area. So with the brightest future in front of us, why not enjoy the year end with some refreshment and food? My very dependable friend Joe Hudson and our secretary Patty Robertson concocted the drinking menu, a tasty punch made from wine and liquor. We all chipped in for the ingredients, which to the best of my recollection was seven gallon (milk cartons) of punch. After combining the items (such as hobo wine), Joe put the jugs in his freezer. As we approached Friday before Christmas, more plans were made as to the proper time to toast a few glasses. We in the division decided on 1400 hours in the afternoon, that way if there was any special requirements that came up we would be capable enough to handle the correspondence or problems and still have a friendly party. Somehow the word spread like wildfire and outsiders began to gather around 1300 hours. The punch was thawing in the punch bowl when guests from various directorates were coming in early. One technical sergeant was real friendly, picked up a six-ounce plastic cup, filled it up and said, "Cheers" and drank it down like it was water. Needless to say he didn't have solid legs for very long. They become "bungee cord" legs and very wobbly. The white juice was "White Lightning" in disguise; "WOW", it was potent. I had several meetings to attend, as well as numerous other chores involving people, so it was drop in, do your thing, then go to the next meeting and get everything accomplished so there would not be any ASE equipment problems. Finally it was in the late afternoon and all of the party attending people said take a cup of "White Lightning", and behold, it was in my hand. Then they proposed a toast. That broke the ice and I enjoyed it. But I could not indulge too much because if any immediate situations would come up it could cause some embarrassment if a person was under the weather. Whereas I could protect my workers by taking calls, meetings, etc., in that way my people had no trouble in enjoying themselves. I made sure that they all had designated rides home, whereby no accidents from any drunken drivers could occur. Then to enhance the morale of my people I allowed them all to put in for either Christmas or New Year's Day leave. Most of my people decided to work on the ASE Systems and take only the specific holiday off. All of you can see why I had a "Winner" division of dedicated personnel supporting me.

Since my accomplishments within the ASE-PM office was on an excellent status for the fifty-one projects that had life cycle management, I had six excellent civilian workers who were really responsible for the workload, whereby I applied Executive Management reasoning to keep all projects on course. This was also done with the help of our field ASE-PM office located in the United States Army Electronic Command at Fort Monmouth, New Jersey.

Colonel Keaton presented me with a Certificate of Achievement Award on 12 December 1978 and an ASE scenic picture. Only high ranking officials received it. It was an excellent gesture of friendship, of being a member of the ASE team personnel from all of the ASE Division's signed the picture. [Colonel Keaton presenting My Award 9-12], [Picture Certificate or Achievement 9-13], [Picture Colonel Keaton—Wayne Kuschel 9-14]

My good friend Joe Hudson lost a son being hit by a drunk driver while he was riding a bicycle on the right side of the road and with the flow of traffic. His bicycle's rear wheel had the impression or dent of the car bumper that killed him. Most of my people attended Joe's son's funeral to show our respect. Joe was a councilman in the town of Fairview Heights, Illinois City. Joe never sloughed off any system work and took on additional work to assist my position. I can only give him praise.

I began having more medical or health problems. My hypertension was really giving me fits. Dr. Buttons, full Colonel with the United Service Public Health Service was my doctor. Oh! She was well qualified being a top notch Flight Surgeon. She was sharp and well experienced in the medical profession. Dr. Buttons began treating me for hypertension. No previous doctor had diagnosed my condition that drastic, as having hypertension. I had many changes of different medications to assist in relieving the hypertension part. This was to no avail. No change in my heart rhythm pattern.

Dr. Button's after all my tests, finally told me there wasn't any more that could be done to improve my heart problems mainly hypertension and that she was putting me in for retirement of course my heart felt like I had dropped and stepped on it so at the happy old age of 55 my application for retirement was submitted.

My wife Marie's health was deteriorating so fast that four medical doctors advised me to send her to a desirable (minimum) humidity area. With the four superior heart-lung specialists expertise it was determined that San Diego, California would be the best weather for her. [Letter on Wife's health problems 9-15]

So the fall season of 1978, she was transported to San Diego, California for what she thought was a rehabilitation period for her health. She progressively declined in health and on 4 October 1979, while under treatment at United States Naval Hospital, Balboa Park, she passed away. My suggestion to all you people smoking is to consider giving up the cancer sticks. Because of her medical condition, the United States Navy autopsy showed that Marie had the worst pair of lungs that they had ever autopsied.

If you smoke, stop smoking because the cancer sticks will get you in the end and your health problems are really going to mount up. In addition, health care plans will be mighty expensive.

To complete the last sentence of my book "All or Nothing" my retirement was approved by Department of the United States Army with an effective date of 10 July 1979.

However on Christmas Eve of 24 December 1986 I had my first heart attack, and on 4, 6 and February I had 3 in one-week, thinking it was a reflux problem because of my Hiatus Hernia operation in 1981 which was a big, huge mistake on myself.

TO ALL SMOKERS OUT THERE PLEASE LISTEN READ CAREFULLY IT MAY HAPPEN TO YOU

My wife Marie had been going to the heart/lung specialists at Scott Air Force Base, Illinois, Eleven (11) years. This appointment day she was having a hard time breathing, so the doctors put her up leaning, against a machine to measure her lung capacity. She passed out before the information came out of the machine. The doctor told me she had <u>less than 10%</u> lung capacity and they gave me a prescription for oxygen to be implemented immediately. I called for an emergency oxygen issue from a St. Louis firm. Within an hour, the oxygen specialist was briefing her on how to administer the oxygen. The wife would wake up screaming about "steel bands" around her chest and they were squeezing tighter all the time. She would huff and puff trying to get more air into her lungs even while on Oxygen. Come to find out the test and blood gases put the doctor onto emphysema as the culprit causing her problems. When I met her in July 1945 she was smoking about a pack a day. She never did smoke more than a pack and a half per day, but it was enough to begin showing up at her young age of forty seven. This ordeal would haunt her for six more years. Donnie, my son, would come to St. Louis and pick his mother up and take her to a drier climate in New Mexico or San Diego for about six or eight months each and every year. No exceptions to this problem and no sound solutions were in sight. I purchased Marie a small car to use in her moving around since she wasn't one hundred and ten percent disabled, so she said. I felt real sorry for her and there wasn't anything that I could do other than support her in any way that I could. So I became the caretaker of Marie, cooking, wheelchair, chauffeur, dishwasher and anything to keep her morale up. She knew that she was dying because of her heart-lung condition from smoking, which Marie gave up in 1968 cold turkey. She never smoked a cigarette again, but it was too late. The damage was done to her lungs and heart. Since my wife's health was deteriorating so fast, I had to make up my mind to retire to become her keeper for as long as it took and keep her happy, as fragile as she was.

I applied for retirement during October 1978 and the United States Army Civil Service Commission approved it on 19 November 1978. Full retirement would be on 10 July 1979, but I had to stay on with the ASE-PM to ensure a Logistics Chief was in place. When personnel in the ASE-PM office heard of my retirement date all the office had a "goodbye party". [Notification of Personnel Action: Retirement 9-16]

ARADCOM determined my Chief of Logistics warranted a higher position, GS-15, but I couldn't stay around very long because the doctors at San Diego Navy Station were asking for my immediate assistance to care for my wife's health problems.

When my retirement paperwork was in my hands, I turned in, my 30 Plaza Square key to apartment 201 and headed west on a highway towards Spring Valley, California. Marie passed away a short time later. I know the Good Lord helped to end her health hurts and pains.

By the way, with the new Research and Development reorganization for the Project Management it made my position qualified for a GS-15 rating. It did not deter my mind one bit. I gave it up so someone else could enjoy the tremendous workload and extra hours of work to accomplish all systems for the Life Cycle Management. Good luck to whoever fights to become the new Logistics Chief. I gave my all with a total of 33 years of Federal Service. I did accept a "disability 3" from the Civil Service Commission. I had somewhere around $21,000 in sick leave coming. My retirement pay would start near $1,000 per month until all data was established and a firm amount was provided. That was for a period of one year, then a recomputed regular paycheck would begin to arrive.

For the readers information, I had my 33 ½ year service career behind me and I kept thinking to myself, I should be able to write this book on my unique United States Army Civil Service experience and have my family members enjoy it. It began in 1923 when I was born, up to when I had "Against All Odds" published in 2004.

To reiterate, I joined the Infantry in 1940 when I was 16 years of age. In 1943 I was accepted into the United States Army Air Corp as a private, I was appointed August 1943 as an assistant crew chief on Major General Gerald C. Brandt's UC-45 aircraft. He got me into the pilot program, I swapped that position, and I was commissioned a 2nd Lieutenant, qualified United States Army Air Force B-29 Flight Engineer in July 1945.

Then while at Wright Field, Ohio I requested pilot training and again I was accepted into pilot Class 48-C and received my wings 18 October 1948 in the newly formed United States Air Force (USAF), (Established 18 September 1947).

I earned 5 silver wings, flew in 50 different aircraft, and had 24 permanent changes of stations in 20 years. I was promoted from Private to Major (never made Staff Sergeant) and retired at age 36 in 1960.

I'm hoping this book is as exciting as "Against all Odds" with Trafford Publishing assistance they are going to write a nice story on my life and marvelous careers and publish them in the Readers' Digest. Both of my books will be illustrated, to expand the content to the public for excellent reading material.

I can truthfully say I also had a remarkable Department of the Army Civil Service career from 1966 to 1979. I was sworn in at the Department of Army Aviation Systems Command 6 June 1966 as a GS-11, earned an instructor rating on three types of gas turbine engines, spent one year in the Republic of Vietnam and promoted to GS-12. I held numerous executive management positions, promoted to GS-13 in 1969, assigned as YO-3A Project Officer and promoted to GS-14 March 1972 as Chief

Logistics Division in AVRADCOM. I retired 10 July 1979, so I have had an exceptional career and feel that other people should read about what I accomplished in this short time span compared to what some may achieve or accomplish in their career. KEY WORDS—be positive, get your college degree, then a master's degree and finally a PhD and be on top of the world doing something that you enjoy and then it becomes second nature to you and your end results will be positive. (P.S. I did not follow these rules acquired a college degree only).

One last item, I want to thank Lui Monsanto for all the assistance from her and to "Aim High and Hit the Mark" for her Grandfather, who fought for the Phillipines independence.

9-1 Picture of CH-47 (Chinook)

9-1 Picture of CH-47 (Chinook) photo 2

DEPARTMENT OF THE ARMY
US ARMY AVIATION SYSTEMS COMMAND
PO BOX 209, ST. LOUIS, MO 63166

AMSAV-G(SA(E&P))

4 DEC 1968

MEMORANDUM FOR: All Employees

SUBJECT: Reorganization of AVSCOM

1. During the past year I have kept you informed of the progress made by my Management Study Group. In my recent speeches, I spoke to you in detail of the reorganization. The purpose of this letter is to reinforce certain key points.

2. Over the past ten years, we have seen a doubling of our aircraft inventory; this increase in numbers will continue into the foreseeable future.

3. Our former organizational structure and way of doing business got the job done, but we had a lot of stresses and strains. With continued foreseeable increases in the volume of our work, it is inevitable that these pressures would have multiplied.

4. Our solution, then, to the known needs of the present and the foreseeable needs of the future, was a total reorganization which would enable us to be even more responsive to the needs of the combat soldier; and at the same time, be able to effect this response more efficiently and expeditiously.

5. With regard to you as an individual--while there will be many name changes of organizations, some shifting of furniture and move- ment of people, no one will be without a position commensurate with his skills and capabilities. In fact, it is my firm belief that this reorganization will vitalize the various career programs and open up more opportunities for advancement than have existed in the past.

9-2 Reorganization of AVSCOM

6. I know that any reorganization has an unsettling effect on the people
involved. I ask that each of you accept this temporary unsettling and
movement with good humor and understanding. For out of our discom-
fort of the moment will emerge an organization that will stand the test
of time and offer you even greater challenges than you have met--and
conquered--in the past.

JOHN NORTON
Major General, USA
Commanding

2

9-2 Reorganization of AVSCOM page 2

AMSAV-GS(SA)

Requirements for Establishment of New Organizations

LTC Straughan, SIMO
Mr. Ball, ASH
LTC Crowell, CH-47
LTC Sternat, RPV

Sp Asst to Chief of Staff

6 Mar 74
LTC Parker/db/2911

1. Reference the attached Bullet from Colonel Browne. As of today, I will have accomplished the coordination of the Mission and Functions with the exception of ASH. Grade structure, grade limitations, and agreements thereof have been accomplished with PT&FD. TDA draft will be submitted this day.

2. Per conversation with Ms. Ottolini this morning, immediate detail actions can be accomplished with the submission of a SF 52 for each detail position, in which it should request detail to the functions of the position within SIMO or the particular organization, i.e., ASH, CH-47, RPV. This is to imply that although job descriptions are imperative and should be completed as expeditiously as possible, the detail actions can begin without benefit of job descriptions.

3. A SF 52 should be prepared to establish and recruit the secretarial, stenographic and clerical positions listed in our agreement of 5 March.

4. The remaining accomplishments then, are Mission and Functions from ASH, a prioritized detail request from each element and job sheets for all positions as soon as possible.

1 Incl
as

MURRY E. PARKER
LTC, GS
Sp Asst to Chief of Staff

CF:
Chief of Staff

9-3 AVSCOM Reorganization updated

AMSAV-SIU

MEMORANDUM THRU: CHIEF, WEAPON SYSTEMS MANAGEMENT

TO: COMMANDING GENERAL, USAAVSCOM

SUBJECT: Recommended TDA Changes for Utility WSMO

1. This study is in response to comments made during the UH-1 WSM briefing
to MG Hinrichs on 6 Nov 74 that the Utility WSM was reviewing developed
management areas and would submit, to the Command Group, a proposed structure/
grade change to the present TDA. Since the onset of the WSM Concept in
May 74, there has been inadequate intelligence or experience available to
determine appropriate staffing of each WSM requirement. With the increasing
emphasis of management, based on the expanding program size and complexity
of the UH-1/VH-1N fleet, it is indicative that this realistic manpower
evaluation based on management workload should be accepted. Since the WSM
Concept has been implemented, this office has been acquiring management
control from the various directorates where program fragmentation existed.
There were numerous minute tasks being managed at very low levels within
the directorates' functional elements which, when combined and elevated
to this office, have multiplied the overall aspects of tasks/units to manage.

2. In addressing this TDA change proposal, sufficient experience and
knowledge have been gained to ascertain what areas and career fields are
affected and additional manpower/grades that will be required to adequately
manage the various complex programs which are: planning and coordinating for
the projected procurement of UH-1 class aircraft for worldwide programs
(DoD, USAF, Navy, Marines, Grant Aid, and Foreign Military Sales cases);
correlating utility weapon system plans; integrating engineering systems/
subsystems; propulsion, logistic programs; reviewing, coordinating and
executing budget inputs, i.e., APA, O&MA, ASF, and RDT&E, etc., from
functional elements and supporting Major Subordinate Commands, exercising
control over assigned funding operations; evaluating, analyzing, and advising
on any impacting problems/adjustments for assigned programs; reviewing and
evaluating program accomplishments against planned objectives; recommending
corrective action to WSM/functional elements; controlling and coordinating
all UH-1 Product Improvement Programs within AVSCOM with ECOM, WECOM, Army
Security Agency, and other sister services; managing weaponization and
avionics areas as they pertain to the UH-1 weapon system; developing data
for presentations and briefings; chairing all Utility WSM Team meetings;
coordinating with higher echelons, supporting Major Subordinate Commands,
other services and agencies on procurement/maintenance/supply/engineering
matters/aircraft distribution pertaining to the utility helicopter end item.

9-4 Recommended TDA Changes for WSMO

DEPARTMENT OF THE ARMY
HEADQUARTERS, US ARMY AVIATION SYSTEMS COMMAND
PO BOX 209, ST. LOUIS, MO 63 66

AMSAV-GS   29 March 1974

SUBJECT: Letter of Commendation

THRU: Chief of Staff, AVSCOM

TO: Mr. Wayne A. Kuschel
          SIMO

1. I wish to take this opportunity to commend you for your
assistance in preparation of the Weapon Systems Management
Study and briefing.

2. Your efforts are especially commendable when considering
the atmosphere surrounding the development of the AVSCOM
Concept. The attitudes of many Middle Managers was mirrored
in the attitude of the rank and file who were not necessarily
in tune with your efforts. The ability to persevere and
accomplish the required tasks in this somewhat hostile atmosphere, and yet be able to accomplish them within a compressed
time frame, to the satisfaction of the Commanding General,
is most praiseworthy.

3. Please accept my sincere gratitude for your willing
cooperation, enduring enthusiasm, and your many contributions
to the accomplishment of the effort. May your future endeavors be as rewarding to those who put faith in you as they
have to me.

4. A copy of this will be placed in your personnel file.

                              MURRY E. PARKER
                              LTC, GS
                              S/A to Chief of Staff

9-5 Letter of Commendation

354

9-6 Picture of UH-1 (Huey)

9-6 Presidential UH-1N Army One

CONFIDENTIAL STATEMENT OF EMPLOYMENT AND FINANCIAL INTERESTS - DEPARTMENT OF DEFENSE PERSONNEL
(Special Department of Defense Employees Use DD Form 1555-1)

1. NAME *(Last, first, middle initial)*	2. TITLE OF POSITION
KUSCHEL, WAYNE A.	Logistican Specialist GS-13

3. DATE OF APPOINTMENT IN PRESENT POSITION	4. AGENCY AND MAJOR ORGANIZATIONAL SEGMENT
15 April 1974	USAAVSCOM, ATTN: AMSAV-SIU 12th & Spruce Streets, St. Louis, MO 63102

PART I. EMPLOYMENT AND FINANCIAL INTERESTS. List the names of all corporations, companies, firms, or other business enterprises, partnerships, nonprofit organizations, and educational, or other institutions: (a) with which you are connected as an employee, officer, owner, director, member, trustee, partner, adviser, or consultant; or (b) in which you have any continuing financial interests, through a pension or retirement plan, shared income, or other arrangement as a result of any current or prior employment or business or professional association; or (c) in which you have any financial interest through the ownership of stock, stock options, bonds, securities, or other arrangements including trusts. If none, write NONE.

NAME AND KIND OF ORGANIZATION *(Use Part I designations where applicable)*	ADDRESS	POSITION IN ORGANIZATION *(Use Part I(a) designations, if applicable)*	NATURE OF FINANCIAL INTEREST. e.g., STOCK, PRIOR BUSINESS INCOME *(Use Part I(b) and (c) designations, if applicable)*
NONE			

PART II. CREDITORS. List the names of your creditors other than those to whom you may be indebted by reason of a mortgage on property which you occupy as a personal residence or to whom you may be indebted for current and ordinary household and living expenses such as household furnishings, automobile, education, vacation, and similar expenses. If none, write NONE.

NAME AND ADDRESS OF CREDITOR	CHARACTER OF INDEBTNESS. e.g., PERSONAL LOAN, NOTE, SECURITY
Mart Credit Union, PO Box 209, St. Louis, MO	Personal Loan

PART III. INTERESTS IN REAL PROPERTY. List your interest in real property or rights in lands, other than property which you occupy as a personal residence. If none, write NONE.

NATURE OF INTEREST. e.g., OWNERSHIP, MORTGAGE, LIEN, INVESTMENT TRUST	TYPE OF PROPERTY. e.g., RESIDENCE, HOTEL, APARTMENT, FARM, UNDEVELOPED LAND	ADDRESS *(If rural, give RFD, or county, state, and Zip Code)*
NONE		

PART IV. INFORMATION REQUESTED OF OTHER PERSONS. If any information is to be supplied by other persons, e.g., trustee, attorney, accountant, relative, please indicate the name and address of such persons, the date upon which you requested that the information be supplied, and the nature of subject matter involved. If none, write NONE.

NAME AND ADDRESS	DATE OF REQUEST	NATURE OF SUBJECT MATTER
NONE		

REMARKS

I CERTIFY THAT THE STATEMENTS I HAVE MADE ARE TRUE, COMPLETE, AND CORRECT TO THE BEST OF MY KNOWLEDGE AND BELIEF.

DATE	SIGNATURE
7 JUNE 74	WAYNE A. KUSCHEL

DD FORM 1555 ¹ MAR 65

9-7 Confidential Statement DD Form 1555

AMSAV-SIU (15 Jan 75) 1st Ind
SUBJECT: Letter of Appreciation

Headquarters, US Army Aviation Systems Command, PO Box 209, St. Louis,
Missouri 63166   30 January 1975

TO: Mr. Wayne Kuschel, Utility Helicopter Division, Weapon Systems
     Management Office

1. I am happy to forward attached correspondence and add my sincere
thanks for your outstanding contributions. Your personal and technical
competence are great assets to this Office and this Command.

2. A copy of this correspondence will be placed in your Official
Personnel Folder.

U. S. LARGE, JR.
LTC, GS
Utility WSM

4

9-8 Letter of Appreciation 15 January 1975

DEPARTMENT OF THE ARMY
HEADQUARTERS, US ARMY AVIATION SYSTEMS COMMAND
PO BOX 209, ST. LOUIS, MO 63166

AMSAV-G   2 2 JAN 1975

SUBJECT: Letter of Appreciation

THRU: Chief, Weapon Systems Management Office

TO: Lieutenant Colonel Ulysses S. Large, Jr.
          UH-1 System Manager
          Weapon Systems Management Office

1. General Hinrichs asked me to forward the attached letter from
Mr. John W. Starke, Chief, Aviation Section, Special Projects Division of
the United States Department of Justice, Drug Enforcement Administration,
regarding the outstanding support you provided during Operation Buccaneer.

2. The General was indeed pleased to receive such favorable comments and
indicated that performance meriting such recognition is indicative of your
competence and does much to enhance the image of AVSCOM.

3. Again thanks for a job well done and best wishes for continued success
in all future endeavors.

FOR THE COMMANDER:

1 Incl   *Jerry F. Wade*
as   JERRY F. WADE
                                            Major, GS
                                            Executive Officer

9-8 Letter of Appreciation 15 January 1975 page 2

UNITED STATES DEPARTMENT OF JUSTICE
DRUG ENFORCEMENT ADMINISTRATION
Washington, D.C. 20537

Major General Frank A. Hinrichs, USA   JAN 15 1975
Commander, Headquarters
U.S. Army Aviation Systems Command
P.O. Box 209
St. Louis, Missouri   63166

Dear General Hinrichs:

Subject: Operation Buccaneer Final Situation Report

The attached message is the final situation report (SITREP)
from the United States Embassy, Kingston, Jamaica, regarding
Operation Buccaneer. Ambassador Sumner Gerard included a
congratulatory paragraph to all the United States Agencies
involved in making this project possible. Indeed, without
the assistance of the Department of Defense and the personal
interest shown by those individuals who contributed their
time and energies to this project, Operation Buccaneer could
not have been as successful. Among the major contributors
were:

        OASD (ADMIN)
        OASD (I & L)
        Under Secretary of the Army
        DAMO-MS (SPD)
        HQ US Army Aviation Systems Command
        Military District Washington
         CDR, HQTRS Davison Army Airfield
         Flight Training Division
        Corpus Christi Army Depot
        US Air Force, Director of Procurement
        Oklahoma City Air Logistics Command (PPWCB)
        US Air Force, Director of Transportation

9-8 Letter of Appreciation 15 January 1975 page 3

As the Drug Enforcement Administration Liaison Officer
to the Department of Defense and as the Air Operations
Project Officer and Logistics Staff Officer for Operation
Buccaneer, I wish to extend my personal thanks to each
of you in the offices and activities within the DOD for
you cooperation and assistance. You have proved that
the United States Government agencies can work together
quickly and effectively on short notice. The statistics
in the SITREP speak for themselves. Each of you contributed significantly to those statistics, and Ambassador
Gerard was made aware of your efforts and contributions
during my tour in Jamaica as Acting Project Manager. It
was a gratifying experience to work with a group of people
who unselfishly extended their talents and efforts on
behalf of the mission of the Drug Enforcement Administration.

Letters of Appreciation/Commendation will follow through
appropriate channels.

Sincerely yours,

John W. Starke
Chief, Aviation Section
Special Projects Division

9-8 Letter of Appreciation 15 January 1975 page 4

```
***********************************
*                                 *
*           UNCLASSIFIED           *
*                                 *
***********************************
```

IONINTS-MTL/DISTR   ROUTER-DWC   COPY 1
OIMTL-MTLMGT DIR SIM-SIMO   COC-CND OP CEN

UZYUW RUFAOWDR224 1931954-UUUU--RUWTFFA.
UUUUU
219407 JUL 74
DA WASHDC //DALO-AV//
RUERRFA/CDRAMC ALEX VA //AMCSU-SC/AMCAV//
O RUWTFFA/CDRUS&AVSCOM STL MO //AMSAV-ONDS/AMSAV-OMA//
I/DRUG ENFORCEMENT ADMIN WASHDC (MAIL)

LAS
J: SUPPORT OF DRUG ENFORCEMENT ADMINISTRATION (DEA), DEPARTMENT
JUSTICE
DA LTR DTD 27 JUN 74 FROM OFC OF THE UNDER SECRETARY TO THE
IG ENFORCEMENT ADMINISTRATION.
  REF A HAS COMMITTED THE ARMY TO SUPPORT THE DRUG ENFORCEMENT
TINISTRATION WITH 3 UH-1H AND 1 OH-58 FOR SIX MONTHS AND THE
VISION OF A SIX-MONTH INVENTORY OF SPARE PARTS FOR THE
ICOPTERS.
  IN ACCORDANCE WITH PARA 1 ABOVE, REQUEST AMC TAKE ACTION TO
VIDE 3 UH-1H, 1 OH-58 ON LOAN FOR A SIX-MONTH PERIOD TO DEA
H TOTAL REIMBURSEMENT TO THE ARMY FOR ALL COSTS ASSOCIATED
H THE LOAN AND RETURN OF THE HELICOPTERS. SUPPORT AGREEMENT
TO INCLUDE SIX MONTHS INVENTORY OF REPAIR PARTS. SPECIFIC
:F 2 RUFAOWDR224 UNCLAS
IVISIONS SHOULD BE INCLUDED TO MAKE CLEAR THE UNDERSTANDING
IT ALL MARKINGS (INTERIOR/EXTERIOR) WHICH IDENTIFY THE HELICOPTER
U.S. ARMY PROPERTY BE REMOVED FOR THE DURATION OF THE AIRCRAFT
IN.
  CONSIDERATION SHOULD BE GIVEN TO AMENDING THE EXISTING LOAN
IEEMENT BETWEEN AVSCOM AND DEA FOR 9 T418 AIRCRAFT. MR. PINGREE,
.COM, AUTOVON 698-3191/2727 IS THE POC FOR THE EXISTING AGREEMENT.
  DARECT COORDIFATION WITH ALCON IS AUTHORIZED. POINTS OF
ITACT ARE:
            DA   OTC CHARLES B. ORAM   AUTOVON 22-704
  DEA   FR. ROBERT T. ALBRAGI   202-382-5725
         (CONTROLLER)
            DEA   MR. JOHN M. STARKE   202-382-2963
         (AVIATION SECTION)
  AMC   MR. PAUL BEARD (DIST)   AUTOVON 284-8632
  AVSCOF OTC U. S. LARGE   AUTOVON 698-3281
         (UH-1H)
  AVSCOM MAJ H. MELENDEZ   AUTOVON 698-2921
         (OH-58)
```

324
JN


```
***********************************
*                                 *
*           UNCLASSIFIED           *
*                                 *
***********************************
```

9-8 Letter of Appreciation 15 January 1975 page 5
```

AMSAV-SIU (2 Jun 75)   1st Ind
SUBJECT: Letter of Appreciation

Headquarters, US Army Aviation Systems Command, PO Box 209, St. Louis,
Missouri 63166   16 June 1975

TO: Mr. Wayne A. Kuschel, Utility Helicopter Division, Directorate for
     Weapon Systems Management

1. The attached correspondence from the Army Vice Chief of Staff and
the USAAVSCOM Commanding General is forwarded in recognition of your
outstanding contributions during the recent UH-1 program review.

2. This endeavor has received considerable praise from the AVSCOM
Command Group and staff members. While these letters generally indicate
your dedication and professional competence, it is important that your
total contributions toward the overall management of a highly complex
program be recognized. Thank you again for your accomplishments as a
key member of the UH-1 Team.

3. A copy of this correspondence will be placed in your Official
Personnel File.

1 Incl   U. S. LARGE, JR.
as   LTC, GS
                                UH-1 WSM

2

9-9
Letter of appreciation General Walter T. Kerwin, Army Chief of Staff

AMSAV-G   2 JUN 1975

SUBJECT: · Letter of Appreciation

THRU: Chief of Weapon Systems Management Office

TO: Lieutenant Colonel Ulysses S. Large, Jr.
          Utility Division
          Weapon Systems Management Office

1. It is a pleasure to forward the attached letter from the Army
Vice Chief of Staff.

2. I add my appreciation and congratulations to you and your staff
for the time and effort expended in preparation for General Kerwin's
recent visit to AVSCOM. Without the dedicated assistance of many
individuals the successful accomplishment of this mission would not
have been realized.

3. Please express my personal thanks to the members of your staff
who contributed to the planning and preparation of General Kerwin's
visit to AVSCOM.

1 Incl   FRANK A. HINRICHS
as   Major General, USA
                               Commanding

9-9 Letter of appreciation General Walter T. Kerwin,
Army Chief of Staff page 2

15 May 1975

Dear General Hinrichs:

I appreciated the opportunity to see and visit with you and your staff yesterday. The briefings were most interesting and well done. Please pass on my appreciation to the members of AVSCOM for a professional job.

Many thanks for your generous hospitality during my stay in St. Louis. The luncheon was most enjoyable.

Sincerely,

WALTER T. KERWIN, JR.
General, United States Army
Vice Chief of Staff

Major General Frank A. Hinrichs
Commander
U.S. Army Aviation Systems Command
St. Louis, MO 63166

9-9 Letter of appreciation General Walter T. Kerwin, Army Chief of Staff page 3

STANDARD FORM 50 Rev. Dec. 1965 Approved Exception
U.S. CIVIL SERVICE COMMISSION
FPM CH. 296
FPM SUPPLEMENT 292D

NOTIFICATION OF PERSONNEL ACTION

(EMPLOYEE — See General Information on Reverse)

APN   25 OF N27CEJ40440

1. NAME (CAPS) LAST - FIRST - MIDDLE MR. - MISS - MRS.	2. (FOR AGENCY USE)	3. BIRTH DATE (Mo., Day, Year)	4. SOCIAL SECURITY NO.
HERSCHEL, WAYNE A MR	56-74	12/06/23	

5. VETERAN PREFERENCE	6. TENURE GROUP	7. SERVICE COMP. DATE
2 1. NO 2. -5 PT. 3. -10 PT. DISAB. 4. -10 PT. COMP. 5. -10 PT. OTHER	1	02/01/56

8. FEGLI	10. RETIREMENT	11. (FOR CSC USE)
1 1. COVERED (reg. only-declined opt.) 2. INELIGIBLE 3. -WAIVED 4. -COVERED (reg. and opt.)	1 1. -CS 2. -FICA 3. -FS 4. -NONE 5. -OTHER	

12. CODE	NATURE OF ACTION	13. EFFECTIVE DATE (Mo., Day, Year)	14. CIVIL SERVICE OR OTHER LEGAL AUTHORITY
702	PROMOTION	12/07/75	REG 335.102

15. FROM: POSITION TITLE AND NUMBER	16. PAY PLAN AND OCCUPATION CODE	17. (a) GRADE OR LEVEL (b) STEP OR RATE	18. SALARY
LOGISTICS MANAGEMENT SPECIALIST POSITION NO. 14350	GS 346 (00)	13/08	PA $28,254.00

19. NAME AND LOCATION OF EMPLOYING OFFICE

US ARMY AVIATION SYSTEMS COMMAND, HEADQUARTERS
DIRECTORATE FOR WEAPON SYSTEMS MANAGEMENT, UTILITY DIVISION
ST LOUIS   MO   63166

CC AC   EMP 6   PARA 04   LINE 01   CLC 233

20. TO: POSITION TITLE AND NUMBER	21. PAY PLAN AND OCCUPATION CODE	22. (a) GRADE OR LEVEL (b) STEP OR RATE	23. SALARY
SUPERVISORY LOGISTICS MANAGEMENT SP- ECIALIST POSITION NO. PA 1476450	GS 346 (00)	14/05	PA $30,441.00 SYBX

24. NAME AND LOCATION OF EMPLOYING OFFICE

USA AVSCOM OFFICE OF THE PRODUCT MGR ACFT SURVIVABILITY EQUIP.
LOGISTICS MANAGEMENT DIVISION
ST LOUIS   MO   63166

CLC 056

25. DUTY STATION (City-State)	26. LOCATION CODE
ST LOUIS MO	29-7080-510

27. APPROPRIATION	28. POSITION OCCUPIED	29. APPORTIONED POSITION		STATE
5QX	1 1 - COMPETITIVE SERVICE 2 - EXCEPTED SERVICE	(FROM:) 1-PROVED 2-WAIVED	(TO:)	

30. REMARKS:
☐ A. SUBJECT TO COMPLETION OF 1   YEAR PROBATIONARY (OR TRIAL) PERIOD COMMENCING _____
B. SERVICE COUNTING TOWARD CAREER (OR PERM) TENURE FROM: _____
SEPARATIONS: SHOW REASONS BELOW, AS REQUIRED. CHECK IF APPLICABLE: ☐ C. DURING PROBATION

DA CAREER REFERRAL NUMBER   4231F   DATED 01/23/75.

31. DATE OF APPOINTMENT AFFIDAVIT (Accessions only)	34. SIGNATURE (Or other authentication) AND TITLE FOR THE APPOINTING OFFICER
32. OFFICE MAINTAINING PERSONNEL FOLDER (If different from employing office)	
33. CODE EMPLOYING DEPARTMENT OR AGENCY 00	CIVILIAN PERSONNEL OFFICER 12/03/75 2203

9-9a Promotion to GS-14

DEPARTMENT OF THE ARMY **JOB DESCRIPTION**	1. INSTALLATION OR HEADQUARTERS OFFICE US Army Aviation Systems Command	2. JOB NUMBER P(A)14,764-S
3. CITATION TO APPLICABLE STANDARD AND ITS DATE OF ISSUANCE FLSA Exempt	4. TITLE Supervisory Logistics Management Specialist	
	5. PAY SCHEDULE GS	6. OCC. CODE 346	7. GRADE 14

8. EVALUATION APPROVAL Title, pay schedule, code and grade of this job have been fixed in accordance with Department of the Army official policy and grade level standards.	SIGNATURE ANTON IMHOF, JR	DATE 21 Oct 74

9. SUPERVISORY CONTROLS, DUTIES, AND WORKING CONDITIONS (Indicate percent of time for each duty, where pertinent.) (Continue statement of duties, etc., on reverse side if necessary.)

SUPERVISORY CONTROLS

Works under the general direction of the Project Manager and his Deputy who define broad objectives and policies and rely on incumbent to independently exercise mature judgement and expertise in carrying out the total logistics functions of the office. Work is reviewed for overall effectiveness and successful achievement of program objectives.

MAJOR DUTIES

Serves as Chief of the logistics management element of the Product Manager's Office for Aircraft Survivability Equipment (ASE). Supervises accomplishment of the total logistics function and is the top expert on logistical matters for ASE. Incumbent has responsibility for logistics management planning and evaluation of the most complex ASE systems throughout the entire life cycle. This requires expert integration and interface of logistics matters with other PM functions such as: engineering, design and development, maintenance engineering, procurement and production, test support, programming and budgeting, configuration management and quality assurance. Serves as advisor and principal logistics representative at higher headquarters, AVSCOM, with contractor personnel, and representatives of other Government agencies. Exercises a thorough knowledge of the overall Army supply and maintenance system, logistics support policies, regulations and procedures, management techniques and performance and uses of assigned ASE systems to perform the following typical duties:

1. Plans, directs, coordinates and evaluates the work of a staff engaged in performing logistics projects involving Integrated Logistics Support (ILS) and maintenance support planning and control. Work is accomplished by a staff of

10.	JOB CONTENT APPROVAL (Complete on organization file copy only.)
ORGANIZATION LOCATION	

THIS STATEMENT ACCURATELY DESCRIBES THE WORK REQUIRED IN ONE POSITION OR IN EACH OF A GROUP OF POSITIONS IN THE ABOVE ORGANIZATION.	THE ABOVE DESCRIPTION, WITH SUPPLEMENTAL MATERIAL, IS ADEQUATE FOR PURPOSES OF EVALUATION.
SIGNATURE OF APPROVING SUPERVISOR	SIGNATURE OF ANALYST Joseph M Stunni

11.	REAUDIT APPROVAL						
DATE							
SUPERVISOR'S APPROVAL							
ANALYST'S							

9-9a Promotion to GS-14 page 2

approximately 5-10 technical and clerical support personnel in grades through GS-13. Analyzes workload, objectives, and requirements, to assure the highest degree of proficiency in the development and execution of assigned projects and to determine personnel and administrative funds required. Establishes work methods and procedures to assure that assigned functions and projects are being properly coordinated with other functional programs within the Product Manager's Office, with appropriate contractors, DA, DOD and other government activities and installations. Reviews, approves, and revises actions in order to insure proper balance, emphasis, accomplishment of objectives and timely response to requests of higher echelons and other agencies. Continuously evaluates program effectiveness in light of objectives and requirements. Identifies and directs corrective action in deficient areas of performance. Makes internal adjustments to accommodate fluctuations in workload resulting from initiation of new programs, current programs being phased out, changes in priorities and the like. Provides management guidance and assistance to subordinates on matters of a policy or highly controversial nature. Executes personnel actions, selects subordinates, and evaluates performance. Reviews periodically position structure to assure that positions are established to provide optimum balance among economy, efficiency and skills utilization. Approves leave, effects minor disciplinary actions and recommends action in more serious cases. Determines needs and provides for employee training.

2. Evaluates overall program effectiveness by review and analysis of statistical and/or narrative reports, by discussion with subordinates, and through conferences with appropriate personnel. Evaluates elements' performance against approved program plans, objectives, schedules and forecasts. Directs the development and implementation of measures to correct problem areas and improve or further facilitate overall operations. Advises Product Manager on problems involving the relationship of work in assigned areas of responsibility to broader programs and resultant impact on such programs. Makes decisions and provides management direction on policy matters affecting assigned programs. Provides to the Product Manager, interpretation, advice, and recommendations which affect the uniformity and management control of maintenance and inventory of supplies and equipment and which have a direct bearing on the logistical and maintenance support of the assigned project aircraft.

3. Conducts design trade-off analyses for subsystems and components at any level of the work breakdown structure to optimize support quality, minimize support cost and obtain the best possible support cost data and estimates of life cycle support cost through the application of an analytical Computer model such as the PLANET type. Assure updating of the total life cycle cost model and validation of support cost characteristics by the same test procedures that apply to other vital system characters.

4. Represents or participates with the Product Manager at conferences with representatives from higher echelon Army commands and/or other military services, industry and other government agencies to formulate plans and discuss broad program requirements and matters affecting both assigned program areas. Is accorded authority to make commitments for the Product Manager and is held totally responsible to the PM for the accuracy and full justification for all actions, decisions and commitments relative to assigned responsibilities.

9-9a Promotion to GS-14 page 3

Performs other duties as assigned.

(Title, series, and grade are established in accordance with position classification standards and guides. These materials are available for your review in the Civilian Personnel Division.)

NOTE: The duties and responsibilities of the job require the incumbent to exercise judgement in making or recommending Government decisions or actions which have an economic impact on the interests of non-Federal enterprises as defined in Section II, AR 600-50, and incumbent must, therefore, file a statement of employment and financial interest as required therein.

"This position is included in the Civilian Career Program for Material Maintenance Management and Supply Management by decision of the appointing officer on 21 Oct 74."

9-9a Promotion to GS-14 page 4

PROJECT MANAGER
COLONEL
JACK L.
KEATON
3961/3962

CHIEF, PROGRAM MANAGEMENT DIVISION
MS. THYRA A. BONDS
3964/3106

DEPUTY PROJECT MANAGER
MR. JAMES C. KATECHIS
3961/3962

CHIEF, LOGISTICS MANAGEMENT DIVISION
MR. WAYNE KUSCHEL
6496/6497

CHIEF, TECHNICAL MANAGEMENT DIVISION
MR. HEBERT B. MURCH
6746/6747

CHIEF, PRODUCT ASSURANCE DIVISION
MR. JERRY DETIMER
6888/6889

PROCUREMENT & PRODUCTION OFFICER
MRS. FRANCINE HOUSMAN
2386/2387

ASSISTANT PROJECT MANAGER FIELD OFFICE FT. MONMOUTH, NJ★
LT. COLONEL KENNETH HERBERGER

Telephone Numbers:
Autovon — 698-XXXX
Commercial (314) 268-XXXX
Address: Hq, AVRADCOM
ATTN: DRCPM-ASE, P.O. Box 209
St. Louis, MO 63166

9-10 Photos of ASE-PM

DEPARTMENT OF THE ARMY
HEADQUARTERS US ARMY MATERIEL DEVELOPMENT AND READINESS COMMAND
5001 EISENHOWER AVE., ALEXANDRIA, VA. 22333

The lethality of weapons found on the modern battlefield dictates that survivability be an essential characteristic of all combat materiel. Since the US Army must be prepared to enter the next war out-numbered, we cannot afford anything approaching equal attrition exchange ratios. To ensure our success, we must have not only superior fire power, but also greater survivability. The DARCOM goal for materiel survivability is to remain capable of decisively engaging and re-engaging the enemy even after absorbing attacks we cannot prevent.

The Army Aviation aircraft survivability program (ASE) is one of our most successful. Survivability features and countermeasures equipment are carefully woven into the design of each aircraft in such a manner as to optimize its survivability and ensure its "staying power" on the high threat battlefield. As a result, the ASE program could well serve as a model for all others.

In addition to its obvious contribution to aviation combat effectiveness, I am particularly proud of this program on two other counts. First, it is truly a living, working example of Tri-Service cooperation and equipment commonality. Second, but of equally high importance, it is a program whose success and rapid progress have resulted from the Army's close partnership with and the technical excellence of American industry.

JOHN R. GUTHRIE
General, USA
Commanding

9-11 General John R. Guthrie comments on ASE program

9-12 Colonel Keaton presenting my Award

DEPARTMENT OF THE ARMY

CERTIFICATE OF ACHIEVEMENT

AWARDED TO

WAYNE A. KUSCHEL

FOR ACCOMPLISHING THE ASSIGNED DUTIES AS CHIEF OF THE LOGISTICS MANAGEMENT DIVISION OF THE AIRCRAFT SURVIVABILITY EQUIPMENT PROJECT IN A MOST COMMENDABLE AND ENVIABLE MANNER. HIS SKILLS IN PERSONNEL MANAGEMENT ARE SOUGHT OUT AND HIS ADVICE IS WELCOMED BY ALL EMPLOYEES AND. MANAGEMENT WHICH HAS MADE A POSITIVE CONTRIBUTION TO MORALE. HIS INITIATIVE IN ACCOMPLISHING URGENT MISSIONS AND ABILITIES IN ADJUSTING RESOURCES TO ACCOMPLISH THE OVERALL MISSION HAS BEEN DEMONSTRATED CONTINUOUSLY. MR. KUSCHEL'S PERFORMANCE AND CONTRIBUTION ARE A CREDIT TO ASE, AVRADCOM AND THE U. S. ARMY.

12 DECEMBER 1978

JACK L. KEATON
COLONEL, FA
Project Manager for
Aircraft Survivability Equipment

9-13 Certificate of Achievement

9-14
Wayne Kuschel and Colonel Keaton

DEPARTMENT OF THE ARMY
WILLIAM BEAUMONT ARMY MEDICAL CENTER
EL PASO, TEXAS 79920

ATZC-MDDM

22 July 1977

TO WHOM IT MAY CONCERN:

Mrs. Gussie M. Kuschel, D/W of Ret USAF Major Wayne,
has been evaluated by our Pulmonary Disease specialists here at
William Beaumont Army Medical and found to have severe chronic
lung disease documented by pulmonary function testing and measurement of arterial blood gases. It would most definitely be to her
benefit if arrangements could be made for her to reside permanently
at an altitude of less than 1000 feet above sea level.

JAMES H. COOKE, JR., M.D., CPT, MC
Internal Medicine Clinic
William Beaumont Army Medical Center

CONCUR:

MICHAEL B. YOUNG, M.D.
LTC, MC
Assistant Chief, Int Med Cl

CLEARED FOR RELEASE   26 JUL 77

M. S. Bell
GILBERT ROSALES
DEP CH. PNT ADM DIV

J. LOREN PITCHER, M.D.
COL, MC
Chief, Department of Medicine

9-15 Letter on Wife's health problems

○ **NOTIFICATION OF PERSONNEL ACTION** ◔

(FOR AGENCY USE)

6

1. NAME (CAPS) LAST – FIRST – MIDDLE MR. – MISS – MRS.	2. (FOR AGENCY USE)	3. BIRTH DATE (Mo., Day, Year)
KUSCHEL, WAYNE A. MR.		12-06-23

5. VETERAN PREFERENCE		6. TENURE GROUP	7. SERVICE COMP. DATE
2	1. – NO 3. – 10 PT. DISAB. 5. – 10 PT. OTHER 2. – 5 PT. 4. – 10 PT. COMP.	1	02-01-56

9. FEGLI		10. RETIREMENT	11. (FOR CSC USE)
1	1. – COVERED (reg. only declared opt.) 3. – WAIVED 2. – INELIGIBLE 4. – COVERED (reg. and opt.)	1	1. – CS 4. – NONE 3. – FS 5. – OTHER 2. – FICA

12. NATURE OF ACTION	13. EFFECTIVE DATE (Mo., Day, Year)	14. CIVIL SERVICE OR OTHER LEGAL AUTHORITY
301 RETIREMENT – DISABILITY CODE	07-10-79	

15. FROM: POSITION TITLE AND NUMBER	16. PAY PLAN AND OCCUPATION CODE	17. (a) GRADE (b) STEP OR OR LEVEL RATE	18. SALARY
SUPERVISORY LOGISTICS MANAGEMENT SPECIALIST POS NO. RP15164 SE	GS-346	14/06	PA $37,847.00

19. NAME AND LOCATION OF EMPLOYING OFFICE

USA AVRADCOM OFC OF THE PROJ MGR ACFT SURVIVABILITY EQUIPMENT
LOGISTICS MANAGEMENT DIVISION
ST. LOUIS,   MO   63120
TDA DATA XB/WJCNAA/004/01   CLC 056

20. TO: POSITION TITLE AND NUMBER	21. PAY PLAN AND OCCUPATION CODE	22. (a) GRADE (b) STEP OR OR LEVEL RATE	23. SALARY

24. NAME AND LOCATION OF EMPLOYING OFFICE

25. DUTY STATION (City–State)	26. LOCATION CODE
ST. LOUIS MO	29-7090-510

27. APPROPRIATION	28. POSITION OCCUPIED 1 – COMPETITIVE SERVICE 2 – EXCEPTED SERVICE	29.	APPORTIONED POSITION (FROM:) (TO.) STATE 1 – PROVED 2 – WAIVED
643711.6530012	1		

30. REMARKS:
☐ A. SUBJECT TO COMPLETION OF 1   YEAR PROBATIONARY (OR TRIAL) PERIOD COMMENCING _____
☐ B. SERVICE COUNTING TOWARD CAREER (OR PERM) TENURE FROM. _____
SEPARATIONS: SHOW REASONS BELOW, AS REQUIRED. CHECK IF APPLICABLE: ☐ C. DURING PROBATION

EXEMPT--FAIR LABOR STANDARDS ACT
3-DIGIT COST CODE: 9QF.
EMPLOYEE UNABLE TO PERFORM THE DUTIES OF HIS JOB.
NO OTHER WORK AVAILABLE.
SF-8 ISSUED TO EMPLOYEE 07-10-79.
SF-2815 COMPLETED AND COPY PROVIDED TO EMPLOYEE 07-10-79.
FORWARDING ADDRESS: P.O. BOX 33263
                     SAN DIEGO, CALIFORNIA 92103

31. DATE OF APPOINTMENT AFFIDAVIT (Accessions only)	34. SIGNATURE (Or other authentication) AND TITLE FOR THE APPOINTING OFFICER
32. OFFICE MAINTAINING PERSONNEL FOLDER (If different from employing office)	E.J.WRIGLEY
USA TRADCOM PO BOX 209 ST LOUIS MO 63166	
33. CODE EMPLOYING DEPARTMENT OR AGENCY	CIVILIAN PERSONNEL OFFICER
AR 00 DEPARTMENT OF THE ARMY	35. DATE 07-09-79 2898

4 PART
50-154-14

4. PERSONNEL FOLDER COPY

9-16 Notification of Personnel Action: Retirement

2009 HENRIETTA TEXAS

Since I started writing this book, I've visualized a lot of things that I wish I had the answers to. One of those things is that I wish Chief Warrant Officer Robert Graves was available to ascertain if in the Green Beret movie with John Wayne if A-107 camp wasn't at Tay Ninh near the Cambodia border. The building visible to me looked like the operations building where we flew in and held maintenance meetings to resolve gas turbine problems. I don't know if I'm right or wrong but my mind sure believes I'm correct. Playing that movie again, sure brings back memories of what the Republic of Vietnam was all about. I know I never earned a Purple Heart or any other distinguished medal outside the ones authorized for our special duties, but I felt pain on seeing a member of our Armed Forces that did not make it into tomorrow, and I mean all of the personnel who did not make it back for freedom in the United States of America.

I want to thank our Good Lord for allowing me to achieve a flawless and remarkable Department of the Army Civil Service career for thirteen years. Somehow I maintained a set of records on all of my episodes in a literalist sense, which by the way constitutes almost page for page in "All or Nothing". I'm wondering how I will place the pages of words with all the back-up material, and how the end results will be?

ACRONYMS

USAF	United States Air Force
TDY	Temporary Duty
AVSCOM	Aviation System Command
AAMTAP	Army Aviation Maintenance Technical Assistance Program
ARADCOM	Army Research and Development Command
AVRADCOM	Aviation Research and Development Command
RVN	Republic of Vietnam
LTC	Lieutenant Colonel
CID	Criminal Investigation Division
VC	Viet Cong
DAC	Department of the Army Civilian
PMO	Project Manager's Office
CO	Commanding Officer
SAC	Strategic Air Command
CONUS	Continental United States
USPHS	United States Public Health Service
ASE	Aircraft Survivability Equipment
DEA	Drug Enforcement Agency
RIF	Reduction in Force
WEI	Western Electronics Institute
FOD	Foreign Object Damage
ASAP	As Soon As Possible
PFC	Private First Class

DOD	Department of Defense
AFPRO	Air Force Procurement Office
SIMO	Special Items Management Office
AAF	Army Air Force
WSMO	Weapons System Management Office

I really need this list of acronyms to be able to write the abbreviated words and sayings in this book. My mind has an error of spelling the words out faster than I can write them down, so use this system of short cuts to helps my ability. (Thanks to all who perfected this page)